Westminster Abbey

Westminster

Abbey

Published by The Annenberg School of Communications with the co-operation of Weidenfeld and Nicolson

Printed in Italy
ISBN 0 297 99535 9

In the early months of my tour of service in this country I found Westminster Abbey to be a sanctuary of peace and comfort. As I reflected on the difficulties, the trials, and the burdens of those whose remains are forever associated with this historic building, I recognised how insignificant were the problems which confronted me. It became my overwhelming ambition to honour what to me is a debt of gratitude; and to commemorate this unique institution, with all its artistic, cultural and historic associations. This ambition is achieved with the publication of this volume. My own feelings for the Abbey are nowhere more completely expressed than in a work published more than one hundred and fifty years ago.

Its remote antiquity, its edificial beauty, the character and variety of its architecture . . . give it a superior distinction. But when the eye is turned from its general form and features, and the mind contemplates all that it contains: when it is regarded as the Mausoleum of our Kings; as the Sepulchre of Princes and Nobles; as guarding the dust of so many men who have, by their courage and virtue, their learning and eloquence, their science and piety, adorned the times in which they lived, and have left examples for imitation to succeeding ages: when it is also considered as the scene of that august, constitutional ceremony which places the crown on the heads, and delivers the sceptre to the hands of British sovereigns; such a combination of characteristic circumstances cannot fail to excite those emotions which are most honourable and improving to the nature of man. Of what materials must his character be composed, who does not feel his best sensibilities awakened, his piety animated, his thoughts dignified, his sense of public duty enlarged, and his moral tendencies strengthened, by reflecting on those objects which this structure presents to his contemplation?

Westminster Abbey, Harrison and Leigh 1812

Walter Annenberg   *Winfield House London 1972*

Contents

5   Dedication *by Ambassador Annenberg*

13   Foreword   *Dean Eric Abbott*

15   Prologue   *John Betjeman*

37   The Abbey in the history of the Nation   *A. L. Rowse*

147   The Art and Architecture   *George Zarnecki*

197   The Tombs and Monuments   *John Pope-Hennessy*

255   Epilogue   *Kenneth Clark*

259   Chronology

260   Biographical Notes

262   Index

264   Acknowledgments

Foreword
by Dean Eric Abbott

We owe this book to the vision and determination of the American Ambassador, and I wish to express the gratitude of the Dean and Chapter of Westminster and indeed of the whole of our 'Abbey Family' for this splendid production. For it is something more than a luxury volume. It has been produced because Mr Annenberg was convinced that a multitude of people should be enabled to see Westminster Abbey as it really is, that they should be able to understand how during the centuries it has drawn into itself the history of a nation, how it has laid under tribute the best that artists and craftsmen could offer, in stone and wood and metal and glass, so that now it stands both as a symbol of a nation's continuing life and as a living church and household of faith. I know that the Ambassador's hope has been that through this book the Abbey will, as it has so often done in the past, speak a relevant word to this generation, and that we may glimpse afresh how beauty and holiness and truth stand undismayed in the uncertainties of our time.

It must be expected, and fully accepted, that men and women will come to Westminster Abbey from every part of the world and that they will come out of a great variety of motivations. Some will come because it is the Coronation Church, some will come for the music (for the Abbey remains one of the great centres of the tradition of English church music), some will come to see historical monuments and memorials, some will come because they know that extraordinary beauty is here, created by craftsmen of brilliance and devotion, and some will come as worshippers and true pilgrims. Each of these motivations is valid. How, otherwise, could we have called our theme for the Abbey's 900th anniversary in 1965 'One People'?

Nevertheless, it is fair to say that in two respects our visitors to Westminster Abbey tend to be deprived. In the first place, they rarely see the Abbey as it really is, in its architectural detail and splendour. They have insufficient time to gaze on it, it cannot at one visit reveal all its secrets (which take many years fully to discover), they do not always know *how* to look at it, such are its historical riches and, I fear, so great may be the crowds who are trying to see it. This book will provide a long look at the Abbey and, through the pictures and through the words of our distinguished authors, will be, I trust, a real revelation.

In the second place, unless our visitors come to the Abbey as worshippers, unless they rest in St Faith's Chapel for quietness and meditation, they cannot experience the spirit of the Abbey in its fullness. The Benedictine spirit and ideal are not dead. Daily the Holy Eucharist is offered at our altars, daily the Morning and Evening Prayer are said, hourly the Short Prayer is said with the visitors, constantly the Abbey is filled for special services, as it ministers to an ever-widening number of those who wish to bring their concerns into the Church and commend them to our Creator. This aspect of the Abbey, which is its primary *raison d'être*, no book, however magnificent, can fully convey. But it is this which is the Abbey's 'soul', and has been through the centuries, whatever may have been the unworthiness of those who have served it, before and after the Reformation.

But that Westminster Abbey, in its multiplicity of attractions, spiritual, historical, architectural and aesthetic, may be more fully understood through this book, is my earnest hope and prayer; and to its compilers, its publishers, and again to Mr Annenberg himself, I offer our sincerest thanks.

John Betjeman

Prologue

Westminster Abbey is different things to different people. To the *dévoué* it is the shrine containing the bones of its founder, St Edward the Confessor. Annual pilgrimages are made to it not only by members of the Church of England but by Roman Catholics, whose cathedral is Bentley's magnificent basilica further down the road towards Victoria Station. For all the English it is the place where every monarch since William the Conqueror (except for Edward v and Edward vIII) has been consecrated with oil and crowned. For antiquaries it is Thorney Island. There are stone vestiges of St Edward the Confessor's original Saxon Abbey. For architects the present church and its great octagonal Chapter House are an exemplar of the Gothic style. Here in Nave, Transept and Cloister is the tall French architecture of the reign of Henry III when England was an integral part of Christendom. It is purest Early English, started in 1245 and continuing to be used in the building of the Nave until 1528, a remarkable survival of a strong plain style triumphing over fashion. At the east end is the last exuberant Tudor outburst of Gothic in Henry vII's Chapel, fan-vaulted English Perpendicular within, sheltering elaborate early Renaissance coloured monuments and gilded ironwork. Outside from across the Thames, Henry vII's Chapel must have looked like an elaborate galleon, for its pinnacles were topped with little gold pennons and vanes.

To the boys of Westminster School 'up Abbey' means going to the Abbey for their school chapel. In it they have daily services. The monks who served St Peter's Abbey, which the Confessor founded, were Benedictines and a teaching order. Boys were first taught by the monks, it is said, in the Western Cloister. There was also a grammar school west of the Abbey in the precincts. Queen Elizabeth I refounded the two schools as a single institution which is the present Westminster School. The Dean is *ex officio* Chairman of its Governors. In the Abbey at Coronations its scholars have the right to acclaim the monarch first. In the eighteenth century it was the greatest public school in England, and it is still one of them. For those interested in monumental sculpture the Abbey is unrivalled in the kingdom. It has the handsomest tombs of every age from the mediaeval to the present. To the liturgiologist the services of the Abbey and its customs make it a unique survival. The late minor Canon and Sacrist, Jocelyn Perkins, wrote three volumes for the Alcuin Club on Westminster Abbey, its worship and ornaments (1938–52). The Dean, Canons, minor Canons, and Sacrist in their enviable houses about the precincts are the successors of the Benedictine monks. The surveyor, organist, vergers, masons and those concerned with the fabric are the equivalent of the lay-brothers of the mediaeval community.

For historians it is the burial place of our kings, queens, courtiers, statesmen, lawyers, writers, generals and particularly admirals and naval officers. Though one could not say that the poets buried in Poets' Corner run the whole gamut of Palgrave's *Golden Treasury*, they are a memorable group.

Joseph Addison in a paper to the *Spectator* for Friday 30 March 1711 said:

Upon going into the Church, I entertained myself with the digging of a Grave; and saw in every Shovel-full of it that was thrown up, the Fragment of a Bone or Skull intermixt with a kind of fresh mouldering Earth that some time or other had a place in the Composition of an human Body. Upon this, I began to consider with myself what innumerable Multitudes of People lay confused together under the Pavement of that ancient Cathedral; how Men and Women, Friends and Enemies, Priests and Soldiers, Monks and Prebendaries, were crumbled amongst one another, and blended together in the same common Mass; how Beauty, Strength, and Youth, with Old-age, Weakness, and Deformity, lay undistinguished in the same promiscuous Heap of Matter.

There have been many books about the Abbey since the Reformation and it has bred its historians from the seventeenth century until today. The most famous authority of Westminster School and Abbey, Mr Lawrence Tanner, CVO, was himself born and first educated in Westminster. W. R. Lethaby, the craftsman architect who was surveyor from 1906 to 1928, produced two books on the building's craftsmen. H. F. Westlake's two volumes (1923) based on the Abbey muniments has the fullest information about the mediaeval monastery. In 1924 the Royal Commission on Historic Monuments produced an inventory. The most authoritative and handsome Victorian book was the fifth edition of the *Historical Memorials of Westminster Abbey* by the famous Dean, Arthur Penrhyn Stanley. The most useful and portable book on the Abbey is the current Official Guide. It originated from the Westminster Abbey Guide compiled in 1885 by two daughters of Dean Bradley and is revised every few years by the Dean and Chapter. The second of these daughters died in 1946. The present double-column, much illustrated and well-indexed Official Guide is written in that dry, wry, informative English which tells a lot in a little space. On a larger scale is Canon Edward Carpenter's handsomely illustrated Official History, *A House of Kings*, which was first published in 1966.

What was I to do in the face of all this learning when I was summoned by Ambassador Annenberg to the United States Embassy and asked to contribute to a book about the Abbey?

> Mortality, behold and fear!
> What a change of flesh is here!
> Think how many royal bones
> Sleep within this heap of stones:
> Here they lie, had realms and lands,
> Who now want strength to stir their hands.

Refuse? I wasn't at school at Westminster. My affiliations are all with the City of London. I was overawed and disturbed. I realized that although I knew nothing much about the Abbey, it had grown into my subconscious over the years. I knew it deserved a splendid-looking book to commemorate it. The last such rich publication,

Right: The façade of the North Transept, with the entrance portal below, and the great rose window above.

The exterior of Henry VII's
Chapel, with its rich and
undulating silhouette provided
by the curved flying buttresses
anchored to octagonal turrets
surmounted by ogival caps.
Every part of the stonework
is enriched by ornament, including the arms and symbols
of Henry VII – the portcullis
of Beaufort, the Tudor rose,
and the fleur-de-lys – pro-
claiming the English claim to
the throne of France.
Originally, statues of saints
occupied the niches but they
have disappeared over the
centuries.

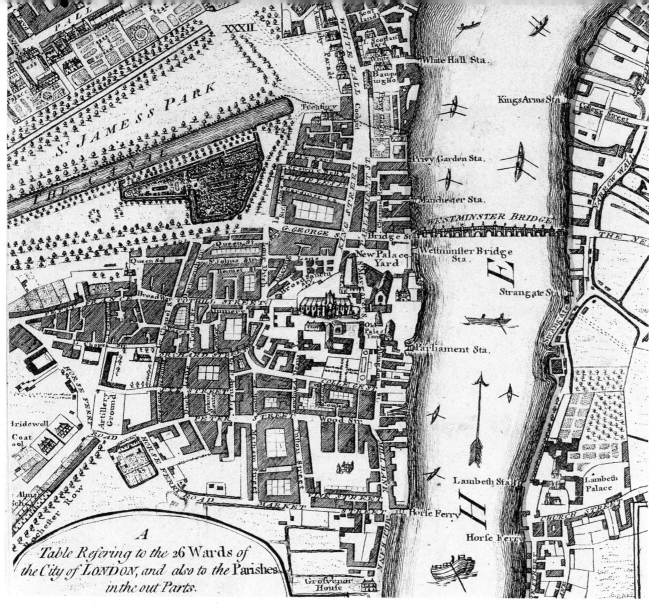

Far left: The entrance portal to the North Transept, which was originally called 'Solomon's Porch' but was largely re-modelled by Sir Gilbert Scott in the late nineteenth century. It shows Christ in Majesty surrounded by angels and apostles, bestowing benediction upon figures representing kings, clergy, statesmen, men of letters and science.

Left: Seventeenth-century plan showing the City of Westminster, with the Abbey and the Palace.

Below: The Palace, Hall and Abbey at Westminster; drawing by Wenceslaus Hollar, *c.* 1630.

Westminster Abbey in the
late seventeenth century,
without the Western Towers
which were added by Nicholas
Hawksmoor. The engraving
shows Solomon's Porch, the
entrance into the North
Transept, before it was re-
modelled by Gilbert Scott in
the nineteenth century.

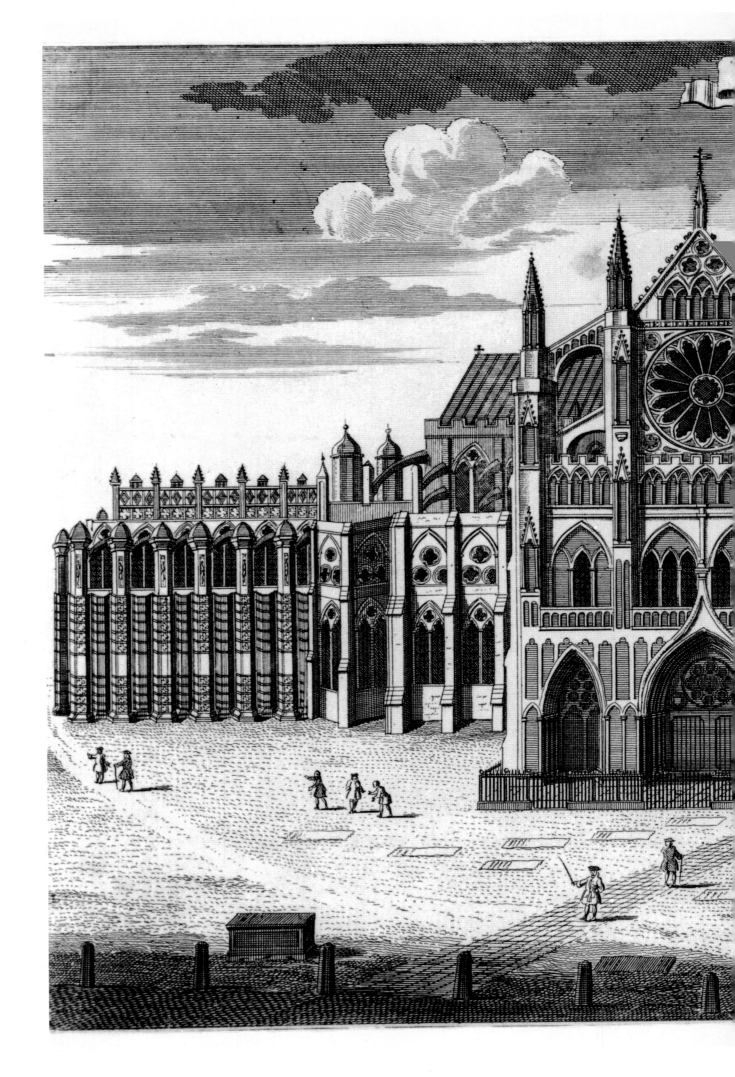

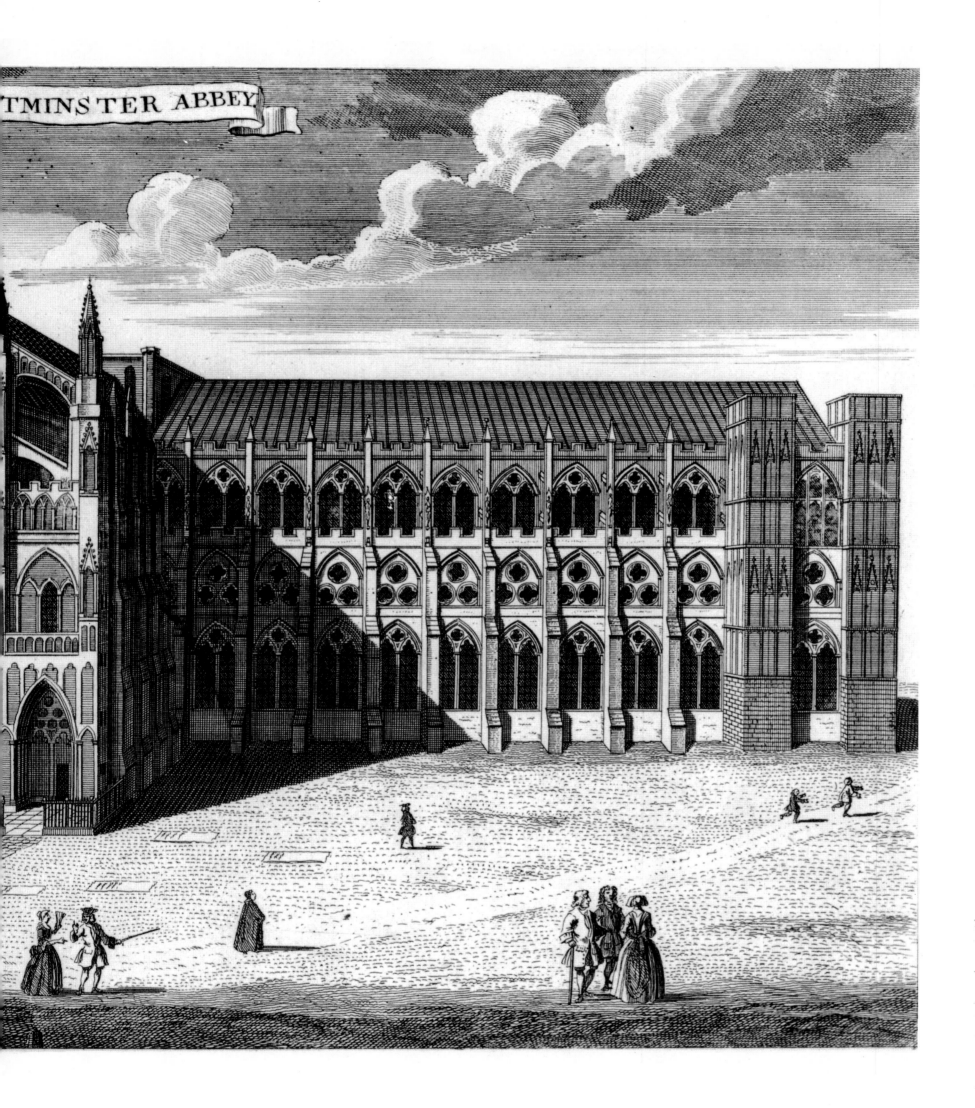

Ackermann's engraving of the
interior of Henry VII's Chapel,
1812. This view shows the
stalls without their normal
draperies, crests and standards
of the Knights of the Bath. In
the centre is the bronze-
gilt grille of Henry VII's tomb.

which depended on magnificence of production, was Ackermann's two-volume *History of the Abbey Church of St Peter's, Westminster* (1812). This, bound in morocco, with its broad margins, gilt edges, thick creamy paper and coloured aquatint plates, glowing in the finest golden sunset of Georgian book production, could never be faithfully reproduced. The smell and the texture would be missing. The nearest equivalent to that sort of book in our own age is the handsome memorial album with plenty of illustrations, which it is hoped this will be. That is why the text of this book is not by one writer only but is a series of studies by some who find in the Abbey subjects for their enthusiasm.

As I left the US Embassy and walked into the streets, I recalled Max Beerbohm's essay on the Abbey's wax effigies 'The Ragged Regiment' from *Yet Again* (1909).

Certainly, such of us as reside in London take Westminister Abbey as a matter of course. A few of us will be buried in it, but meanwhile we don't go to it, even as we don't go to the Tower, or the Mint, or the Monument. Only for some special purpose do we go – as to hear a sensational bishop preaching, or to see a monarch anointed. And on these rare occasions we cast but a casual glance at the Abbey – that close packed chaos of beautiful things and worthless vulgar things. That the Abbey should be thus chaotic does not seem strange to us; for lack of orderliness and discrimination is an essential characteristic of the English genius. But to the Frenchman, with his passion for symmetry and harmony, how very strange it must all seem!

The only contribution I can make personally to this book is to describe the impression the Abbey has made on me as a Londoner; I will write of it as a gradual unfolding to me in sixty years.

I suppose I was five when I first saw it. At that age there was the impression that it was only the South Transept. For most visitors, until recently, this was the chief entrance open to the public. One glanced in, the crowds were great, the place was tall and dark and surprisingly short for something so tall. I did not walk as far as the tower-crossing nor did I look down the Nave nor up to those three exquisite arches behind the High Altar. It was not until I was nine or ten that I was taken to the royal tombs and Henry VII's Chapel. These did not seem as interesting to me then as the Tower of London and Traitor's Gate. There were not enough ghosts. In those days I did not know that the bodies of Cromwell's government had been disinterred at the Restoration and thrown into a deep pit outside the Abbey and their decapitated heads displayed over Westminster Hall. I thought that anything really old and to be revered, had to be round-arched and Norman. As for the kings and tombs and effigies, they were a spate of words of vergers or schoolmasters or guides and too many to be taken in.

At the age of sixteen or seventeen one reacts against the opinions of one's parents. Mine admired the Gothic and the Abbey particularly, because it was Gothic and historic, two qualities of perfection. I was already tending towards the Georgian and had begun to admire the Baroque sculpture of Roubiliac and the pioneer investigation by Mrs Esdaile of eighteenth-century monuments. Partly to annoy my parents and old-fashioned schoolmasters, and also partly within myself, I then preferred St Paul's. When I came to work in London, after the usual two-year period of teaching in preparatory schools, my friend John Edward Bowle, the historian, had been made sixth-form history master at Westminster School. Thus I was able to discover the Armoury and the Little Cloister with its splashing fountain and its unforgettable view of Barry's Victoria Tower. I also discovered the Main Cloisters. As to the Canons and clergy, I knew none of them; they seemed to me semi-royal. The precincts of the

Abbey, though they are blessedly open during most of the day, still have a forbiddingly private look.

As a journalist on the *Architectural Review* in Queen Anne's Gate, I found the Abbey a dominating presence. Those two Western Towers completed by Nicholas Hawksmoor, in his own version of Gothic, were to be seen every day down Tothill Street. A reproach to them, we modernists must have felt, was Charles Holden's London Transport Building, built in 1929, with its plain square tower in the latest modern unadorned functional style, and carved insets by Henry Moore, Eric Gill and others. This seemed the true Gothic. All the same there was the deeper call of the truer Gothic, when all ten bells rolled out on state occasions and when the lesser smaller melodious ring could be heard after fashionable weddings in St Margaret's.

In those days the interior of the Abbey was dark and dingy. The great Lethaby seemed to have concentrated on keeping the structure standing, and I have been told that his only artistic contribution was the rather inadequate brass electroliers. There were many things for a forward-looking architectural journalist to criticize. For instance the lettering on the Unknown Warrior's grave seemed a very long way from Eric Gill. It still seems so, and must have come from a monumental mason and been ordered by the foot and acquiesced in by the Dean and Chapter, who were only interested in the wording. But now I do not know that art is all that important in an inspired idea like this. In a way, this famous slab typifies the Abbey and that touch of the commonplace and the numinous which make it different from anywhere else.

Since the war the Abbey has been transformed inside and has flowered. The new Surveyor, Stephen Dykes Bower (appointed in 1951), first cleaned the stone and we realized that the grey Purbeck of the Henry III columns was designed to contrast with the cream-coloured Caen stone. The paintings on the vaulted roof became visible, including arabesques designed by Wren around the bosses. The early Renaissance monuments were startlingly restored to their full colour, which brought back the swagger and delightful vulgarity of the New Learning. The monument to Henry Carey, 1st Baron Hunsdon, in St John the Baptist's Chapel off the north ambulatory, must be the biggest in any church in England. The cleaning of the walls showed up the splendour of the eighteenth-century glass, particularly that in the West Window. The noble, white marble statues of Georgian and Victorian days were cleaned.

The internal glory has been almost wholly restored, yet the heart of the Abbey, the shrine of its founder, is a caricature of a shrine. It was despoiled in 1540, and though the relics are still inside it, the mosaics have been picked out from the stonework and its columns damaged. All this could easily be restored to what it was like when Henry III rebuilt the shrine. The Cosmati work with which it was adorned could be put back by modern craftsmen.

One of the first of the Victorian restorers of the Abbey was Edward Blore, who designed the Choir Screen in 1834. Greatly daring, the present Surveyor applied full colour to this screen and to the stalls within the Choir, which had later been restored by Sir Gilbert Scott, whose masterpiece is the restored Chapter House.

This lightening of the former dinginess of the Abbey shows up how good Victorian work can be. Its proportions and detail are emphasized by bright-coloured paint and they are well suited to their surroundings, as is the restored stained glass in the Chapter House. Let us hope that this book will bring about the completion of the interior restoration of the Abbey. For the floors of Nave and Transepts, at present of inferior

Opposite: One of Hawksmoor's Western Towers, showing how well he matched his own version of Gothic to the mediaeval body of the Church.

Right and below left : Details from the gates of Henry VII's Chapel, showing the badges which recur in every part of the Chapel: the portcullis of the Beauforts; the root of daisies of Henry's mother, the Countess of Richmond; the initials 'RH' surmounted by a crown; the Welsh dragon; the Tudor rose; and the fleur-de-lys. The gates closely resemble the screen around Henry VII's tomb *below right* and *below opposite*, which was executed by Thomas Ducheman. The screen, or 'closure' of bronze was erected shortly after the King's death in 1509. Some of the statues from the niches have disappeared but the royal badges, the dragon of Wales and the greyhound of Richmond are still preserved.

Right: Two details of the thirteenth-century stained glass now in the Abbey Museum. They depict the beheading of St John the Baptist (*left*) and the stoning of St Stephen (*right*).

Plate 52

Right: Ackermann's engraving of
Henry v's Chantry Chapel,
1812. The chantry was built by
John Thirske in the 1440s.
The Chantry Chapel, flanked
by octagonal stair turrets, lies
above the tomb and contains
an altar of Annunciation
dedicated to the Virgin, where
prayers were to be said for the
King's soul. The figures of
St Edward the Confessor and
St Edmund can be seen flanking a vacant niche, which
probably contained a
representation of the Trinity.

Far right: Stone corbel in the
form of an angel, flanking the
entrance to 21 Dean's Yard. The
angel is holding the arms of Pre-
Reformation Westminster, with
the crozier and mitre of the
Abbot.

Overleaf: Engraving of
Westminster Abbey in the
early eighteenth century, with
the newly-built towers at the
western end of the Church, and
St Margaret's Westminster,
to the left.

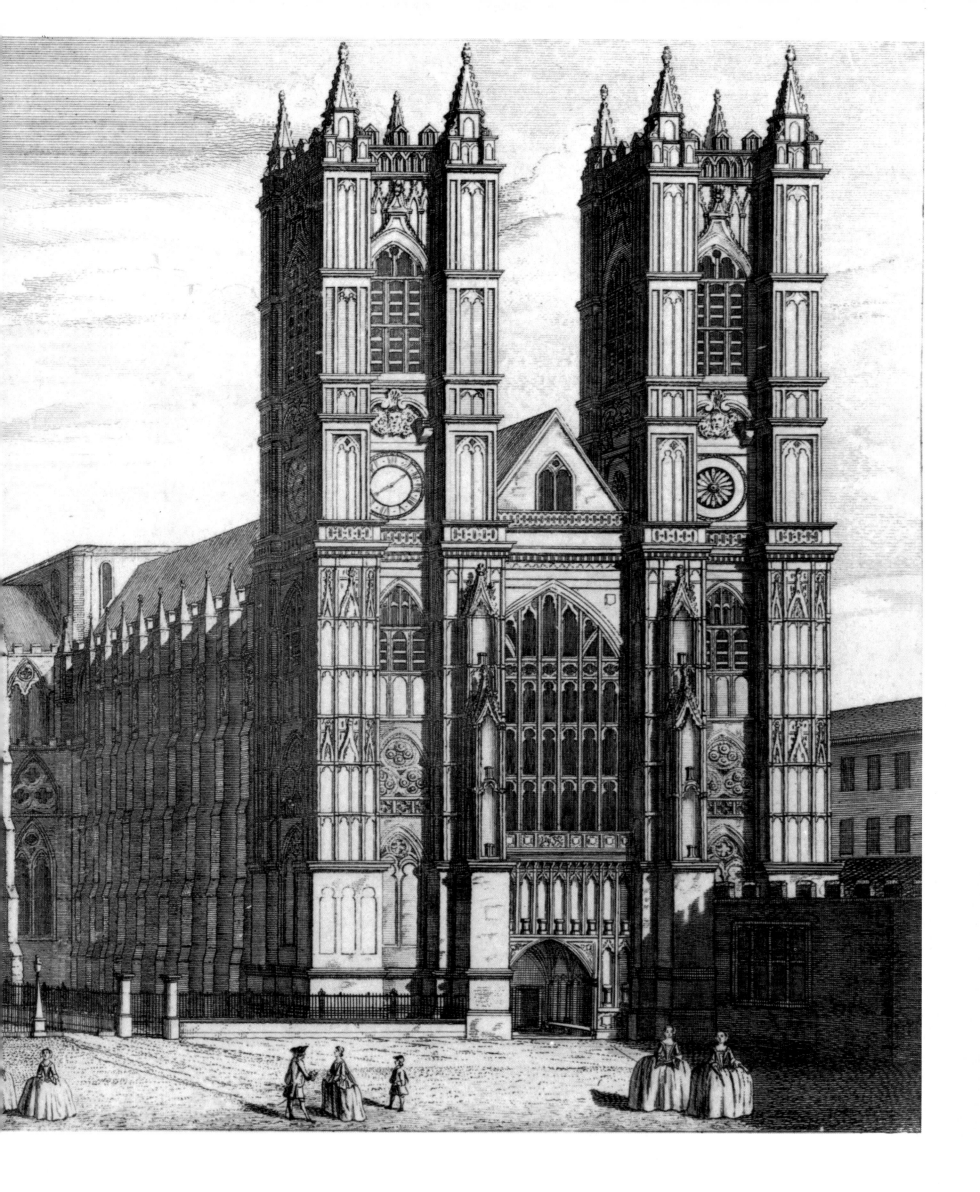

Portland stone, should be of more durable material, such as marble, to withstand the onslaught of thousands of shoes.

The chief delight of Westminster Abbey for the Londoner can be its daily services. I remember with embarrassment some satirical verses I wrote before the war on official religion connected with the Abbey. After the war, when I deteriorated into becoming a committee man, I sat on a Commission whose offices were close by. After these painful and often boring sessions, it was a relief to come out into the open air. More often than not the two bells were ringing for Evensong, then I would go in to the service and be ushered into a seat near the Choir. The evening light would fade from the stained glass. Softened electric light threw mysterious shadows. The well-known prayer-book phrases were read by priests in canopied stalls. An anthem by Lawes or Weelkes or some unrecognized Victorian musician soared to the vaulting. The Commission and the arguments fell into proportion and ceased to irritate. The traffic roar in Parliament Square, the 11s and the 24s, were muffled by the buttressed building. Even more than state occasions and memorial services, these weekday Evensongs have impressed me. The Abbey is more of an ancient abbey still at an 8 am Communion Service in one of the side chapels, with only a few there.

For the purpose of writing this introduction, I was taken a final tour of the place by the Archdeacon, Canon Carpenter. It was a summer evening after the church had been shut. I walked to his house just as the gas-lights were being turned on in the Cloisters and cobbled passages of the royal surroundings of the Abbey. I was in the London of Dickens. As we passed the Chapter House, I remarked on how strange it was that this building, so well restored by Sir Gilbert Scott, was in the care of the Department of the Environment, and not of the Dean and Chapter. He pointed out that it had been the scene of the first English Parliament in the Royal Palace of Westminster and that it represented what the Abbey stands for, the tension between the present and the past. As we came into the Nave by the South-West Door, someone was playing the organ. There was a lay brother (i.e. a verger) on duty. The stained glass in the West Window, gold, blue, dark red and silver was at its Georgian armorial grandest. I saw the point of those crystal chandeliers, which were presented to the Abbey by the Guinness family in 1965. The lay brother turned them on and they gradually swelled in brightness, though there was never a glare. We walked round the tombs, up to St Edward's shrine, over the engineer's new bridge leading to it. This is as inoffensive as it is practical. We went into Henry VII's Chapel, and had a look at the praying hands of Margaret Beaufort. The lights were turned down into semi-darkness as we came out into the gas-lit mystery of the Cloister and past the Hall of Westminster School close by the Deanery – that Hall inside looks like a Georgian aquatint of the hall of a Cambridge College.

As I write these final sentences in a City of London precinct near the Norman church of Rahere's Priory of St Bartholomew the Great, the Corporation of London dust-cart is making a hellish noise under my window. There is always a tension between the past and the present. In Westminster Abbey the tension for most of us is created by the thousands of tourists of all nations and faiths who queue, apparently without comprehension, through a place which means much to us. But do they not understand? I think they do. Their shuffling presence remains after the doors are shut. Finally, at the south end of the South Transept hidden away, is the chapel of St Faith. This is for me the part of the Abbey where tension between past and present ceases.

The great Gothic flying buttresses which spring from the clerestory of the Nave.

A. L. Rowse

The Abbey
in the history
of the Nation

WESTMINSTER ABBEY – which is the inheritance of all English-speaking peoples – is a unique institution. Other countries possess famous places of royal burial – Saint-Denis in France, the Escorial in Spain. Other cities possess shrines where some of the greatest spirits of their people rest, notably Santa Croce in Florence, or the Pantheon in Paris. But there is no building in the world that brings together both these functions and is also so intimately interwoven with the political and constitutional development of a nation – is in some sense its birthplace, the cocoon of the chrysalis; or, again, is a microcosm of so many aspects of a people's activity, architectural and artistic, literary and scientific, social and personal, in a word, exhibiting to the perceptive eye the record of a nation's whole cultural life.

So many streams have contributed to it. There is, first, its religious inspiration and origin – though this was associated, even in its earliest legends, with the government of a people, the welding together of a society. This last was spectacularly enforced by the Norman Conquest, from the moment the Conqueror asserted his right, by his coronation in the Abbey, as the inheritor of the Confessor's Anglo-Saxon kingdom. William I was supported on one side by his Norman (originally Lombard) Archbishop, Lanfranc, on the other by the English Bishop, Wulfstan, the rite expressing the dual nature of the nation henceforth.

Under the Normans the native English element was continued in the cult of the founder, Edward the Confessor, until the adoption of St George in the later Middle Ages, the patron saint of the English people. This was underlined by the burial, as the first royal personage after the Confessor, of Henry I's English wife, Maud (originally Edith), granddaughter of Edgar the Atheling and thus descended from King Alfred. We see in the burial of Chaucer, in 1400, the first of the long line of poets in the language we all speak today – the London dialect of the original Midlands Mercian – whether in Britain or America, Canada, Australia, or wherever our stocks have settled overseas.

Other, earlier elements enter in. With the Stone of Scone, for example: no one knows precisely how far it goes back, but there is no doubt that it is the stone upon which the ancient Celtic kings of Scotland were crowned according to primitive folk-custom. The Celtic element was emphasized by the Tudor Henry VII, descendant of Llewelyn and, as he wished people to think, of Arthur of Britain, with his banner of the Red Dragon of Wales prominent in his Chapel as it was at Bosworth Field.

By Henry VII's farsighted marriage of his daughter Margaret to James IV of Scotland, the ground was laid for the union of the island kingdoms. It was through that fortunate marriage that the Stuarts – and, through them, the present royal line – got the English throne. And, by one of those curious proprieties of history that make its study so delightful, when the burial-place of James I was lost sight of for some centuries, it was ultimately found to be the tomb of Henry VII. The first of the Stuarts lay alongside his progenitors, the first of the Tudors and Elizabeth of York, to whom his line owed their accession.

All the elements in the varied stocks that creatively forged the English-speaking people are there: not only Anglo-Saxon but their predecessors in these islands, Welsh, Scots, Irish. Even a small people like the Cornish have their representatives in the Boscawens, Killigrews, Godolphins who lie there. When one thinks of all the history that has surged through those grey walls, the great events, joyous in coronations, sorrowful in funerals, the high festivals and quiet celebrations at dawn or nightfall, the dramatic confrontations, all the human stories gathered about the dust of so many passionate, heroic lives – no wonder a famed American statesman, Daniel Webster, on first entering the Abbey, looked around him and burst into tears. Thousands of ordinary visitors of no fame, but capable of generous feeling – the spark of imagination the least of us possesses – have known the same emotion.

At the end of the splendid rites of the last coronation, in essence the same as those of the first on that spot, close on a thousand years ago, I watched the most famous citizen of both Britain and America, Sir Winston Churchill in full panoply, pausing before

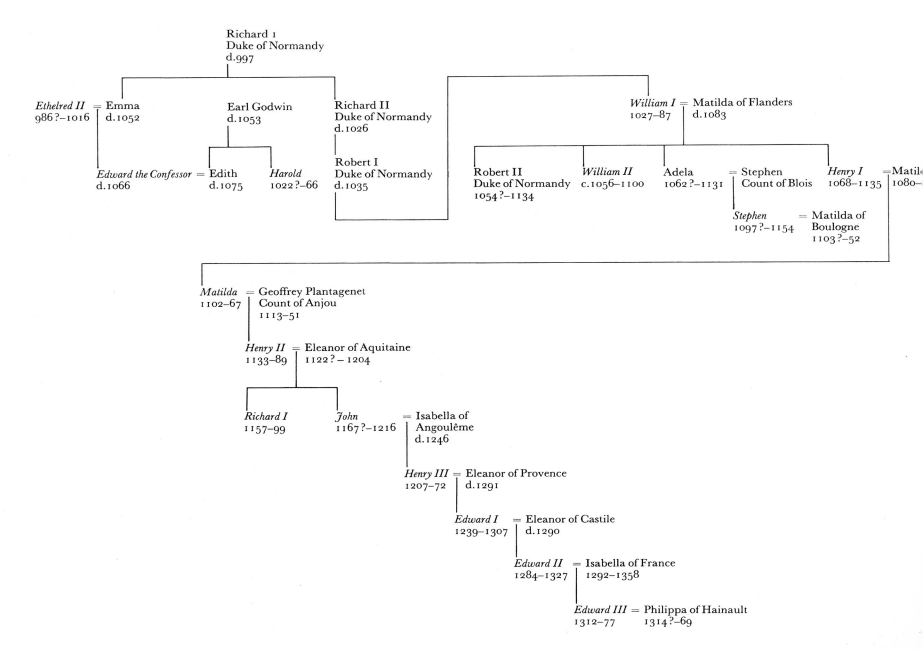

Edward
the Confessor
and the
Normans

taking his place in the procession to turn round and look up to the Sanctuary, to register before departing the significance of all that happened there, in that place so full of imprints on the mind for anyone with a feeling for history.

We may properly study, then, the most famous church in the English-speaking world as a microcosm of the history of our people, the changes and revolutions, the memories of a millennium.

Geography, as usual, determined the site. Here among the marshes and streams running into the Thames rose the island which the Saxons called Thorney. But it had its importance before they came to Britain, for the Roman Watling Street crossed here, following an ancient track, before there was any bridge lower down the Thames at the Pool (the 'lyn' element in the Celtic name London). We can still recognize something of Watling Street in Park Lane and the Edgware Road, as we see one of the original creeks of the Thames in the lake in St James's Park. Legends concerning a Roman temple on the site probably grew simply from the rivalry that has always subsisted between London and Westminster. St Paul's certainly grew up on a Roman site – the east minster in rivalry with which Westminster got its name.

As against the commerce, the shipping, the citizenry of London, Westminster was a royal residence. We must visualize the whole area so familiar to us today, with the Abbey, the Houses of Parliament ('the Palace of Westminster', with Old and New Palace Yards), Westminster Hall and Parliament Square, as one large precinct, defended by its ditches and gates, the river to the south-east. Here, in embryo, Church and State grew up together, inseparably linked.

There was a church here, a St Peter's, as against London's St Paul's, centuries before Edward the Confessor, whose foundation was thus a re-foundation. The Confessor's devotion to St Peter enabled his church to be surrounded in time with a garland of legends – now depicted around the cornice of his shrine – which the mediaeval mind did not distinguish from historical fact. (The devotion of St Peter still remains with us under the name of Battersea, with which the Abbey was endowed: it means Peter's island.)

King Edward intended to build something spectacular and new, the grandest church in his kingdom. It is impossible apparently to arrive at the truth with regard to his personality, so buried under the accretions of monastic legend. One thing is indubitable – he had luck with him to have gained the kingdom at all, after long exile, and he was not without the capacity to hold on to it, in critical, barbarous times, for a reign of over twenty years. He was the last king of the royal line of Wessex, already the most historic in Europe, going back to the fifth century and its probably British ancestor, Cerdic, since this is a Celtic name (Welsh, Ceredig). The ancient Englishry of his stock must have been an element in the cult of the Confessor that grew up under the Normans: it would have had an appeal for a suppressed people.

Perhaps Edward is best summed up by the Norse poet and historian, Snorri Sturluson: 'He was nicknamed Edward the Good, which describes him well. By the English he is regarded as a saint.'

Actually his own tastes were Norman, more sophisticated than his Saxon environment. His mother was Norman and he had spent the formative years of youth and young manhood in Normandy. Almost his sole concession to Anglo-Saxon tastes was his long hair and beard, though he knew the language, which his Norman successors thought it beneath them to learn.

His church, then, was to be a splendid monument of Romanesque architecture and art: of stone, the first cruciform church in England, with a central tower and two western towers. We have a representation of it in the Bayeux Tapestry, woven to depict the Conqueror's claim to succeed as heir to the Confessor. Fragments of the Confessor's building, some piers of the Undercroft, survive: the Church was almost as large as the existing Abbey, except for the eastern end with Henry VII's Chapel.

Some fifteen years in building, the Minster was at last ready for consecration as the King's life was closing. Minster means a monastic church, and the monks were largely recruited from the westernmost diocese of Exeter. Worn out by the struggles going on around him, between the Scandinavian house of Godwin, of which Harold was heir, and the Normans, Edward hurried forward the dedication of the Abbey, 28 December 1065, but was too ill to be present. He himself died on 5 January in the new year of destiny: 1066.

On Christmas Day of that year took place the first coronation in the Abbey: that of William the Conqueror. Having had to conquer his kingdom by force of arms, William was determined to exert the rights of the old English royal house to coronation as its heir, and that in his cousin Edward's minster. It was a moment of crisis, rendered unforgettable by the scene that ensued. The recognition of the King by acclamation is an element of the coronation rite from Saxon times to today. When William's Norman horsemen on guard without the Abbey heard the clamour within, they panicked and trampled on the crowd; the congregation rushed forth from the Church into the turmoil. William was left alone with the prelates and clergy; trembling with apprehension, he pressed on the shortened ceremonies to emerge as an anointed and crowned King.

It was the Normans who fixed the coronation ceremony at Westminster – hitherto there had been no fixed place for the Saxon Kings. Since then, every English sovereign has been crowned on that spot – with the exceptions of the boy-King, Edward V, who was murdered shortly after his uncle, Richard III, usurped his throne; and, more recently, Edward VIII.

Following the Normans, the Angevins – who began with Henry II – in turn set down the tradition of their coronations at Westminster. William Rufus, son of the Conqueror, did not forego what sacrosanctity might accrue to him from being crowned there, followed by his brother, Henry I, and the easy-going Stephen. Henry II had his son, the young Henry, crowned in his own lifetime, in the course of his violent quarrel with Thomas Becket. Since the Archbishop was in exile, the coronation was performed by the Archbishop of York in 1170. Becket promptly excommunicated the leading prelates who took part in it, and a tragic sequence of events unfolded: his own murder at the end of that year, the death of the young Henry, the suicidal quarrels within Henry II's family, leading to the loss of Normandy under John.

Underneath the harsh rule and violent tempers of Normans and Angevins, the cult of the Confessor continued and was encouraged: it was a mode of propitiating English sentiment and assuaging the sense of their identity. Henry II had the Confessor canonized at Rome and the body underwent its first translation. It was left to his

grandson, Henry III, to complete the process by providing the new saint with a gorgeous shrine, and rebuilding the Church on an altogether grander scale in the new Gothic style, of which its soaring interior remains one of the finest expressions. We owe the Abbey as we know it today mostly to Henry III; strangely enough, and contrary to usual mediaeval practice, when the Nave was finished in the following centuries, the builders adhered to Henry's intention and completed it in his chosen style.

Henry III was no great warrior like his famous uncle, Richard Coeur-de-Lion – the universally admired embodiment of chivalry – or even much good at politics. Henry was an aesthete: he has left us a finer and more lasting inheritance – the Westminster Abbey we know. More interested in objects of beauty than in the weary round of political struggle, he was, in 1252, forced to swear, somewhat ignominiously, to the observance of Magna Carta in his rising fane. Putting the best face on the matter, he took part in the excommunication of those who transgressed the Great Charter, no one dashing his candle to the ground more demonstratively, or asseverating 'Amen, Amen' more loudly than himself, at whom the ceremony was aimed.

He devoted the resources that his opponents thought should have been expended on the purposes of government (or on them) to the building and decoration of his church. Nothing was too good or too costly for it; everything was to be of the best, in the most sophisticated foreign taste of the time: marbles and mosaics from Italy, images, paintings, jewels from the finest craftsmen, while the design of the building was French in inspiration with its aspiring Chevet and radiating chapels, even if the elongated Transepts were an English feature.

Henry's devotion to the Confessor – whose memory had come to overshadow the original dedication to St Peter – was genuine. He erected the exquisite shrine that we have left to us today, in spite of the ravages of the Reformation: the only shrine of its kind in this country to survive. We can imagine its former splendour, the sparkle and glitter, the rose, green and gold of its mosaics in their pristine colour. Henry's own effigy reposes upon a tomb hardly less splendid, though the whole Church is in a sense his memorial. An historian of the Middle Ages describes for us the personality of:

... the refined, distinguished figure represented upon Peter Cosmati's lovely tomb. Henry's great passion was for building, decorating and the collection of beautiful things of every kind. A connoisseur to the finger-tips, [we see his outstretched hands with the long fingers in propitiation upon his tomb] he enjoyed nothing so much as the buying or getting made images, jewels, plate, relics, pictures, and rich stuffs of all kinds. The nature of the cloth, the setting of the jewel, the style of the ornamentation he would specify with minute care. These treasures were for the most part destined as gifts for the shrine of St Edward, the ardent focus of his religious life. He built madly, to his own impoverishment and our perpetual gain.

He is said to have spent something like one-tenth of the wealth of his kingdom on it all. If so, we have something still to show for it, after seven centuries, unlike the outpouring upon trivial objects of consumption, without much significance or lasting value, in contemporary society.

The great vault of the Chapter House springing from the central pillar. The Chapter House, begun in 1250 and completed three years later, was probably supervised by an English mason, Master Alberic.

Beside the Church, and all round it, a vast congeries of monastic buildings – of which a fair part of those on the south side remain to us – was growing up in close proximity to the Palace. We observe again the intertwining of Church and State, of secular and religious functions. The nation's Treasury was within the Abbey walls, in the Chapel of the Pyx (a term of art for a box), no doubt to secure the sacrosanct guardianship of both St Peter and St Edward. The nineteenth-century historian of the Abbey, Dean Stanley, writes of it with the appropriate awe with which Victorians approached questions of finance:

In the eastern cloisters is an ancient double door, which can never be opened except by the officers of the Government or their representatives (now the Lords Commissioners of the Treasury), bearing seven keys that alone could admit to the chamber within. That chamber ... is no less than the Treasury of England. A grand word, which – whilst it conveys us back to the most primitive times – is yet big with the destinies of the present and the future: that sacred building, in which were hoarded the treasures of the nation, in the days when the public robbers were literally thieves or highwaymen: that institution, which is now the keystone of the Commonwealth, of which the Prime Minister is the 'First Lord', the Chancellor of the Exchequer the administrator, and which represents the wealth of the wealthiest nation in the world.

Here speaks the complacency – well justified – of the High Victorian Age.

In the Middle Ages there were kept here not only the regalia but the standard coins of the realm by which the purity of those in circulation was tested at 'the trial of the pyx'. Centuries later, with the increasing secularization of society, this trial was shifted to the Royal Mint. Other buildings in the monastic precincts came in handy for state occasions when there was a large assembly. Henry III used the big hall of the Refectory for a council of state in 1244. His son, Edward I, used it for a special assembly of clergy and laity to call for a subsidy for his war against the Scots. Here the Commons met, under *his* son Edward II, to impeach the King's favourite, Piers Gaveston; and it was used on several state occasions in the succeeding reigns.

But the grand meeting-place was the lofty-vaulted Chapter House, one of Henry III's finest legacies, eight-sided with its complex groining, the arches springing gracefully from a central pillar. An early Parliament was summoned here, before the Commons were called in to aid the proceedings with their presence – or, rather, to provide the funds from the country at large: the knights to represent the shires, the burgesses the towns. Contemporaneously with the rising of the white walls of the new Abbey Church, Henry's reign saw the shaping of Parliament in embryo, with the calling of the Commons to be part of it. From the reign of Edward III the Chapter House became their regular meeting-place for the next two centuries up to the Reformation.

It was here, ironically enough, that the Commons pushed forward the Statutes of Provisors and of Praemunire, which pared the powers of the Church. Here, too, as we shall see in Henry VIII's reign, the Acts of Submission of the Clergy and of Supremacy effected the subordination of the English Church to the State. In 1540, after the suppression of the Abbey, the Chapter House became in fact state property. In 1547, with the death of Henry VIII and the flood-gates of the Reformation fully open, the Commons transferred themselves to the secularized St Stephen's Chapel within the Palace of Westminster. The Chapter House became the Rolls Office, where such manuscript treasures as Domesday Book and important state records were kept.

Thus it was that at the end of the Elizabethan Age a distinguished band of scholars and antiquaries gathered round this treasury of learning, where the records were kept by Arthur Agarde. William Camden, first of Elizabethan historians, was for most of his life Master or Head Master of Westminster School, which had taken over part of the monastic buildings, and brought up a whole generation of scholars – foremost among them, Ben Jonson. Sir Robert Cotton occupied a former Dean's house. They made a learned and agreeable society there. At the end of the seventeenth century, in the time of William III and Queen Anne, the voluminous Thomas Rymer was in charge, whence his *Foedera* appeared in twenty volumes, invaluable for the purposes of historical research. The last Keeper to hold the fort, in the Victorian Age, was the eminent Jewish mediaevalist, Sir Francis Palgrave, whose classic *History of Normandy and England* owed much to these surroundings.

From Henry III to Henry VII

Hence forward the historic impetus Henry III gave to his Abbey gathered strength in its dual functions: the crowning and the burial of kings, the setting for great events in Church and State. Not only royal personages were buried around the shrine of St Edward, abbots in the Choir, monks in the Cloister where they had lived their quiet lives, but private persons began to be buried and, from the time of Richard II, their monuments also to be erected there. The Abbey was becoming more representative of the nation at large. The burial of Chaucer, in 1400, may be taken as an indication, forerunner of the long line of poets:

> These poets near our princes sleep,
> And in one grave their mansion keep.

Edward I carried on something of his father's work: he brought back from his Crusade the porphyry and marble for Henry's tomb, the beginning of the series of royal sepulchres, with the life-like bronze effigy by Torel which starts the sequence, among the finest remaining monuments of mediaeval art. But Edward was an inveterate campaigner, who spent his energies on war against the Welsh and Scots, rather than finishing his father's Church. In 1290 he held here the council that expelled the Jews from England, a significant event in its historic consequences. His conquest of the Welsh enabled him to hang up the gold circlet of their Prince Llewelyn at the shrine of the unconquering Confessor. From his Scots campaigns, though victory eluded him, he brought back the sacred Stone of Scone, and proceeded to enclose it in the Coronation Chair which he was having made and decorated.

Since then every sovereign has been crowned upon that stone. Such was its aura that when Oliver Cromwell became Lord Protector in Westminster Hall, the Stone was carried out of the Abbey for him to be installed upon – one would hardly expect Puritans to be so observant of the numinous and anthropological. It is said that in the staid times of good Queen Anne, an old gentleman remarked, looking at the Coronation Chair: 'The last time I saw that Chair I sat in it.' It was Richard Cromwell, who had briefly succeeded his father as Lord Protector.

The Abbey suffered along with the rest of the country from the ravages of the Black Death – in 1348 the abbot and twenty-six monks were dead. This must have held up the completion of the Nave, as it held up works all over England. But twenty years later Archbishop Langham left a large bequest for finishing the Nave, and thenceforth work went forward right up to the Reformation.

This was very much to the mind of Richard II – an aesthete like his ancestor Henry III, and even less good at rule. Such time as he could spare from the neglect of good government and quarrelling with his uncles, he put into the rebuilding of Westminster Hall. But he had a particular devotion to the Confessor, and formed the habit

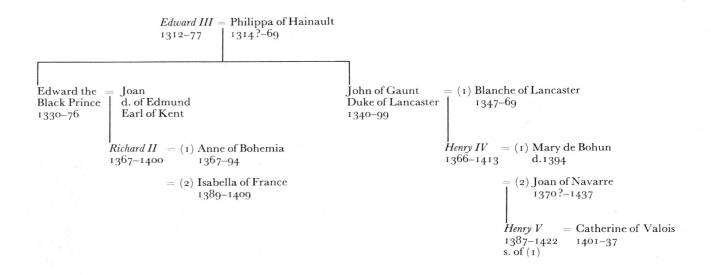

Edward III = Philippa of Hainault
1312–77 | 1314?–69

Edward the = Joan   John of Gaunt = (1) Blanche of Lancaster
Black Prince d. of Edmund   Duke of Lancaster   1347–69
1330–76   Earl of Kent   1340–99

Richard II = (1) Anne of Bohemia   Henry IV = (1) Mary de Bohun
1367–1400   1367–94   1366–1413   d.1394

      = (2) Isabella of France   = (2) Joan of Navarre
          1389–1409   1370?–1437

                                              Henry V = Catherine of Valois
                                              1387–1422 1401–37
                                              s. of (1)

of coming to pray at the Confessor's shrine for guidance in his troubles. At the height of the Peasants' Revolt in 1381 he rode to the Abbey to kneel there, 'since human counsel had altogether failed'. Richard was generous in his gifts to his favourite Church. A state portrait of himself, crowned and seated in the Coronation Chair, came to the Abbey; one of the principal relics of mediaeval portraiture, though somewhat abraded by the wigs of successive Lord Chancellors in the stall where it was placed.

The Church was the scene of a characteristic bit of neurotic behaviour on the King's part. He displayed hysterical grief at the death of his wife, Anne of Bohemia, ordering the manor where she died to be razed to the ground. At her funeral in the Abbey a leading baronial opponent, the Earl of Arundel, failed to join the procession and turned up late merely to ask permission to withdraw. The King seized a baton from an attendant and struck the Earl to the ground. On account of the effusion of blood the funeral ceremonies were delayed till nightfall, for the office of cleansing. However, before his own sinister death at Pontefract, he seems to have finished the tomb for Anne and himself, on which we see still near life-like appearance in their bronze effigies.

John of Gaunt's son, Henry Bolingbroke, a far abler ruler, was called to the throne by the will of the nation, so far as it could be expressed, by Parliament and the Church. But he was borne down by the anxieties of his reign, the persistence and strength of his combined opponents, perhaps gnawed by secret remorse for making away with an anointed King, and before his short reign was over he was a sick man, the hand of death upon him. As a brilliant young prince he had been on Crusade, and even, briefly, in Jerusalem. He was much under the influence of a prophecy that he would die there, and as his strength ebbed his thoughts kept returning to it. He suffered from a succession of small strokes, the last on 20 March 1413 as he was praying at the shrine of St Edward, patron of the royal house and of England. It is well known – for Shakespeare has made a wonderful scene of it – how the King was carried into the Abbot's withdrawing parlour, known from an early scene depicted on its walls as the Jerusalem Chamber, and there that same night he died: in Jerusalem at last.

The night of his accession the young Henry v spent alone in the Abbey with a religious recluse. In the precincts, between Solomon's Porch, the grand state-entry into the North Transept, and St Margaret's Church, there stood a hermitage, usually

Right: The genealogy of Elizabeth I from Hatfield House, showing *above*, Egbert, King of the West Saxons, and *below*, displaying William the Conqueror's claim to succeed to the English throne.

Below: Thirteenth-century seal of Westminster Abbey, showing Edward the Confessor holding a model of his Church.

Top : Edward the Confessor
enthroned and holding his
sceptre, from the Bayeux
Tapestry.
Bottom : The funeral procession
of Edward the Confessor,
showing his body being borne
into his newly-built Abbey at
Westminster in January 1066.
This detail from the Bayeux
Tapestry provides a unique
view of the Romanesque
Church, which was demolished
by Henry III to make way for
his Gothic building.

Details from the frieze of the fifteenth-century screen on the west side of the Confessor's Chapel. These were executed in 1441, at the same time as Henry V's Chantry Chapel, and show the principal events – historical and legendary – from the life of Edward the Confessor. *Top:* Edward sees in a vision the shipwreck of the King of Denmark, who was drowned on his way to invade England. To the right is a small ship with a figure falling into the sea. *Bottom:* The dedication of the Abbey Church which took place on 28 December 1065.

Illustration from Matthew
Paris' *Historia Anglorum*,
showing Henry III enthroned,
holding in one hand his sceptre,
and in the other a model of his
new Abbey Church at
Westminster.

Henry III with his masons at work on the building of Westminster Abbey from Matthew Paris' *Lives of the Two Offas*.

Right: The Stone of Scone, traditionally regarded as the stone upon which Jacob rested his head at Bethel. Legend says that it was carried to Egypt, Spain, Ireland and finally to Scotland where it was placed in the monastery of Scone. Whatever its origin, it was held in great veneration by the Scots, who crowned their kings upon it. In 1296, Edward I seized the stone and had the Coronation Chair made in order to enclose it.

Below: Panels from the reverse of the Wilton Diptych. The chained white hart on the right was the personal symbol of Richard II, while his crest and arms are shown on the left. Richard had a particular devotion to the Confessor and quartered his arms with the martlets – by tradition the arms of the Confessor.

The left-hand panel of the
Wilton Diptych depicting
Richard II kneeling in prayer
to the Virgin, with behind his
three patron saints – Edmund
the Martyr, Edward the
Confessor holding his ring, and
St John the Baptist.

Top: Henry IV usurped Richard II's throne, claiming that he had forfeited it by bad government. Henry was accepted as King by Parliament and the Church. In this illustration from the chronicle of Monstrelet, Henry is shown dressed in black with the bishops and abbots to the left, and the lay lords to the right.
Bottom: The coronation of Henry IV, which took place in the Abbey on 13 October 1399. His son, the future Henry V, is shown carrying the sword of justice.

Right: The Ampulla and Anointing Spoon, which were used at the coronation of Henry IV. The Ampulla was filled with sacred oil blessed by the Pope and sent to Henry specially for his anointing.

The body of Richard II being brought back to London from King's Langley on the orders of Henry V in December 1413. He was placed in the magnificent tomb at Westminster that he had prepared for himself and his first Queen, Anne of Bohemia.

Detail from the Chantry
Chapel of Henry V, showing
the anointing of the King at his
coronation in 1413. On the
frieze and cornice are the
King's personal badges – the
cresset, the collared antelope
and the chained swan of the
de Bohuns.

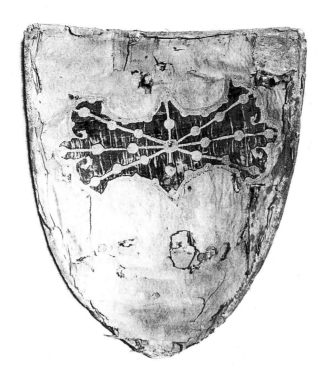

Left: The shield of Henry v with the arms of his step-mother Joanna of Navarre. This shield was purchased specially for the King's funeral and was probably carried on the cortège.

Below left: The oaken effigy of Henry v, which was originally covered in plates of silver gilt. The head, sceptre and other regalia, all of silver, were stolen in 1546.

Below right: The wooden funeral effigy of Henry's Queen, Catherine of Valois. This was dressed to imitate life, with painted face and wig, and was carried before the funeral procession to the grave. After the burial it would be set up under a hearse or temporary monument.

Left : Henry VI became King of England at the age of nine months, in September 1422 and was crowned in Westminster Abbey on 6 November 1429. This silverpoint drawing is taken from the *Life of Richard Beauchamp, Earl of Warwick.*

Below : Henry VI was anxious as to where he was to be buried in the Abbey, and made several visits to decide on the place. This manuscript contains the depositions of witnesses concerning the King's choice of his tomb. In the event, Henry was not buried at Westminster, but in St George's Chapel, Windsor.

occupied by an anchorite. Though there had been nothing disreputable in the Prince's conduct – even in his youth he was all for soldiering and politics – on assuming the responsibilities of the Crown he seems to have undergone something of a conversion. He became a dedicated man: he meant the conquest of France as a stage on the road to Jerusalem. At the time of his death at only thirty-five, after Agincourt and all his victories, he had borrowed from his aunt, Joan Beaufort, *The Chronicle of Jerusalem* and *The Journey of Godfrey de Bouillon*. There was his inner dream of leading Europe in a last Crusade: he might have been just in time to save Constantinople.

Henry IV was buried at Canterbury, perhaps to avoid the Ricardian associations of Westminster. But Henry V resumed the special feeling of the royal house for the Abbey. He is said to have had the body of Richard – for whom he had a tenderness, for Richard had been kind to him as a boy – brought back and placed in his tomb. On his last visit to England he presided in the Chapter House at a large assembly to reform the Benedictine Order. For he was a reformer, one for having everything in order: a most able ruler, there was something daunting, withdrawn, unapproachable about his personality. Though dying young, all the arrangements were made: he alone of the Kings was to have a chantry, where Masses might be offered up for him for ever. He had chosen the place: a platform was to be raised at the east end of the Confessor's Chapel, high enough for his tomb to be seen from the Choir where *Te Deum* had been solemnly sung for Agincourt. He had been good to the Abbey, promoted the work on the Nave, given lands to advance it and fat bucks to cheer the monks at high festivals. Now he was to rest in a new chapel above the Plantagenet graves, his effigy plated all over with gilt, the head of solid silver. Around him were scenes and figures from his short and crowded career of glory: his coronation, and his battles in France. In the event, his effigy has suffered more than any other monument in the Abbey. At the time of the Dissolution the head was carried off, and all the silver plating has disappeared.

His widow, Catherine of Valois, had even worse treatment. During all the troubles of holding on to France in the minority of the child-king, Henry VI, Catherine made a private marriage with a Welsh squire of her late husband, Owen Tudor, and by him became the ancestress of the Tudor line. She died in some obscurity and was buried in a rude tomb in the Lady Chapel. When this was destroyed to make way for her grandson, Henry VII's, royal chapel, her coffin was placed beside her first husband. It fell into disrepair in the course of the next two centuries, so that prying Mr Pepys was able to look in, on 23 February 1669. 'And here we did see, by particular favour, the body of Queen Catherine of Valois. And I had the upper part of her body in my hands, and I did kiss her mouth, reflecting upon it that I did kiss a Queen, and that this was my birthday, thirty-six years old, that I did first kiss a Queen.'

From the funeral effigy of her we can still see the long, graceful neck, the slender narrow features that she bequeathed to her grandson, Henry VII.

Meanwhile her child, Henry VI, was growing up to his life of trouble. If any king was a saint, he was: humble of heart, he could not bear the panoply of royal robes and would make contrition by wearing a hair-shirt underneath; charitable, compassionate, merciful – in an age of violence, the Wars of the Roses, which his incapacity as a ruler brought on – well read in history and the Scriptures, caring much for education, founder of Eton and King's, slightly daft. Several efforts have been made at his canonization: I have never understood why they were not successful.

Henry VI had much in common with the Confessor, after whom he named his only son, Edward, by his wife Margaret of Anjou. She was another disaster to him, the most spirited and unwisest of women married to a *roi fainéant* : she did everything to alienate the Yorkists and drive them into irreconcilable opposition, eventually to claim the Crown. In the crisis of the war, between the battles of St Albans and Wakefield, workmen several times saw the anxious King come to the Abbey to choose his place of burial. He had been crowned there thirty years before, a mere child of nine, raised on a platform that all might see him, while he sat 'beholding all the people sadly and wisely'. Now he was coming to the end of his journey. By torchlight he went round the Confessor's Chapel with the Abbot, who suggested moving Eleanor of Castile, Edward I's queen. Henry would not hear of it. Then he went into the Lady Chapel, hoping to find a place beside his mother. On another visit he settled for a humble grave beneath the pavement, as near as might be to St Edward : 'Is it not fitting I should have a place here, where my father and my ancestors lie, near St Edward?'

But he was not to rest at Westminster. He was murdered by the Yorkists in the Tower on the night of 21 May 1471 – when Richard, Duke of Gloucester, is known to have been there. Henry's body was ultimately given burial in the Yorkist mausoleum of St George's, Windsor. They thought that they had got rid of the whole Lancastrian dynasty, but there remained the Lady Margaret Beaufort, undoubted heiress to the claims of John of Gaunt.

Thus the Yorkist Kings were not buried at Westminster, though they needed to be crowned there. Edward IV claimed the throne by right of inheritance, but he won it by his victories in the field. He was simply acclaimed King, at first by his army on 1 March 1461, then three days later in St Paul's by the citizenry of London, who wanted above all good government and order. Thence Edward marched to Westminster Hall, where he was enthroned, and went in procession to the Abbey, where St Ed-

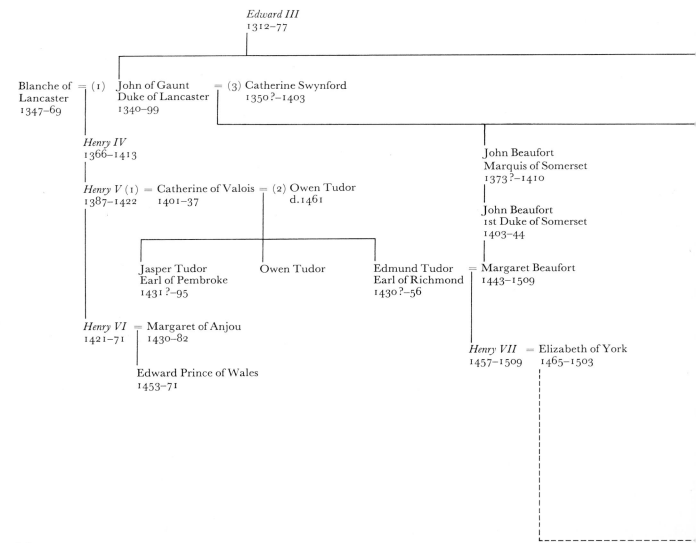

ward's sceptre was placed in his hands. It was not a coronation: for that he would have to fight. The fate of the country lay in the balance; it was settled in the far North at Towton, later that month. There was a terrible slaughter of the Lancastrian nobility; Margaret escaped with King Henry over the Border into Scotland.

Edward IV came south to his coronation at the end of June. Not much is said about it: the country was breathless from the speed of events, the change of dynasties, the chops and turns of fortune during the crisis years, 1459–61. Money was short; cash for the coronation festivities had to be raised by the obliging Archbishop Bourchier exacting a tenth from the Convocation of Canterbury. (It met sometimes at Westminster, but more usually at St Paul's.)

Edward lost the throne temporarily in 1470–1, partly by offending the powerful Warwick the King-maker by his marriage to Elizabeth Woodville. Warwick brought poor King Henry out of the Tower, paraded him through the streets to St Paul's, and returned him to his old apartments at Westminster, where daily 'much people and in great number' came to partake of his charity. He always remained popular, who wished ill to no man and did good to many. Edward fled overseas; his Queen took refuge in the Sanctuary of the Abbey. Here Edward's ill-fated son and heir, for a brief space Edward V, was born, with the Abbot as his godfather, on whose bounty the little family lived until Edward's return and his victories at Barnet and Tewkesbury. During her restored prosperity, in the next dozen years, Edward's Queen added a chapel to the Lady Chapel, that of St Erasmus, evidently as a thank-offering. It was pulled down shortly after, with the rest, to make way for her son-in-law Henry VII's great structure.

Elizabeth had to take Sanctuary in the Abbey a second time, in more sinister circumstances that worked out tragically. After proving a successful ruler, Edward IV failed his house by dying unexpectedly at forty, in 1483. He left two young boys, Edward and Richard, aged thirteen and eleven respectively. The elder was at once

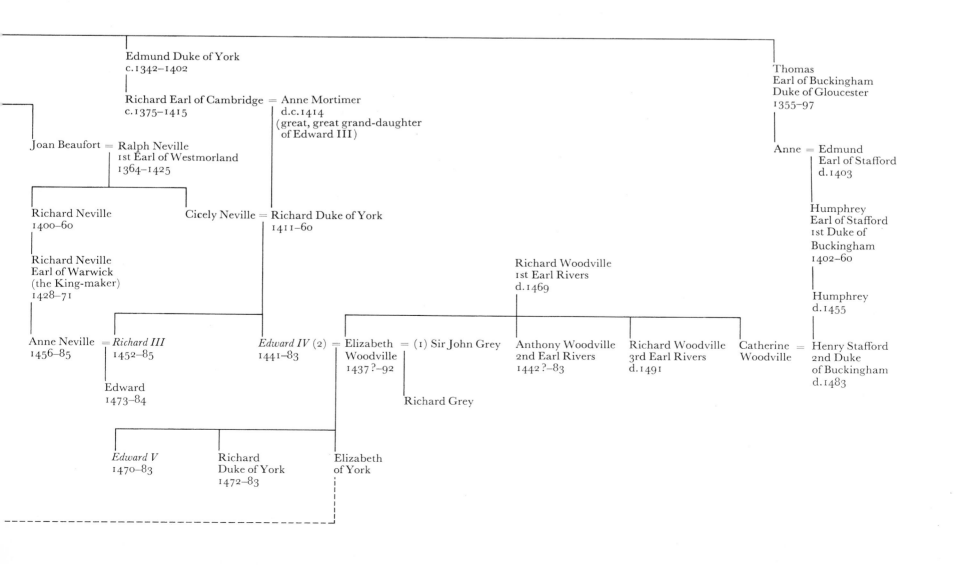

recognized as King Edward V, but on his way to London from Wales fell into the hands of his uncle, Richard of Gloucester, who escorted him to the Tower, which he never left again alive. Edward's widow, alarmed, took refuge again in the Abbey with her remaining children, Richard of York and several daughters. Preparations were going forward for the young King's coronation in the Abbey. Meanwhile his uncle, Gloucester, got the younger boy out of the custody of his mother on the plea that his brother needed his companionship in the Tower.

Richard now had both the boys in his power. On 13 June he had Lord Hastings, his late brother's closest friend, summarily executed, followed by the Queen's brother, Earl Rivers, and Richard Grey, her son by her first marriage. At the end of the month he had not only Edward IV's marriage declared invalid and his children illegitimate, but he also had his brother Edward IV himself bastardized. A petition was arranged from a gathering of Lords and Commons that Richard assume the Crown. Next day, Richard's leading supporter, Buckingham, presented the petition to Richard before a meeting of London citizens. With a proper show of reluctance Richard assented. He then rode to Westminster Hall and usurped the throne. Speed had been the essence of the *coup d'état*.

The preparations that had been made for his nephew's coronation for 22 June, were now available for the uncle's on 6 July, by which time large forces from Richard's sphere of power in Yorkshire had arrived and no counter-*coup* was possible. The ceremony, to make up for the dubiety lingering over it, was of splendour and marked by exceptional rewards. Richard's henchman, John Howard ('Jack of Norfolk') was created Duke of Norfolk, his son Earl of Surrey – such was the beginning of the almost regal family of the Howards. But Richard's coronation was even more heavy with latent drama – in this sense it was the most truly dramatic to take place in the Abbey. For the poor Queen Anne's train was borne by the Lady Margaret Beaufort, who undoubtedly regarded herself as rightful Queen, sole heiress now of the royal house of Lancaster. (When her son became King, she used to sign herself, if rather improperly, as 'Margaret R'.) What must they have thought as they all took their parts in the magnificent ceremony? It was ordered by Buckingham, but his Woodville wife was not there. Neither was Queen Elizabeth Woodville, though she was not far away – still in Sanctuary, with her daughters, in the Abbey precincts. Her two sons, the little Princes, were in the Tower, not yet dead.

When the coronation was over the leaders of society dispersed: Buckingham to Wales, where he had been rewarded with virtually vice-regal dominion, Richard to go on progress and show himself to the people in the South and West, where he was not well-known. Sir Thomas More, who was a man of the utmost truth, tells us what happened. He was also in a position to know: several of his friends had lived through these events, his father had been Sheriff of London, his friend Richard FitzJames its Bishop, who had been Edward IV's Chaplain, and there were others who were informed. More tells us that the order to murder the boys went out from Warwick – and we know that Richard was at Warwick on 8 August 1483. The boys were never seen alive again after August 1483; it was two whole years before Richard met his end at Bosworth Field. If only he could have produced them in these two last agonized years of his life, it would have been well for him.

When the back staircase to the royal apartments at the Tower was being demolished in 1674, the bones of the two boys – of about thirteen and ten or eleven years of age

– were discovered exactly where Sir Thomas More said they were buried, 'at the stair foot, meetly deep in the ground under a great heap of stones'. Thence they were brought to be reburied in the Abbey, in the north aisle of Henry VII's Chapel, the urn designed by Sir Christopher Wren : *iniectisque culcitris suffocatos* ('suffocated by pillows thrust down upon them').

In April 1484 – eight months after the murder of the princes – Richard's only boy, another Edward, died ; and in March next year, Anne Neville, his wife. Richard hardly knew where to turn, certainly not whom to trust. Thus it was that when he reached the end at Bosworth Field, 22 August 1485, he was not simply defeated but betrayed by his own side. Richard's gold circlet was picked up on the battle-field and brought to Henry on the summit, still known there as Crown Hill. Henry VII ordered the depiction of this famous incident in the stained glass of his Chapel at Westminster.

His coronation there, on 30 October 1485, was no very grand affair : Henry regarded himself as the rightful occupant of the throne, but the complaisant Cardinal Bourchier, Archbishop of Canterbury, came forward – this was his third time out – to sanctify him in it. Henry's marriage to Elizabeth of York necessitated a papal dispensation, for they were related ; but the Papacy blessed not only the marriage but the settlement arrived at. The wedding was splendidly celebrated, and the Queen was always popular. Not so Henry : his personality was too subtle and *recherché*, too politic and wise, for the populace to appreciate. He was careful to postpone his wife's coronation for a couple of years, to make it clear that he did not occupy the throne through any claim of hers. In ordering his tomb he laid down that he was to be represented holding the Crown, 'which it pleased God to give us with the victory of our enemy at our first field'.

Respectability had returned to the royal family. Henry VII and Elizabeth of York lived happily together, joined more closely by their grief at the early death of their son and heir, Prince Arthur. Then, in 1503, Elizabeth died in child-bed, aged only thirty-eight.

Young Thomas More wrote her elegy :

> Where are our castles, now where are our towers?
> Goodly Richmond, soon art thou gone from me ;
> At Westminster, that costly work of yours,
> Mine own dear lord now shall I never see.
> Almighty God, vouchsafe to grant that ye
> For you and your children well may edify.
> My palace builded is, and lo now here I lie.

It seems likely that the 'costly work' More refers to is Henry's Chapel, the foundation-stone of which had been laid a few weeks before the Queen's death. It was natural that, with his Lancastrian and Valois descents, Henry VII should concentrate his attention on, and wish to do something very grand for, the Abbey. Throughout all the tumults of the Wars of the Roses, his old uncle, Owen Tudor, had lived quietly on, a monk of the Abbey, amid the family tombs, close to his mother, Catherine of Valois. He was her third son. Edmund the eldest, Earl of Richmond, had married the Lady Margaret when she was a girl of thirteen. At fourteen, some months after her husband's death, she gave birth to Henry – by so narrow a squeak did the Tudor dynasty come into being. Jasper, Earl of Pembroke, was a very fly customer, always popular in Wales, whence he evaded all the nets the Yorkists laid for him, to look after his nephew's interests and conduct him safely to the throne. Owen must have been feeble to have been made a monk. In 1498 we find his nephew, the King, giving him a gratuity of £2; four years later one of Henry's Welsh retainers buried the old man. He was given a knell from St Margaret's Church – a link with all that past.

Henry VII was no warrior: he was a man of peace and politics, interested in business, money, statecraft, planning ahead, developing the country's real resources, backing the Cabots' exploratory voyages across the Atlantic to America. His character is visible in the terracotta bust of him that survives, and in the remarkable effigy that the Abbey possesses. There are the deep-sunken eyes, the ascetic features, the care-worn expression of watchfulness. With little exaggeration, he once told Polydore Vergil, his historian, that the first twenty-eight years of his life had been spent either in confinement or in exile. Life had made him very wary and reserved; an introvert type, he over-compensated his sense of insecurity by piling up money, looking to the future.

But he was not cheese-paring about the Abbey: he planned the grandest monument of late mediaeval architecture in England, originally as a shrine to Henry VI, if his canonization might be obtained. When the proceedings failed, the chapel became Henry VII's own memorial. One is reminded of the contemporary chapel in which Ferdinand and Isabella lie in Granada, the great candle burning for ever between them. With its nave and aisles, its grouped chapels at the east end, Henry VII's Chapel is a separate church in itself; in the stalls a company of priests were to sing 'as long as the world shall endure'. Within the wrought screens, as in a new shrine, he lies with his Queen upon the bronze and plated tomb made by Pietro Torrigiano. The tomb itself bespeaks the close of the mediaeval world, the foreshadowing of another; for where the idiom of the Chapel is Gothic, vernacular English Perpendicular, the tomb is Renaissance, by a colleague of Michelangelo. These works in the Chapel, with the neighbouring effigy of the Lady Margaret, are the finest works of the early Renaissance in England: they point to a wonderful flowering in the future, but they have never been surpassed.

The Lady Margaret's effigy, almost monastic as it is, gives one her character too: beside the asceticism of her features, there is a masculine determination. Henry owed his throne to her not only by right of descent, but by her advice and politic support through all the bad days. For she united the abnormal piety of the Lancastrians to the politic brain of the Beauforts. She would say that, if only Europe would unite in a Crusade, she would gladly serve as a washerwoman with the army. She was a more than royal foundress, though here too one sees a new world coming to birth, for her wealth went mainly upon education: not so much chantries to sing Masses to the world's end, but professorships at the universities and her two noble colleges at Cambridge, Christ's and St John's. She died at Westminster in the Abbot's house, not long after her son.

Thus Henry lies, surrounded by his family and descendants. His grandson, Edward VI, was buried in Torrigiano's Renaissance altar within the enclosure, subsequently destroyed as idolatrous by Civil War Puritans. His granddaughters, Mary Tudor and Elizabeth, lie together in the latter's sumptuous classical monument, Corinthian columns and all, in the north aisle; in the south, another granddaughter, Margaret Countess of Lennox, mother of Darnley, lies beside her son's wife and murderess, Mary Queen of Scots – Henry's great-granddaughter, one is liable to forget. We have already seen that his great-great-grandson, James I, is beside him in his vault. All round are the unnumbered saints of Henry's devotion, including the obscure Breton St Armigil of Ploërmel, to whom Henry considered he owed his safety from shipwreck once in his adventurous life in exile.

In the precincts, close by the Sanctuary, was the Almonry, which Henry endowed with pensions for thirteen poor men, while his mother gave a similar endowment for women – hers went on right up to the Victorian age in a dole of meat and bread to poor folk in the College Hall. In a house in the Almonry in these years, 1476 to 1491, there lived William Caxton, first of English printers, a decisive figure in the development of our literature. The earliest dated English book to be printed was *The Dicts or Sayings of the Philosophers*, 1477, translated by the unfortunate Earl Rivers, Elizabeth Woodville's brother, an educated, cultivated man. There followed an extraordinary number and variety of books from Caxton's press, some hundred or so separate works or editions of works, a number of them specified as printed 'in the Abbey of Westminster'. His shop bore the sign of the Red Pale (a stripe on a shield), and it was next to St Anne's Chapel. Hence the printers' term 'chapel' for a printing-office, or an assembly of printers. Altogether this new development was no less an indication of the ending of the mediaeval world and the transition to the modern than John Cabot's reaching the coast of America.

The Reformation and the Elizabethan Age

WE HAVE SEEN how closely associated with historic events the Abbey was in the Middle Ages, chiefly through its intimate connection with the Kings at Westminster; in the next two centuries we shall see it becoming even more a microcosm of the nation's history. It not only extends its arms to take in the illustrious dead among the nation, widening its scope outwards from the monastic and the royal, but also the Abbey itself reflects the history of the time: Reformation and suppression again, a brief interval as the cathedral of a bishopric; restoration of the monks and their suppression once more; final emergence as a collegiate body under Dean and Chapter, and, in place of the antique monks, the founding of a great school.

Up to the eve of the Reformation the Abbey was still a-building. Building never ceased; then, with the Reformation, they began to pull down. Henry VII's Chapel was finished in about 1519, in remarkably short time for a mediaeval structure. The saving Henry had left plenty of money for it – and for his extravagant son to spend. Abbot Estney, 1474–98, finished the Nave, at last, in Henry VII's time. Abbot Islip, 1500–32, built the lower part of the two Western Towers; but they were not finished for two centuries, until the 1740s. Indeed the Abbey was never finished; Abbot Islip had thoughts of beginning on the central tower, but it has never been built.

Henry VIII, in the pride and exultation of his youth, lost no time after his father's death in fixing a splendid coronation for himself and Catherine of Aragon, at Midsummer, Sunday 24 June 1509. Within the week his Beaufort grandmother was laid to rest, nearing seventy, a remarkable age for a royal personage of the time – her son and grandson died in their early fifties; but she was as tough as she was venerable.

Six years later, on 18 November 1515, took place an ecclesiastical ceremony, possibly a unique one, certainly the last of its kind in England: the reception of a Cardinal's Hat. The recipient was Wolsey. The butcher's son, from Ipswich, was magnificent enough, but Henry VIII was even more anxious to have his minister made a Cardinal – the more honour for himself as King. The new Cardinal was escorted from his new palace of Whitehall – which, in the end, Henry took from him – by a gorgeous procession representing Church and State, archbishops and dukes, bishops and peers, abbots and knights. Archbishop Warham sang the Mass of the Holy Ghost, Bishop Fisher bore his cross. But, when the procession returned, it was observed that the Archbishop of Canterbury no longer had his cross borne before him in the presence of the Papal Legate. A Victorian Dean wrote, 'one almost revolts from writing the fact'. Ultimately, Wolsey's concentration of the powers of Church and State in his hands brought the Church down with him when he crashed. The pattern of reform he set but carried out insufficiently, the suppression of a number of small monasteries for the benefit of schools and colleges, formed a precedent for Henry's later nation-wide Dissolution of the Monasteries.

Wolsey began well enough with genuine intentions of reform, but found himself held up, for all his powers, by age-long privileges and entrenched traditions. In the event Westminster Abbey completely defeated the almighty Cardinal. This was over the question of its privileged right of Sanctuary. Something of a safety-valve in mediaeval circumstances, it was now becoming more of an abuse. Within the Sanctuary, under the shadow of the bell-tower – where now the Middlesex Guildhall stands – there huddled a number of undesirable, if colourful, characters.

When Wolsey became both Lord Chancellor and Legate of the Holy See, uniting all the powers of Church and State in his hands, he mounted an assault in form. He first visited the monastery, investigating the conduct of the monks: 'he peered and pried and turned everything upside down'. The monks had to pay a pretty penny for their sins of omission and commission. He next called the right of Sanctuary in question, and Abbot Islip before Star Chamber to justify it; he even brought the King himself into Star Chamber to overawe opposition. But Abbot Islip produced his charter, which portended to go back to time immemorial. Though a monastic forgery, no one was scholar enough to detect that – and no Englishman, after Magna Carta, could go against a charter. 'After two days of argument, Wolsey was obliged to give way. His was the longest arm England had ever known, but it could not reach over the wall of Westminster Abbey.'

Something of the penalty the Cardinal had to pay is to be seen in the series of satires the poet Skelton directed against him from the shelter of the Sanctuary. Skelton, himself a cleric, was the most famous of early Tudor poets; recognized as 'laureate', his poems and elegies were already hung in the Abbey, and in 1516 he added one for the tomb of Lady Margaret. But in 1522, when Wolsey's involvement in foreign affairs ran into difficulties and his unpopularity soared with increased taxation, Skelton aimed a telling blow with the most outspoken and shameless of all his works, *Why Come Ye Not To Court?* It is perhaps the most famous, as it is the most idiosyncratic, contribution to literature to emerge from the precincts.

Its point of departure is the way in which Wolsey has absorbed all power in his hands:

> The King's court
> Should have the excellence,

Vr lan x nir   Et en apres p fuvent tog

Above : The coronation of Edward IV, which took place in Westminster Abbey on 28 June 1461. William Bourchier, Archbishop of Canterbury, is shown anointing the King.
Right : Richard Neville, Earl of Warwick, 'the King-maker'. Offended by Edward's marriage to Elizabeth Woodville, he, with the King's brother George, Duke of Clarence, changed his allegiance in 1469. He brought Henry vi out of the Tower and returned him to the throne, but this restoration was short-lived, for Warwick was killed at Barnet on 14 April 1471. Illustration from the Rous Roll of the Earls of Warwick.

Right: William Caxton presenting a book to his patroness, Margaret of York, Duchess of Burgundy – the sister of Edward IV and Richard III. This engraving appears in Lefèvres *Recuyell of the historyes of Troye*, printed in Bruges by Caxton and Colard Mansion in 1475 – the first printed book in English.

Below: William Caxton first set up his printing press within the Abbey precincts in 1476, outside the Chapter House, and then in 1483–4 in larger premises in the Almonry. This advertisement was printed by Caxton to make known his press: 'If it plese ony man spirituel or temporel to bye ony pyes of two and thre comemoraciõs of Salisburi use enpryntid after the forme of this preset lettre whiche ben wel and truly correct, late hym come to Westmonester in to the almonelrye at the reed pale and he shal haue them good chepe.' Among Caxton's patrons were Margaret of York, Lady Margaret Beaufort and John Estney, Abbott of Westminster.

RICARDVS · III · ANG · REX

Richard III, who usurped the throne of his nephew, Edward V. The preparations that had been made for Edward's coronation were taken over for that of his uncle on 6 July 1483. Portrait by an unknown artist.

Right : Three saints from Henry VII's Chapel. Above are crouched the dragon of Wales, the lion of England and the greyhound of Richmond and below, angels support the Tudor symbols – the portcullis, rose and fleurs-de-lys.

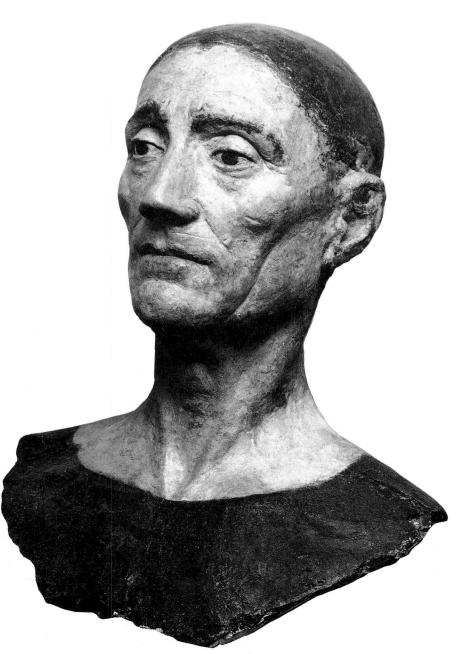

Above: The head of Henry VII, from his tomb which was made by the Florentine artist, Pietro Torrigiano, and completed in 1518. The finely-executed effigy was worked in gilt bronze.
Left: The funeral effigy of Henry VII was a death mask.

Above: The coronation of
Henry VIII, which took place on
Midsummer Day 1509, from
the roll of Abbot Islip, 1532.
Left: Stone carving, believed to
be of Abbot John Islip. Islip
was the Abbot of Westminster
during the reigns of Henry VII
and VIII and laid the foundation
stone for the King's Chapel in
1503. He also completed the
building of the Nave, erected
the Western Towers to roof
level and added the Jericho
Parlour to the Abbot's lodgings.

Right: The coronation of Anne Boleyn, Henry VIII's second Queen, took place amid great pageantry on 1 June 1533. The streets from the Tower to Westminster were filled with decorations and tableaux, and this drawing, possibly by Holbein, was the design for one of the triumphal arches.

Left: The coronation oath of Henry VIII, altered in his own hand at a later date when he declared himself Head of the Church of England. It reads thus (the King's emendations in italics) 'The King shall swear that he shall kepe and maytene the *lawful* right and the libertees of old tyme granted by the rightuous Cristen kinges of England *to the holy Chirche nott preiudyciall to hys jurysdyction and dignitie ryall* . . . And that he shall graunte to holde laws and approved customs of the realme and *lawfull and nott preiudyciall to hys crowne or imperial juris (diction)*.'

Right: Abbot John Islip died on 12 May 1532 and his body was brought to his little Chantry Chapel in the Abbey. A roll of pen drawings, attributed to Gerard Hornebolt, was made to show Islip's life, but was never completed, probably because of the Dissolution. This drawing from the roll shows the Abbot's hearse standing before the High Altar, with the rood screen above.

The coronation procession of
Edward VI, 20 February 1547.
The illustration shows the
procession leaving the Tower,
where the monarch by custom
spent the eve of his coronation.
It passed through the City of
London and along the Strand,
to Westminster, where the
crowning would take place.

K. Edward.

Master Latimer.

Left: Hugh Latimer, Bishop of Worcester, preaching to Edward VI. Latimer was a leading Reformer, famous for his sermons, who, in the reign of Mary, was burnt at the stake at Oxford in 1555. Woodcut from Foxe's *Book of Martyrs.*
Right: Mary I married Philip II of Spain in 1554: they are shown together holding sceptres and orbs within the initial 'P' from the illuminated membrane of the Plea Roll of the Court of the King's Bench for Easter Term, 1556.

The coronation portrait of
Elizabeth I, painted in 1559 by
an unknown artist. This shows
Elizabeth at the age of twenty-
five, dressed in her coronation
robes, holding the orb and
sceptre.

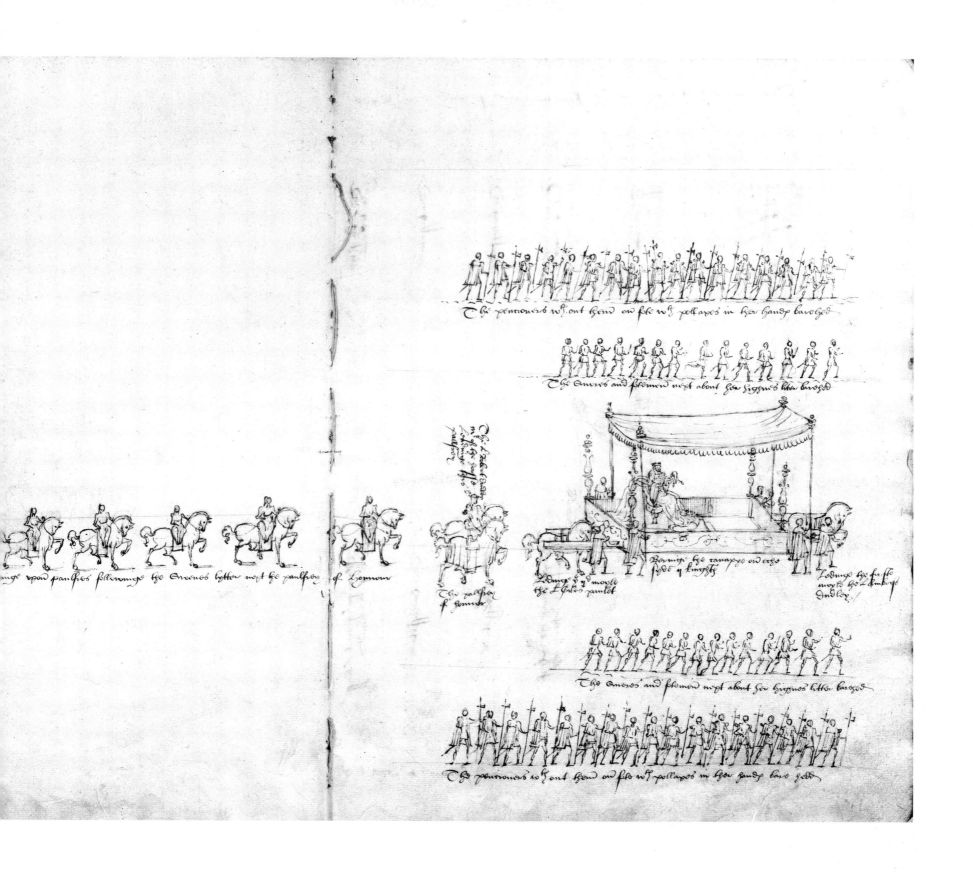

The pentioners without head on fote with pollaxes in their handes bare gold

The Aimers and footmen next about her highnes litter borne

Borninge the canappye on certo fote of knightes

Aimers of ye moyste the Esholes painted

Ledinge the first moyte the Lordenbe Dudley

The master of honour

mge upon panifies following the Quenes litter next the paulfrey of honour

The Aimers and footmen next about her highnes litter borne

The pentioners without head on fote with pollaxes in their handes bare gold

Elizabeth I's coronation procession, which made its way from the Tower to the Abbey on 15 January 1559. This sketch shows the Queen being borne in her litter of cloth-of-gold.

The tomb of Margaret Douglas, Countess of Lennox, daughter of Margaret Tudor, Henry VIII's elder sister. The alabaster effigy of the Countess, upon the sides of which are the kneeling figures of her four sons and daughters. To the right is Lord Darnley, in armour and a long cloak, with a crown over his head, and Charles, Earl of Lennox, the father of Arbella Stuart.

Left: The Darnley Cenotaph, which was painted in London in 1567 for the Earl and Countess of Lennox, to proclaim the guilt of Mary Queen of Scots for the murder of her husband, Darnley. His effigy lies before the altar, while the infant James VI, the Earl and Countess of Lennox, and their second son Charles kneel calling for retribution.
Right: The Coronation Chair made for Edward I to enclose the Stone of Scone, which he had seized from the Scots in 1296. Made of oak, the Chair was painted with birds, foliage and animals on a gilt ground, and faint traces of these remain. At coronations the Chair is removed to the Sanctuary; since 1308 every sovereign of England – except Edward V and Edward VIII – has been crowned on it.

But Hampton Court
Hath the pre-eminence,
And York Place,
With my Lord's Grace.

This was, in fact, unfair; but whenever did a satirist aim at fairness? It goes on to an attack on Wolsey's rule, the expensive waste of his foreign policy, his bullying of secular peers in Council and rating them for their ignorance; it follows up with a scarifying denunciation of his person as a low-born, gormandizing, loose voluptuary:

To weave all in one loom
A web of linsey-woolsey,
Opus male dulce :
The devil kiss his cule !
For, while he doth rule,
All is warse and warse,
The devil kiss his arse !
For whether he bless or curse
It cannot be much worse.

Tudor amenities were not only coarse but very mercurial: next year we find laureate Skelton making it up with a flattering dedication of his *Garland of Laurel* to King and Cardinal both. It was some evidence of Wolsey's good nature that he accepted it – he was really a tolerant man. But it is also evidence that reform was in the air, and being obstructed; after the Cardinal's downfall it would take a far more drastic form with the utter destruction of the monasteries.

Westminster Abbey was, from its position, its associations, and its wealth, the foremost of them all. It reflects in its history – and, alas, in its monuments – the whole process of the Reformation; the violence of the breach with the past, its iconoclasm, the destruction of works of art in the interest of convictions; the brief reaction and attempt to return to the past; its impossibility and defeat, the resumption on a more constructive course and a more moderate basis. Yet not all the changes could efface its name, even when rendered inexact, in the affections of the nation.

Henry VIII's personal problem, the necessity of providing an heir for the succession to the throne, provided the occasion for the breach with Rome. When Anne Boleyn became pregnant in December 1532, he decided that this might be the long-desired son and heir, and was secretly married to her in the following month. On Sunday 1 June, he gave her a magnificent coronation, seven months gone with the child that was to be Elizabeth I. We may say that this was *her* first visit to the Abbey. This was no derogation in Henry's eyes – he wanted people to see that there was an heir on the way, his dynasty at length assured – there was only the small and sickly girl, Mary, of all Catherine of Aragon's children that had survived.

The new Queen Anne was given the full royal treatment: the customary residence in the King's lodgings in the Tower before a coronation; on 31 May a glorious procession through the streets of London to present her to the city, dressed all in white, her long hair falling in virginal fashion over her shoulders. Little did she know that she was as much an appointed victim of state as her discarded predecessor, over

This portrait of Richard II, painted during his lifetime, used to hang over the Lord Chancellor's stall in the Choir, until it was discovered that the wigs of the occupants were damaging it. Some scholars have suggested that it was the work of a French artist, André Beauneveu, court painter to Charles V, who is known to have visited Richard's court in 1398, but it is more likely to be an English work. The King is portrayed full face, enthroned and in his coronation robes.

whom she had triumphed. In the Abbey she was crowned by Archbishop Cranmer with full Catholic rites, anointing and all – the second and last of Henry's wives to receive such an honour. All politics, of course: it was a political necessity to shore up the succession by all possible means.

When an Act was passed requiring people to subscribe to the new succession, everybody was prepared to do so, except Sir Thomas More and Bishop Fisher. More was committed to the custody of the Abbot of Westminster, 14–17 April 1534, on his way to the Tower. The Abbot implored More to subscribe, as indeed everyone else did who wished to save him. More and Fisher were executed in the summer of 1535 for their refusal. Next year, Anne Boleyn followed them on the scaffold in the Tower, and her daughter was declared illegitimate. No one knows whether Anne was guilty of the adultery with which Henry charged her, but he was now free – with the deaths of both Catherine and Anne – to make an undoubted marriage to Jane Seymour in May 1536.

The Reformation impulse was allowed to go forward, though under Henry's firm control. In 1536 the smaller monasteries were suppressed – 'nationalized' would be an appropriate word, since their lands and wealth were annexed to the Crown. From 1538 the larger houses began to be surrendered, until in 1540 the process reached Westminster Abbey itself, one of the last to be taken over. Meanwhile shrines and the veneration of relics throughout the country were suppressed, such as the most popular and richest of them all, that of St Thomas Becket at Canterbury. Even at Westminster the bones of the Confessor were taken out of the shrine and buried apart, so that they should not be worshipped. The images, banners, trophies – including Llewelyn's circlet – were all removed, the golden feretory melted down. The stone structure of the shrine was left to stand, the only one in England, but empty.

Henry intended to devote some of the proceeds of the Dissolution to the creation of a dozen new dioceses; but the vast expense of his last French war, 1543–6, truncated this useful reform and, in the event, only six were established. Westminster was one of them; Thomas Thirlby, a Cambridge *protégé* of Cranmer, became the first, and only, Bishop. Middlesex became his diocese, leaving Essex (and Fulham) to the diocese of London. The last Abbot became the first Dean of Westminster, though he had to turn out of his palatial house to make way for the Bishop. He presided over a Chapter of twelve prebendaries, with an establishment of priests, most of whom had been monks; for full choir-services continued, with three Masses a day, so long as Henry VIII continued.

Henry died in 1547, and was buried, not at Westminster with his father, but more appropriately with his Yorkist grandfather, Edward IV, at Windsor. For Henry VIII was not in the least like his Tudor father, Henry VII. He took after Edward IV: similar figure, large and bulky; an extrovert, with the Yorkist over-confidence in life; an out-of-doors man, given to sport and women; interested in everything to do with war, military and naval; extravagant and exhibitionist, capricious and cruel, a *faux bonhomme*; but an able ruler, with the capacity for leadership and, in spite of everything, always popular, like Edward IV.

With the removal of Henry's heavy hand, and the accession of a boy-King, Edward VI, the Reformation dynamic surged ahead. Redundant churches, chapels, chantries, monastic buildings were destroyed or transformed, put to secular uses. In the Abbey altars were removed, statues destroyed, lights extinguished, some monuments, brasses and paintings defaced or whitewashed. Bronze lecterns, candlesticks, censers, crosses, vestments – works of art – were sold. Dependent chapels in the precincts, like St Catherine's, were unroofed for their lead or were taken down as no longer needed. No wonder Protector Somerset, uncle of the boy-King and ruling in his name, could ask, not in vain, for twenty tons of the best Caen stone, 'if there could be so much spared'. He was building a grand new palace in the Strand: Somerset House. To its building there was devoted not only the stone from Westminster Abbey but that of the Cloister at St Paul's. The old anchorite's house was leased to a bell-ringer, whose appointment was in the hands of the young Princess Elizabeth, being educated with her brother and waiting in the wings.

Even the bishopric was suppressed; Thirlby, not really in sympathy with the Protestant course, but a Henrician, accepted the better offer of Norwich. The Abbot's house was secularized, bought by Lord Wentworth, who had a grand funeral from it in 1551, buried in Abbot Islip's recent chantry. The obituary sermon was preached by Coverdale, a Protestant translator of the Bible. Of the brief bishopric all that has remained to us is the title of the 'City' of Westminster, as anomalous as that of Abbey for a church without abbot or monks.

Henry VIII, obsessed by the problem of the succession, had intended to crown his young heir in his lifetime to make all sure. Preparations were on foot at the time of his death, so that Edward VI was crowned only a month after. Cranmer, who had been involved in the most intimate passages of the late King's life, performed the ceremonies, which were still Catholic. The Archbishop anointed the boy, who was lying prostrate before the altar, on his back; but in his address he was careful to point out that these rites were not sacramental, 'but good admonitions to put kings in mind of their duty to God'; the anointing was but a ceremony, conferring no sanctity through

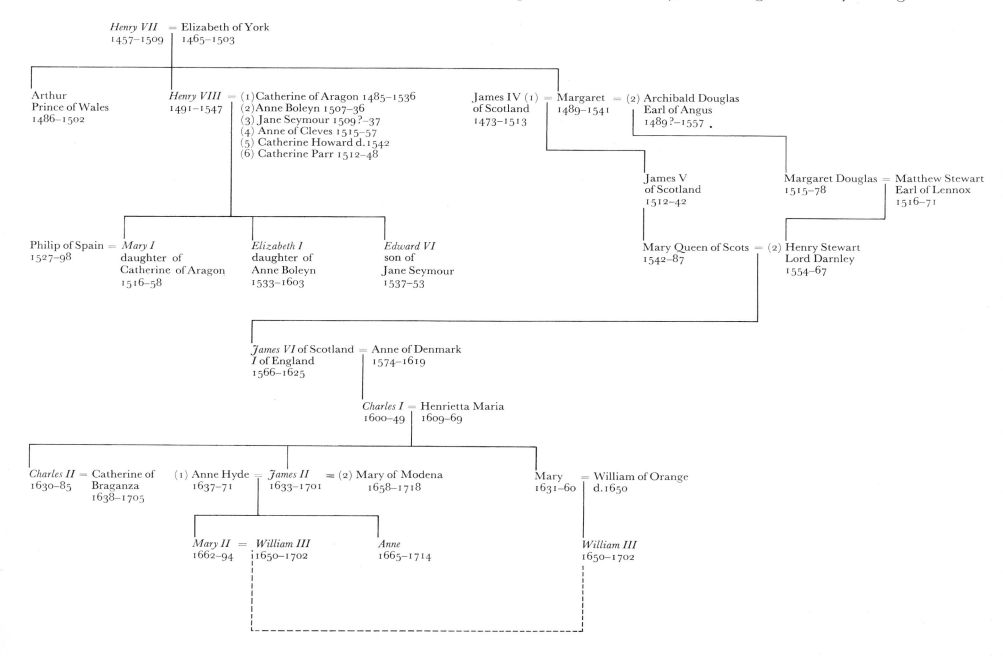

the performing bishop: 'If it be wanting, that king is yet a perfect monarch notwithstanding, and God's anointed, as well as if he was inoiled.'

Six years later, it fell to Cranmer to bury the young King, whom he had baptized and crowned; it was his last public function before his burning. By another swift turn in affairs, Mary, who succeeded Edward, was an extreme Catholic *dévote*. It was with much difficulty that the concession of a Protestant funeral in the Abbey was wrung from her, though it was still the law of the land. She herself attended a requiem for her brother in the Tower.

Mary Tudor was the daughter of Catherine of Aragon, with the religious fixation of that family: she had none of the political brain of the Tudors. Her accession to the throne was unexpected; it was only a few months before that the young King had irrecoverably sickened. The Edwardians had looked forward to a time of promise, a new age: what became the Elizabethan Age was largely created by them – it should have been the Edwardian Age. Meanwhile, there was the fact of Mary's accession, after twenty years of retirement, into a new and unsympathetic world she detested. The Council attempted to get guarantees from her as to the independence of the English Church; but she had no sense of compromise: she was determined to restore the full Roman obedience, and to have things as they had ceased to be.

With the Archbishops of Canterbury and York and the Bishop of London imprisoned, Gardiner, the restored Bishop of Winchester, officiated at her coronation. He had gone all the way with Henry VIII – nearly everybody had; it was Edward's new deal that divided the country. Fearing that the holy oil had lost its efficacy, Mary had a fresh supply, blessed by the indubitable Bishop of Arras, sent over by the Emperor's ambassador. The coronation proceeded. Anne of Cleves, Henry's discarded fourth wife, was present; so was the young Elizabeth, who had been at her mother's coronation, in her womb. At one point she complained to the rival ambassador of France, who sought to be of her party, of the weight of her coronet. 'Have patience,' said Noailles, 'and before long you will exchange it for a crown.' Elizabeth had plenty of patience; she did not have to wait long.

In the interval a great many things happened. Hugh Weston – an inferior Oxford man who was to preside over the trials of those eminent Cambridge men, Cranmer and Latimer – was appointed Dean of Westminster. On 12 November 1554 a Mass of the Holy Ghost was celebrated in state, with Mary and her husband, Philip of Spain, present, to inaugurate the Parliament that was to welcome Cardinal Pole and be received back into the Roman obedience. This last was accomplished a fortnight later in Westminster Hall. The Queen and her cousin, the Cardinal, were not present. Both wished to spare themselves fatigue: Mary thought she was expecting a child, the Cardinal was frail. Neither of them was a good life actuarially.

Parliament might make a formal act of submission and restore Catholic rites in the churches; but it was impossible to restore the lands of the Church or the monasteries. The Queen, out of devotion, and her own resources, did what little she could to set up a few houses of monks and friars in her immediate vicinity; principally, Westminster Abbey itself, though the restoration could only take place gradually. Hugh Weston was removed to Windsor, and a respectable man of humble origin, John Feckenham, was brought in to renew monastic life in the precincts, with only thirteen monks who could be gathered together, four of them from ancient, already ruined, Glastonbury.

The monks were reinstalled, in November 1555, with all possible honours to improve their prestige in a world where the propaganda against monasticism had taken such root. Feckenham was consecrated to his mitred abbacy, which gave him a seat in the House of Lords; Cardinal Pole was there, and Bishop Gardiner, shortly to die. Next month a procession of monks marched before three homicides, young Lord Dacre, a low-born murderer of a tailor, and a Westminster schoolboy who had killed a beggar by hitting him with a stone under the ear. This was probably an assertion of the former right of Sanctuary – in any case, a way of thought outmoded by the time.

So perhaps was the restoration of the bones of the Confessor, after so many translations, taken up and buried once more in the despoiled shrine. Efforts were begun to repair the shrine: evidence remains of the hurried work – displaced fragments of mosaic, and a new cornice. A wooden structure was erected, in place of the golden feretory that had once been there; but this was never finished: Mary's reign was over before it could be.

With Elizabeth I, the daughter of the Reformation, it resumed its impulse, propelling her further to the Left than she wished, so vehement was the reaction against Mary's burnings. She would have preferred something more in the way of a *via media*, of an Erasmian moderation. She had hopes of Feckenham, and others like Archbishop Heath and Bishop Tunstall, who had been moderates. But the bishops had burned their boats as well as Protestants, and could hardly eat their words yet once more. This time they held together – all apparently except Kitchin, Bishop of Llandaff, who had been a monk of Westminster, and was consecrated in the Abbey.

An indication of the way the wind was blowing was given by the new Queen's words to the Abbot and his monks, meeting her in procession before her first Parliament with lighted tapers according to wont: 'Away with those torches, for we see very well.' The coronation took place on 15 January 1559: Mary's Catholic rites were still the law of the land. Cardinal Pole had died on the same night as Queen Mary: the see of Canterbury was vacant; Bonner, Bishop of London, burner *par excellence*, was in the Tower. But the bishops would not crown the Queen without guarantees of Elizabeth's submission to Rome. In the end, Oglethorpe, Bishop of Carlisle, was prevailed upon to do the job. Mass was sung in Latin, but the Litany, as in her father's later years, in English; the Epistle and Gospel in both. At the Elevation the Queen withdrew into her traverse: whatever she did or did not believe, she did not believe in transubstantiation. Of the holy oil, she said, in her commonsense fashion, that it stank. However, she was indubitably and safely crowned, with proper rites.

The next event of any significance to occur in the Abbey was a formal disputation between leading Protestant and Catholic divines as to their tenets, putting their opposing cases before an audience of Lords and Commons, for whose better instruction the proceedings were in English. Instruction, however, was not the main point, but propaganda. The issues of such disputes were settled beforehand; the Edwardians now had the power and saw to it that they had the last word. The Marians may have been out-argued: they were certainly out-manoeuvred. The disputation took place on 31 March 1559: it was all part of the build-up for Parliament's restoration of the Edwardian Second Prayer Book. If Archbishop Cranmer had not been burned, he would have been restored too. The Marian hiatus was over; the Reformation resumed its drive, but more moderately under a conservative, Laodicean sovereign. For her time destruction was over, construction was possible on the basis of settled order.

The Marian episcopate could hardly turn again, though the Queen would gladly have recruited good men like Archbishop Heath and Abbot Feckenham. But these made the chief protests in the Lords against the resumed Edwardian course – though Heath had been one of Henry VIII's bishops and had accepted him as Supreme Head of the English Church. Elizabeth was content with the less demanding title of Supreme Governor in all causes ecclesiastical – and acted more like a supreme governess. Both Heath and Feckenham went briefly to the Tower, but they were not burned; in fact, Heath was allowed to retire comfortably to a house in the country. Feckenham was committed to the care of the Bishop of Winchester, and later that of Bishop Cox of Ely, who had been Feckenham's predecessor as Edwardian Dean of Westminster. When the crisis of war with Spain approached, he was removed, with other recalcitrants, to the security of Wisbech Castle, where he died in 1585, last of the long line of all those Abbots.

At Westminster the work of construction could now go forward – in the perspective of history the most important being the founding of Westminster School on a permanent institutional foundation. The Elizabethan enthusiasm for education and its purpose in training the young for service to society and state is emphasized in the Queen's commendatory letters. This famous school has always regarded Queen Elizabeth as its Foundress. The whole country continued to celebrate the relief of Elizabeth's accession on 17 November with the ringing of church-bells for more than a century after her death; to this Westminster added the ringing in of her coronation day on 15 January, and, up to the Victorian Age, a feast in the College Hall. The College Hall was in fact the former Abbot's, now taken over for the School. The monastic granary became the School Dormitory; the former monks' Dormitory was large enough to contain both the School-room, and the lower part of it the old Library, so nostalgically described by Washington Irving in his *Sketch Book*. Other monastic buildings were made use of for married prebendaries' houses – though the Queen could never bring herself to approve of a married clergy.

This is not the place for a history of Westminster School, distinguished as is its place in the English tradition – the school of Camden and Ben Jonson, Dryden and Cowper, Warren Hastings and his opponent in India, Sir Elijah Impey; for a time, in the later eighteenth century, Westminster surpassed Eton as first of English schools. But we should notice its close connection, not only physically but constitutionally, with the Abbey as a collegiate body. The Dean was the head of the whole establishment; Dean and Prebendaries occasionally dined at high table in hall like the Master and Fellows of an Oxford or Cambridge college. Sometimes the Dean took boarders in his house, and most Deans have taken some interest in the educational side of the dual body. The traditional Latin play in the Dormitory went on from Elizabeth's time to our own barbarous age, when the building was gutted by the Germans – the play now resumed in the open air. The School was closely connected by statute with those other royal foundations – Christ Church, Oxford, and Trinity College, Cambridge – to both of which it continues to enjoy special scholarships. At coronations Westminster scholars have a place of their own, to lead the acclamation of the monarch.

The personality of the Dean, thenceforth, became more important than that of most mediaeval Abbots: the Dean was in a position to leave an imprint on the institution, not only the fabric. The long reign of Dean Gabriel Goodman for forty years, 1561–1601, almost exactly coeval with Queen Elizabeth's, like hers gave opportunity to settle on a sure foundation and build constructively for the future. Dean Goodman, like his contemporary, Dean Alexander Nowell of St Paul's, was one of the best of Elizabethan clerics. Like Nowell, he was a great one for putting things into order, and it was he who put the existing establishment on its feet. He made the allocation of the remaining monastic buildings between School on one side, Dean and Prebendaries on the other. For the School, he secured the necessary 'pest-house', a sanatorium on the river at Chiswick, where the scholars could take refuge in plague-time. He ordered the services in the Abbey, which continued as he laid down right up to the later nineteenth century. Copes and vestments, rendered superfluous, were sold for the benefit of the Library.

Goodman was indeed a scholarly and bookish man, a solid support to Camden in his work. A patriotic Welshman, he hospitably entertained the translator of the Bible into Welsh, William Morgan, during Armada Year, while the latter was seeing his work through the press. The good Dean founded both a hospital and a grammar-school in his native Ruthin, besides leaving benefactions to various Cambridge colleges. He was also the virtual founder of the Corporation of Westminster, of which relics remained into the Victorian age in the twelve burgesses, bailiff and High Steward. Burghley himself held this last, then not solely honorific, office – and was very much on the spot. By no means munificent in *his* foundations – except, of course, of two great families – he left a few almshouses in Westminster and his second wife, something of a bluestocking, gave a few scholarships. Dean Goodman was buried in the chapel of St Benedict, with his impersonal predecessors, the Abbots. One sees him kneeling at his prayer-desk there, a stocky, portly figure, in full flowing gown and leg-of-mutton sleeves, with a long beard and grave profile under his skull-cap.

With the more secular inflexion of the Elizabethan age the Abbey was opened more widely to leading figures in society for burial. In St Nicholas's Chapel there is a large Renaissance monument to Lady Burghley and her unhappy daughter, the Countess of Oxford, who died in the year of the Armada, 1588, her mother the year after. Mildred Burghley was one of the four highly educated daughters of Sir Anthony Cooke, who had been a tutor of Edward VI. They all made good marriages – another to Sir Nicholas Bacon, Lord Keeper, becoming mother of Francis Bacon; a third to Lord Russell, heir of the house of Russell; the fourth to Sir Henry Killigrew, a frequent ambassador abroad. John, Lord Russell, is here too: he died before succeeding to the earldom, to the disappointment of his wife, Elizabeth Cooke; she may have been acquainted with Greek, but was otherwise a preposterous character, to anyone who knows her well. Robert Cecil's wife is here too; also his brother Thomas – the unclever elder son by Burghley's first wife, ancestor of the Exeter Cecils – and his daughter-in-law. Cecils and Russells – we already see something of the age under our eyes.

There are others, hardly less significant. These are the Norrises and, on their monument, their famous soldier sons – 'Black John' and his brothers, who all served in the wars abroad, in France, the Netherlands, Portugal, Brittany, Ireland. Lord Norris was the son of Henry Norris, who had died for Anne Boleyn: no offers would induce him to confess that the Queen was guilty. Elizabeth rewarded his family with her love. There is a magnificent monument to Sir Francis Vere, perhaps the most professional and consistently successful commander in the field: based on the famous monument at Breda, it displays four knights kneeling on one knee, supporting a marble slab on which are the arms and accoutrements of the warrior. The fighting Bingham is here too: 'To the glory of the Lord of Hosts, here resteth Sir Richard Bingham, knight, who fought not only in Scotland and Ireland but in the Isle of Candy (Crete) under the Venetians, at Cabo Chrio and the famous battle of Lepanto against the Turks; in the civil wars of France; in the Netherlands, and at Smerwick where the Romans and Irish were vanquished.'

No less appropriately, the Elizabethans began the burial of the poets in the South Transept, which in course of time formed the popular 'Poets' Corner'. The burial of Edmund Spenser, in 1599, formed a precedent, followed by the longer-lived Michael Drayton and Ben Jonson. The last two lived quieter lives, but Spenser was worn out by his experiences in Ireland when he died at only forty-six. He had, however, already written *The Faerie Queene* and was recognized by all as the great poet of the age, of which that work is both mirror and fantasy. Other poets attended his funeral, and threw the elegies they had written, with their quills, into his grave – a characteristic flourish by way of tribute. He was placed close to Chaucer, with Francis Beaumont still nearer, though there was no money to give him a memorial. A little later a monument by the best of Caroline sculptors, Nicholas Stone, was put up by Anne Clifford, Countess of Dorset, Pembroke and Montgomery, who had a fine care for the past. And a Caroline poet wrote:

> Renownèd Spenser, lie a thought more nigh
> To learnèd Chaucer; and, rare Beaumont, lie
> A little nearer Spenser, to make room
> For Shakespeare in your threefold fourfold tomb.

But the Elizabethans did not think that the first of their dramatists was their first poet: to them, that honour went to Spenser, while Drayton was the laureate. Anne Clifford put up the bust to him, too, as she also did that to Samuel Daniel in the church of beautiful Beckington in Somerset. Six years later there followed Ben Jonson, whose life had so many associations with Westminster, as a schoolboy, through his friendship with Camden and Sir Robert Cotton, and his occupancy of a house in the precincts. All remember the simplicity, and sufficiency, of the inscription:

> O rare Ben Johnson!*

Meanwhile the best known poem on the Abbey had been written by Beaumont:

> Mortality, behold and fear!
> What a change of flesh is here:
> Think how many royal bones
> Sleep within these heaps of stones.
> Here they lie, had realms and lands,
> Who now want strength to stir their hands . . .
> Here's an acre, sown indeed
> With the richest, royalest seed . . .
> Here's a world of pomp and state
> Buried in dust, once dead by fate.

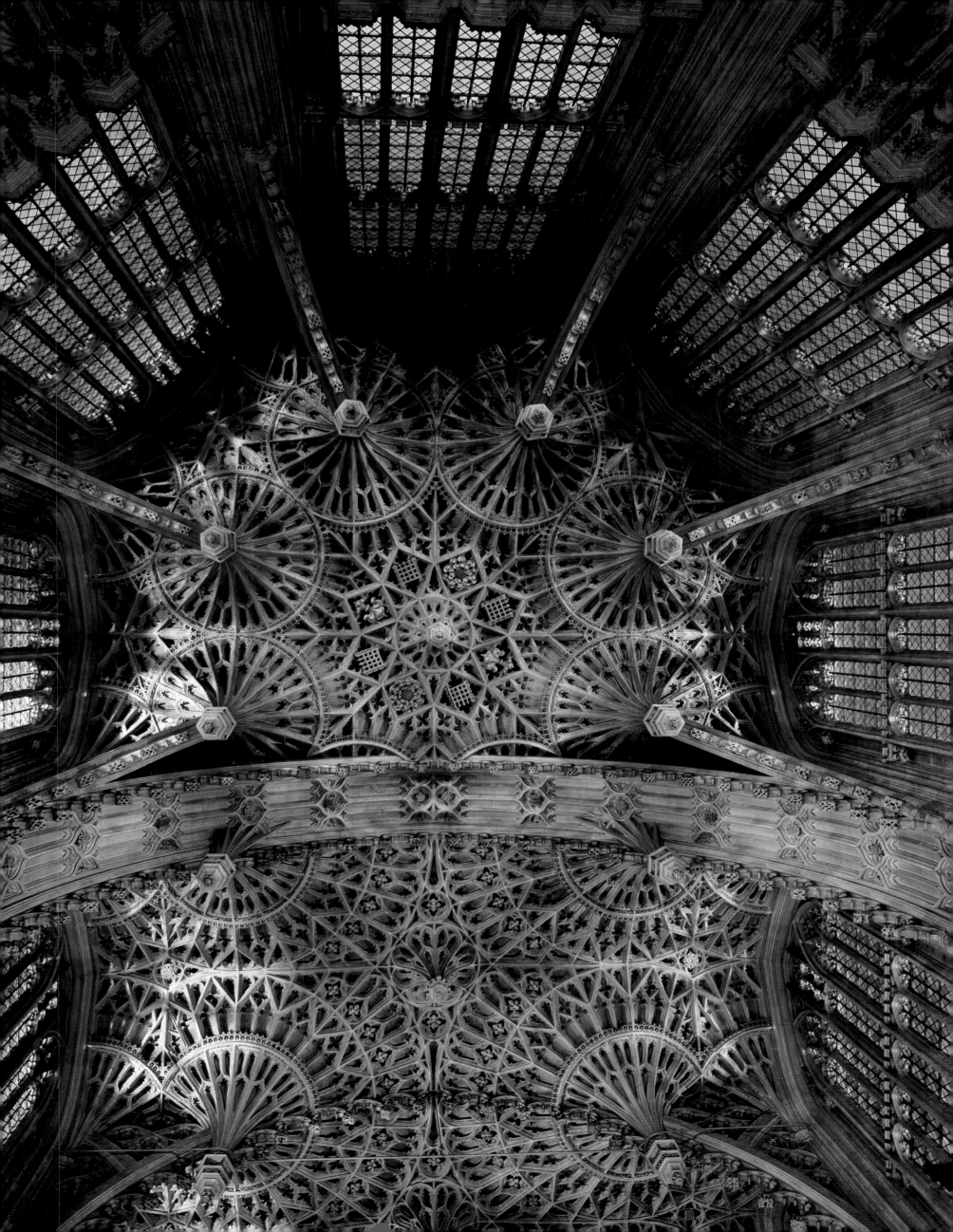

The royal tombs at Westminster were already one of the sights of the capital which foreigners went to see. Dean Goodman, in his care for everything, had provided a keeper of the monuments. Donne describes him:

'At Westminster',
Said I, 'the man that keeps the Abbey tombs
And, for his price, doth with whoever comes
Of all our Harrys and our Edwards talk,
From king to king and all their kin can walk.
Your ears shall hear nought but kings; your eyes meet
Kings only: the way to it is King's Street'.

When Henri IV's companion at arms, Marshal Biron, came over with his suite in 1601, Sir Walter Ralegh took them to see the monuments – though they seem to have enjoyed the Bear Garden more.

Elizabeth I's long reign came to an end, 24 March 1603. A numbness descended on the capital – many people could remember no other ruler, and regarded the future with apprehension. She was buried a month later. When people saw her life-like effigy borne through the streets of Westminster where they had often seen her in life – on her way in state to Parliament or to the Abbey, or coming back to Whitehall from progress – now stiff on her hearse, in the familiar robes, with crown and sceptre, they burst into a tempest of weeping. 'The like has not been known in the memory of man.' Ralegh was present as Captain of the Guard – his last service to her – and shortly to make his memorable acquaintance with the Gatehouse at Westminster.

Elizabeth's coffin was taken to her grandfather's Chapel where she rests in the same vault as her sister – no one had wished to rekindle her memory. Robert Cecil was determined that his sovereign mistress should not go uncommemorated, in spite of the shortage in the Exchequer from her successor's extravagance. Rather than fail in his duty, 'neither the Exchequer nor London shall have a penny left'. A grand monument was erected, designed by Maximilian Colt, a very recognizable portrait figure upon it: the great ruff open to display the bare breast of a virgin, necklace and ear-drops of pearls and jewelled pendant, the tight slender stomacher, hands clasping orb and sceptre. We see again the very Welsh face, with the narrow forehead and high cheek-bones, the sharp determined oval and hawk nose, the reminder of Henry VII and the Valois.

There is no representation of Mary Tudor on the monument; she shares merely in the inscription, not without its irony to those who appreciate all that had gone before: '*Regno consortes et urna, hic obdormimus Elizabetha et Maria sorores, in spe resurrectionis.*' ('Here sleep Elizabeth and Mary, sisters, in hope of resurrection'.)

Not to be outdone, James had his mother, Mary Queen of Scots, translated here from Peterborough, in 1612, after Robert Cecil's death, and an even larger monument erected over her. With an elaborate epitaph recounting her virtues, it was placed in a balancing position in the opposite aisle of her great-grandfather's Chapel, next to the tomb of Darnley's parents. Her portrait, too, is from the life, with its Guise and Valois likeness, reminding one of the ambivalent Henri III.

Owing to the troubles that befell the Stuarts in the ensuing century, and other circumstances, the series of royal tombs in the Abbey concluded with these, as poignant as any in the memories they carry.

The monuments to two daughters of James I, who both died young: Princess Sophia, who died in 1606, and Princess Mary, who died in 1607. These were executed by Maximilian Colt.

The Stuarts: Civil War, Revolution and Restoration

In THE EXCITEMENT, conflicts and disturbances, revolutions and reactions of the seventeenth century, Westminster Abbey is more closely connected with national events than ever before and offers a still more precise mirror.

James I's coronation took place on 25 July 1603: though it was the first to be conducted in English, it followed the old ritual. The famous scholar, Lancelot Andrewes, in whose custody as Dean the regalia were kept, performed the part of the former Abbots in the anointing. The procession was omitted, for the plague was at its height; even so, the ceremonies offered a grave risk. Andrewes was an exemplary Dean, who took a special interest in the School, charging 'all masters that they should give lessons out of none but the most classical authors'.

A new generation brought with it a movement for liturgical reform, a better ordering of services, the return of the altar to its proper place. Laud was the leader of this movement and drove it forward both at Oxford and at Westminster, when he became a prebendary there. It played an increasing part in the storm that was gathering between King and Church on one side, and Parliament, particularly the Commons, on the other. In the course of this the Commons transferred their attendance from the Abbey, 'for fear of copes and wafer cakes', to St Margaret's which henceforth became their church. Another dispute flared up over the Commons' insistence that the Calvinistic Usher should preach in the Abbey.

To this there was added an unedifying squabble between Laud and the Welsh Dean Williams, which grew into a rivalry that helped to split the Church. Williams was as magnificent as he was musical, as extravagant as he was pluralistic (Laud had no music in his soul). Williams' sympathies were Protestant and Parliamentarian, and he was popular. Made Bishop of Lincoln, he refused to give up the Deanery, which, it was said, King James designed for Laud. The King was certainly right (as he was over Donne for St Paul's) in wishing to confine Laud to a deanery, where he could cause less trouble than as a bishop. Laud was Buckingham's confessor and had the confidence of Charles I, from whose coronation he managed to exclude Williams and himself took the place of the Dean in the anointing. Charles I's coronation in 1626 was remembered for the ill omens subsequently remarked on: the refusal of Henrietta Maria, as a Catholic, to attend; the King clad all in white like a sacrificial victim; the sermon preached on a text for martyrdom by a maladroit bishop.

Williams, with all his promotions and benefices, could live on a splendid scale and was a generous soul. He set up a fine Library, still one of the Abbey's best possessions; he provided for four more scholars on the foundation, with a couple of fellowships for them at Cambridge. With the Welsh gift for music – he had a fine tenor voice – he promoted the choir-services, where one of the greatest of English composers, Orlando Gibbons, was organist 1623–5. (He was only forty when he died.)

Other secular occurrences foreshadowed the clash that was to come: notably Sir Walter Ralegh's execution in 1618 outside the Gatehouse, where he had been confined. He turned his last public appearance into a dramatic demonstration against Stuart rule – it is said that both Sir John Eliot and John Pym were in the crowd that saw him die. The great Parliamentary leader Pym one day took an almighty revenge for the death of his fellow Westcountryman. Ralegh was attended the night before his execution and on the scaffold by Dean Townson, who considered that Ralegh was playing a part – as indeed he was. Sir John Eliot wrote of it: 'Our Ralegh gave an example of fortitude such as history could scarcely parallel.' When asked if he wished to be buried facing the east, he replied, with conscious effect: 'So the heart be right, it is no matter which way the head lieth.' His words reverberated far and wide among the growing opposition to the Stuarts.

Williams' prolonged duel with Laud – the Deanery versus Lambeth across the water – reflected the struggle within the Church at large. Nevertheless Williams' popularity with the opposition did not save him from being roughly manhandled by the London apprentices on 27 December 1641, in the thick of the crisis between King and Commons. Next day the apprentices – who were used by Parliamentary leaders to bring pressure on Charles – attacked the Abbey in force. It was manfully defended from within: no doubt it was one of the scholars who aimed a tile from the battlements with such effect that it killed the leader of the onset, Sir Richard Wiseman. The populace gave him as good a funeral 'as if he had deserved well of his country'.

At the centre of the storm the Abbey was bound to suffer with the Puritan victory in the Civil War. All Laud's good work was undone; all who cared for things of beauty, works of art, music, the works of men's hands – often so much more worth-while than what they think – were bound to grieve at what followed: the abomination of desolation. In 1644 a Parliamentary Committee under the Puritan Sir Robert Harley – grandfather of Queen Anne's Lord Treasurer – ordered the destruction of Torrigiano's altar-piece in Henry VII's Chapel and the razing out of the painted images in the windows. In the Sanctuary the High Altar was destroyed, the exquisite mediaeval pavement mutilated. The thirteenth-century tapestries around the Choir disappeared. Copes were torn up, their gold and silver melted down for the benefit of 'the poor Irish', i.e. Irish Protestants.

Next it was the turn of the regalia: the Chapel of the Pyx was broken into, the bad poet Withers dressed up with crown and sceptre and paraded around the Abbey. Subsequently the regalia – crown, orb, sceptre and all – was destroyed. Companies of soldiers quartered in the Church made hay of the place, capering round in surplices, burning the altar-rails, smashing the organs. Puritans hated the divine music of the Church – Tallis and Byrd, Weelkes and Orlando Gibbons; they particularly hated the subtle art of antiphony, 'tossing the ball from one side to the other', they called it, 'nothing but roaring boys and squeaking organ pipes, and the cathedral catches of Morley, and I know not what trash'. What Philistines they were! The choir, with its age-long rendering of the services, was dispersed, the traditional music-books scattered or destroyed; paintings defaced, statues taken down (though there were so many that even the maniac energy of iconoclasts flagged). All lay waste: the Church was ready to be cluttered up with pews turned towards a high pulpit from which nothing but the Word was to be preached.

Over this, however, there was some disagreement. Laud's views may not have been popular, but neither were those of the Puritans who pushed him into the Tower and eventually made a martyr of him – to the ultimate benefit of the restored Church. In 1649, when the King was executed before his own Whitehall, a guard of musketeers had to be posted in the Abbey during sermon-time 'to keep the people from making disturbance'. And though the Archbishop's blood was shed to ratify the Covenant with the Presbyterian Scots, this could never be successfully imposed upon the English people. The attempt, indeed, led to a split within the victorious ranks of Parliament, and ultimately to the unexpected turn of a military dictatorship under one of the greatest of Englishmen, Oliver Cromwell, defended by one of the greatest of poets, John Milton.

Meanwhile, something very important in the history of Presbyterianism in English-speaking countries, particularly overseas, was taking place in the Abbey. A body of Puritan ministers representing the minority within the Church, aided by a small but influential number of commissioners from Scotland, was to draw up a Confession and Directory for Public Worship to take the place of the Prayer Book. The real purpose of Parliament in calling the Westminster Assembly into being was to underwrite its political plea for aid from the Scots. This was the price it had to pay – the imposition of the Scottish Covenant upon England – and the Scots members expected to call the tune. It did not, however, quite work out that way.

The first of over a thousand sessions took place in Henry VII's Chapel, on 1 July 1643; thereafter it met every day of the week except – with Puritan Sabbatarianism – on Saturdays. Of some one hundred and fifty members, only one half attended regularly; when the weather grew cold they met in Jerusalem Chamber, which was 'all well hung and has a good fire, which is some dainty at London' – thus the Scot, Baillie. Seven powerful preachers had been appointed to the Abbey, and Baillie gives us some idea of their Sabbath exercises. Mr Marshall prayed 'two large hours'. Then Mr Arrowsmith preached an hour, followed by a psalm. Thereafter Mr Vines prayed near two hours, and Mr Palmer preached an hour. Mr Seaman prayed near two hours, then a psalm. After that Mr Henderson preached; Dr Twisse closed, as he had begun, with a short prayer; 'thus spending', Baillie said, 'nine to five very graciously'. It must have offered some contrast with the ordered beauty of the Anglican liturgy, the haunting music with its echoes of the ages, the intimations of eternity.

The Assembly had no difficulty in completely Calvinizing the Thirty-Nine Articles, which were more than half way there already, and it urged on the poor Archbishop's trial and execution. By Act of Parliament in January 1645, England was supposedly Presbyterianized. The Assembly had hammered out in debate its Confession of Faith, with the Larger and Shorter Catechisms, but it could never get its Directory of Public Worship, still less the Presbyterian Discipline, imposed upon the nation. Parliament took the line that the Assembly's rôle was simply advisory and that it had no authority apart from Parliament. The Divines wanted to impose the Discipline, excommunication and all; but the English had not escaped the braces of the bishops for the straitjacket of a presbytery.

Meanwhile, outside the Assembly, the issue was being decided – as usual in history – by the facts of power. With the victories of Cromwell and the New Model Army, power was passing to the Independents. Baillie groaned in spirit at the multiplication of the sects, the leaning to 'Anabaptism and Antinomianism: sundry also to worse, if worse needs be – the mortality of the soul, the denial of angels and devils; and cast off all sacraments, and many blasphemous things. All these are from New England.' This was one for Roger Williams, of Connecticut, with his ideas of toleration – the Assembly loathed the thought of toleration.

But such revolting ideas were expressed in their midst, especially by the greatest living scholar, John Selden, a Parliamentarian, but also an Erastian and a sceptic, who saw through both sides and tormented the Presbyterian majority not only by his scholarship but by his sense of humour. He would sometimes deflate their theological absurdities by bringing them up against the real meaning of the Hebrew of the Old Testament, or the Greek of the New. Over an inconclusive dispute as to the distance between Jerusalem and Jericho, eventually decided in favour of the shorter distance because fish was brought to Jerusalem from Jericho, he upset the calculations of the Divines with the question – what if the fish were salted?

Once Cromwell had won the war for them, Parliament was free for a showdown with the Assembly: they were publicly rebuked for stirring up dissension in the City, and told that they had no authority to interpret the Covenant, nor was their opinion required on matters decided by Parliament. Selden rubbed salt in the wound with a series of scholarly inquiries whether elderships and the whole Presbyterian paraphernalia were *jure divino* any more than bishops and by the direct appointment of Christ – if so, they should furnish Scripture proofs. John Milton, incensed by their self-righteous inhibition of freedom of thought, their strictures upon divorce, their hatred of toleration, lashed them with the most contemptuous of his public poems:

> Because you have thrown off your prelate Lord,
> And with stiff vows renounced his liturgy
> To seize the widowed whore, Plurality,
> From them whose sin ye envied, not abhorred:
> Dare ye for this adjure the civil sword
> To force our consciences that Christ set free,
> And ride us with a classic hierarchy
> Taught ye by mere A. S. and Rutherford?...
> By shallow Edwards and Scotch what d'ye call.

And so on to the uncompromising conclusion:

> *New Presbyter* is but *Old Priest* writ large.

Baillie, disillusioned at length, concluded that the English leaders inclined to 'liberty for all religions, to have but a lame Erastian Presbytery', and that the Scots, having served their turn against the King, could now go home. They could, and did – expressing the view that 'the humour of this people is very various and inclinable to singularities, to differ from all the world [i.e. Scotch Presbyterians], and from one another, and shortly from themselves: no people had so much need of a Presbytery, [i.e. the Discipline]'. But Oliver Cromwell had more sense than to attempt to impose it: he knew that the English people would never stand for it. Only the theology of Calvinism was accepted by the victorious minority: the essence of Presbyterianism, the Discipline, was never sanctioned by Parliament, and the new rulers kept Church-government in their own hands. The Assembly, like old soldiers, just faded away.

Yet the Divines had their reward – doubly so. For one thing, they got the preferments from which the Royalist clergy had been driven. At Cambridge alone one hundred and fifty Masters and Fellows of colleges – at Oxford more – were ejected to make way for Puritans. Many of these became pluralists, as Milton unkindly pointed out, like their Anglican predecessors against whom they had created such a relentless propaganda. No wonder Milton was driven to reflect, to what point had been

> ...all this waste of wealth and loss of blood:

he did not mention the destruction of works of art, the poor inoffensive objects of beauty.

Their second achievement was more lasting. Though they failed to impose their form of worship upon England, the Westminster Confession, the Cathechisms and Directory that emerged from their deliberations 'have had the greatest influence on Presbyterian development in the English-speaking world'. They are 'recognized and venerated standards in all the lands where British Presbyterianism has taken root, especially in the United States. The Directory of Public Worship has shaped ... the ritual and atmosphere of Protestant Anglo-Saxon worshippers throughout the world' – with the exception of the Methodists, who sprang out of the Anglican Church and were more affected by the Prayer Book.

All over the English-speaking world one finds that Westminster has given its name to scores, if not hundreds, of Presbyterian institutions and colleges. It is one of the ironies as well as proprieties of history that this should be so.

The Abbey reflected the history of the times in other ways too. When the Parliamentarian leader, John Pym, died, he was given a state funeral and his grave was much visited during the Commonwealth. Members of Cromwell's family were buried there, his favourite daughter Elizabeth, and his able son-in-law, Ireton. The Protector himself paid for the funeral of the scholarly Archbishop Usher and allowed the Prayer Book service for the occasion – it was typical of Cromwell's greatness of spirit. A conscious inheritor of the Elizabethan Age, he had Robert Blake buried there as a deliberate incentive to heroic achievement. We have seen that the Stone of Scone was carried across to Westminster Hall for the Lord Protector's installation, and at his death he was given a regal funeral in the Abbey. It was a pity that, at the Restoration, the bodies of these very great men were disinterred – we could dispense with Judge Bradshaw, who presided over Charles I's trial and whose ghost, Westminster boys said, haunted the gallery next his chamber in the South-West Tower. Meanwhile, the famous Headmaster, Dr Busby, presided over *them*, from 1638 to 1695, through all the changes and vicissitudes of the time.

The excitements of the Restoration and succeeding years we can follow through the amused, and amusing, eyes of Pepys, or the sedate pen of John Evelyn. Charles II returned to his patrimony in the glad Maytime of 1660. On 1 July Mr Pepys went to afternoon service at the Abbey, 'where a good sermon by a stranger, but no Common Prayer yet'. On the Lord's Day, 23 September, we find him laughing at a Puritan preacher there who desired that God 'would imprint his word on the thumbs of our right hands and on the right great toes of our right feet'. In the midst of this enlightening sermon 'some plaster fell from the top of the Abbey, that made me and all the rest in our pew afeared, and I wished myself out'. Evidently the place was much in need of repair. Pepys had seen 'poor Bishop Wren' make his appearance after eighteen years' imprisonment in the Tower – it was his famous nephew, Sir Christopher, who would eventually repair the fabric. In between, Mr Pepys was surprised to discover his Lord, Edward Montagu of that leading Puritan family – a Cromwellian, later to serve Charles II as Earl of Sandwich – 'plainly to be a sceptic in all things of religion, and to make no great matter of anything therein, but to be a perfect Stoic'. In October Pepys went to see the consecration of several new bishops in Henry VII's Chapel. 'But,

Lord! at their going out, how people did look upon them as strange creatures, and few with any kind of love and respect.' Nor did the restored Prayer Book at first appeal to him – his background, we are apt to forget, was Puritan. '7th October, Lord's day. After dinner to the Abbey, where I heard them read the church-service, but very ridiculously, that indeed I do not in myself like it at all.' Curiosity, however, prevailed and later that month there was such a crowd for the consecrating of five more bishops that, though Pepys went round by the Cloisters, he could not get into Henry VII's Chapel. The music completed his conquest: when the organs were restored at the end of the year, there was 'great confusion of people that come there to hear the organs'.

Meanwhile, John Evelyn's 'dear friend' Dr Earles was made Dean of Westminster, and when he received the sacrament, 'the service was also in the old Cathedral music'. When Evelyn communicated at Westminster, he usually dined afterwards with the Dean – he was friends with each of them, Earles, Dolben, and Sprat. In May 1661 he was present at the election of Westminster scholars to Oxford and Cambridge, who 'in themes and extemporary verses as wonderfully astonished me in such young striplings, with that readiness and wit, some of them not above twelve or thirteen years of age'. Good for Dr Busby! But Evelyn, who had spent some years of the Inter-regnum abroad, deplored the old English way of pronouncing Latin 'so that, out of England, no nation were able to understand or endure it'.

This was not Mr Pepys' line of interest, though in December 1661 he sang the service in the Choir, and later went to see the tombs 'with great pleasure' – things were settling down; the Abbey, like Paul's Walk, was a regular meeting place, and Pepys sometimes went there to walk up and down before the sermon, to exchange gossip – or wait for an assignation he had made with a girl. One Lord's Day in September 1664, he 'there wearily walked, expecting her till 6 o'clock from three, but no Jane came, which vexed me'. However, he spent some of the time usefully walking with the musician Blagrave, a gentleman of the Chapel Royal, who explained 'the caution now used against admitting any debauched persons, which I was glad to hear, though he tells me there are persons bad enough'. Next Sunday Mr Pepys spent the whole afternoon in the Cloisters waiting in vain for Jane, and was vexed again. In January, 'I spent the whole afternoon walking into the church and Abbey, and up and down, but could not find her': he was forced to take a coach home to discourse with his wife. And so a fortnight later; he heard a good anthem well sung, but no Jane: 'so being defeated, away by coach home, and there spent the evening prettily in discourse with my wife and Mercer, and so to supper, prayers, and to bed.'

However, we owe to Pepys our finest account of Charles II's coronation, celebrated with exceptional magnificence, to make up for the bleak years. Clarendon took care that everything was done in accordance with tradition, in order 'to discredit and discountenance the novelties with which the kingdom had been so much intoxicated for so many years together'. Since the ancient regalia had been destroyed, new was made – and this constitutes most of the regalia of today. Out came cloth-of-gold copes again among the bishops, the peers in their Parliament robes, 'which was a most magnificent sight'. Mr Pepy's sceptical Lord, now an Earl, carried the sceptre; General Monk, to whom the Restoration was due, now promoted Duke, preceded the King – who had greeted him affectingly as 'Father' on entering upon his kingdom; the King 'in his robes, bare-headed, which was very fine'. Mr Pepys had risen at four, and 'with much ado did get up into a great scaffold across the north end [transept] of the

Abbey, where with a great deal of patience I sat from past 4 till 11 before the King came in'. From his position he could not see the crowning and anointing, however much he craned: the devout Evelyn describes that for us, performed as it was by Archbishop Juxon, now old and infirm, who had attended Charles I upon his scaffold. What memories it must have aroused for all who took part!

The Abbey became more than ever a burial-place for servants of the state – perhaps the Commonwealth had led the way in that. In a few years Monk and Edward Montagu, Pepys's patron, were laid together in the same vault – the armour that was carried at Monk's funeral still survives, and on the occasion a still more historic figure made his first public appearance: young Ensign Churchill, to become Duke of Marlborough, who at the Revolution of 1688 sought to play Monk's rôle of 1660. One day Evelyn heard a fine sermon from one of Henrietta Maria's Capuchin chaplains, become a convert – so that the traffic was not all one way. Another time Evelyn heard the famous preacher, Dr South, who had much amused the Merry Monarch with a description of Oliver Cromwell, 'entering the Parliament House with a threadbare torn cloak and greasy hat, and perhaps neither of them paid for'. 'Odds fish, Lory', Charles said to Rochester, 'your chaplain must be a bishop: put me in mind of him at the next death'. The King it was who died, and was buried in Henry VII's Chapel, where several of his numerous illegitimate children had preceded him.

James II's coronation was considerably truncated, because he did not wish to communicate with the Church of which he was the Supreme Governor. A King of England who drew the line at the Church of which he was the legal head was not long for the job – his intelligent brother had given him just three years on the throne before he was off it. James's sullenness at his coronation was observed, by contrast with his Catholic Queen who responded to the rites devoutly. A curious thing happened at the ceremony. A piece of scaffolding broke open the Confessor's coffin, and from it were extracted his gold cross and chain. These were handed to James, who venerated them as relics; they did not save him, however – nothing could: they were still in the possession of the Stuarts in exile in 1715.

James built himself a fine Catholic chapel at Whitehall for his devotions, designed by Wren. After the collapse of his régime and the Revolution of 1688, the splendid altar-piece, shorn of its more Baroque devotional features, was re-erected in the Abbey. This was one of the few churches in the country where James's Declaration of Indulgence – promoting toleration with special intention on behalf of Catholics – was read, by the accommodating Bishop Sprat (for the Deanery was now held along with the bishopric of Rochester), the admired historian of the early Royal Society. One way and another, James filled the cup of the nation's grievances against him – he was as obstinate as he was foolish, as kings go; and, as they sometimes go, he went.

In April 1689 Evelyn watched the processions to and from the Abbey of James's daughter and son-in-law, Mary and William, who were taking his place. Something was altered in the Coronation Oath to make more specific the monarchs' duty to maintain the Protestant religion. The Whig Bishop Burnet, who had begun as a Scotch Presbyterian, preached 'with infinite applause'; but Archbishop Sancroft, one of the seven bishops who had refused to sanction James's Declaration of Indulgence, excused himself from crowning William and Mary. Here was a pointer to party-conflicts to come – the Non-Jurors against a Whiggish episcopate, High

D. O. M.

GABRIEL GOODMAN SACRÆ THEOLOGIÆ
DOCTOR, DECANVS HVIVS ECCLESIÆ
QVINTVS, CVI CVM SVMMA LAVDE XL ANOS
PRÆFVISSET, ET RVTHINIÆ IN COMITATV
DENBIGHÆNSI VBI NATVS HOSPITALE FVN
DASSET, SCHOLÂQ INSTITVISSET, VITÆ SANC
TIMONIA DEO BONISQ CHARVS IN COELESTĒ
PATRIAM PIE EMIGRAVIT XVII IVNII ANNO
SALVTIS. M D C I. ÆT. SVÆ LXXIII.

The monument to Gabriel
Goodman, who was Dean of
Westminster for forty years
from 1561 to 1601. During his
term of office, Westminster
School was founded; as Dean,
he was the head of the whole
establishment.

The funeral cortège of
Elizabeth I, an illustration from
William Camden. Her funeral
took place cn 28 April, 1603.
This illustration shows the
chariot with the life-size effigy
lying upon the draped coffin
under a black canopy carried
by six knights. The other

Right: The Abbey and Palace of Westminster in *c.* 1555, showing William Rufus's Great Hall on the left, Palace Yard in the centre, and the beginning of Henry VIII's palace of Whitehall on the right. Behind the Abbey are open fields. This illustration is based upon the drawings of a Flemish artist, Anthony van Wyngaerde, who visited London during the reign of Mary Tudor.

Below: The Great Hall of Westminster, where the coronation banquets were held, and other buildings of the Old Palace of Westminster, with the Abbey showing above their roofs. This engraving was made by Wenceslaus Hollar in the early part of the seventeenth century.

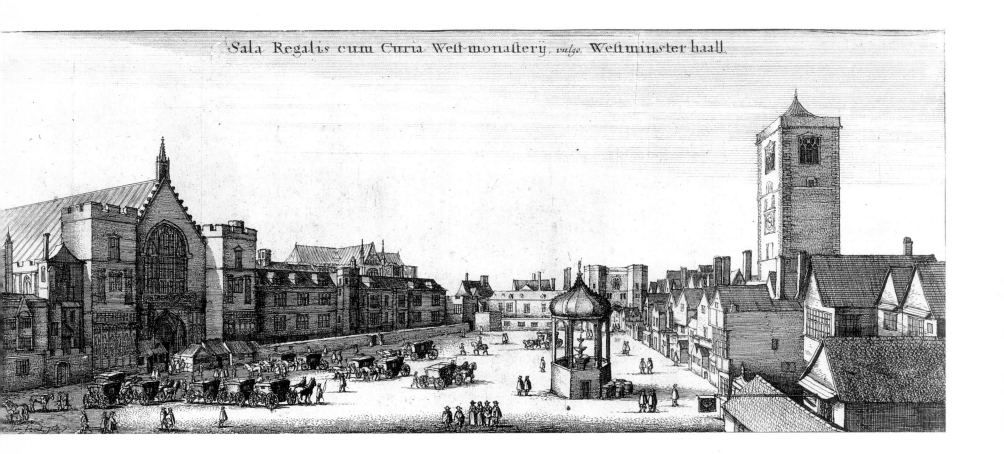

Sala Regalis cum Curia West-monastery, *vulgo,* Westminster haall

The True Emblem of Antichrift: Or,
SCHISM Diſplay'd.

In all its various Colours of Confuſions and Diſſentions, both in *Church* and *State*, Horrid Blaſphemies, Antichriſtian Hereſies, Bloody and Unnatural Rebellions, and utter Subverſions of all Method, Peace, Order and Proſperity in a Chriſtian Kingdom.

O. CROMWELL, the *Fanaticks* and their *Vices* — Chief Head of the Supported by DEVILS.

The coronation procession of
Charles II, which was the last to
be made from the Tower. In the
second row rides the King's
brother, James Duke of York –
later James II – and in the
bottom row the King
surrounded by his Gentlemen
Pensioners. Behind the King
can be seen General Monk,
created Duke of Albemarle at
the coronation.

The coronation of Charles II,
which took place on St
George's Day, 1661.

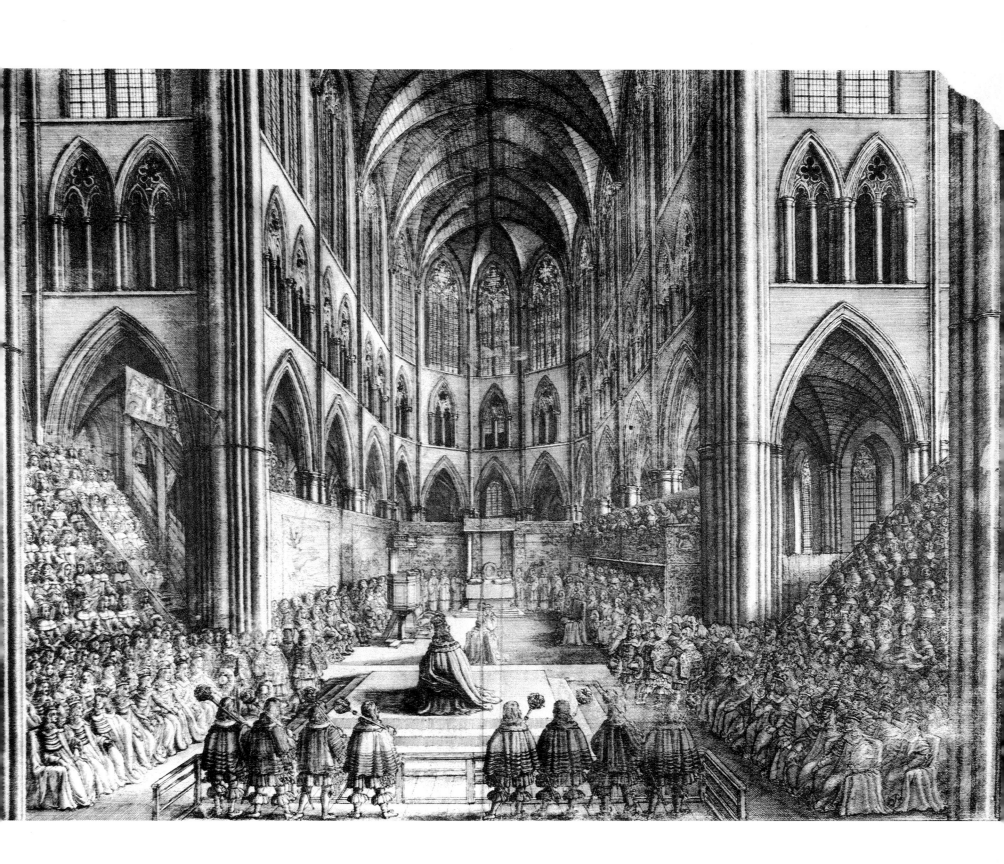

Wax effigy of Charles II, now in the Abbey Undercroft, which is contemporary and a remarkable likeness. The modelling is very fine, and one contemporary wrote 'tis to ye life, and truly to admiration'.

Above: The coronation of James II, on 23 April 1685. His Queen, Mary of Modena, is seated to the left.

Left: The Baroque altarpiece designed by Wren. Originally placed in James II's Catholic Chapel at Whitehall, during the reign of his daughter Anne, the altarpiece was divested of its Catholic features and re-erected in the Abbey.

Dr Richard Busby, the
headmaster of Westminster
School from 1640 till his death
in 1695. His rigid discipline
was legendary. He is now
buried in the Abbey beneath
the black and white pavement
which he presented to the
Choir.

The Great Hall or 'School' at
Westminster, from a lithograph
of about 1845. The hall was
originally the monks'
dormitory and had a fine
hammerbeam roof which was
destroyed by incendiary bombs
in 1941. The names painted all
over the walls – clearly visible
in this picture – were also
destroyed at the same time.
The room is divided by an iron
bar from which used to hang a
curtain to separate the upper
from lower school.

Francis Atterbury, Dean of Westminster and Bishop of Rochester, from a painting by Kneller. He was a King's Scholar at Westminster under Dr Busby. Following the Jacobite Rebellion of 1715 he was sent to the Tower charged with conspiracy to place the Old Pretender on the throne, was deprived of his office and exiled in 1723. He died in Paris nine years later, but his body was returned to his beloved Abbey.

G. Kneller Eq. Bar.t Pinx.

M.r d.r Gucht Sculp.

The R.t Reverend Father in God
FRANCIS *LORD BISHOP OF* ROCHESTER
and DEAN *of* Westminster.

Dart's engraving of the
monument to Admiral George
Churchill, a brother of the
Duke of Marlborough. In
charge of the Admiralty in
Marlborough's war,
he died in 1710.

John Churchill, 1st Duke of
Marlborough, died in 1722 and
was buried in the Duke of
Ormond's vault at the east end
of Henry VII's Chapel. This
illustration shows the order
drawn up by the Duke of
Newcastle to open the vault.
Marlborough's remains were
later transferred to the
mausoleum in the chapel of
Blenheim Palace.

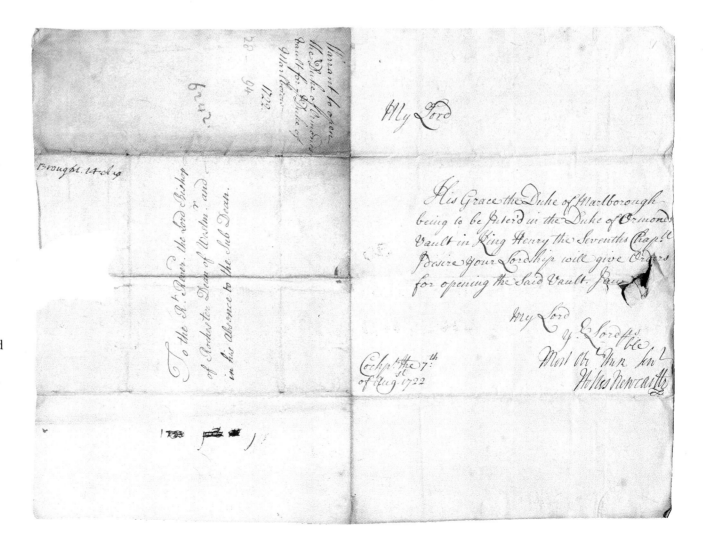

In 1723, John Dart's
*Westmonasterium or the History
and Antiquities of the Abbey
Church* was published. Dart had
been encouraged in his
venture by Dean Atterbury,
though the Dean was by then
in disgrace and exile.
Above: The monument to John
Dryden, Poet Laureate under
Charles II and James II, who
had been educated at
Westminster under Busby. He
was buried on 13 May 1700
near Chaucer's tomb. The
monument was erected in 1720
by Dryden's friend John
Sheffield, Duke of Buckingham.
Dart shows it in its original
state before later alterations.
Above right: Dart's engraving of
the eastern end of the North
Aisle to Henry VII's Chapel,
called 'Innocents' Corner' by
Dean Stanley. Behind, set in
the wall, is the sarcophagus
containing the bones of the
Princes murdered in the Tower.
The urn was designed by Sir
Christopher Wren.

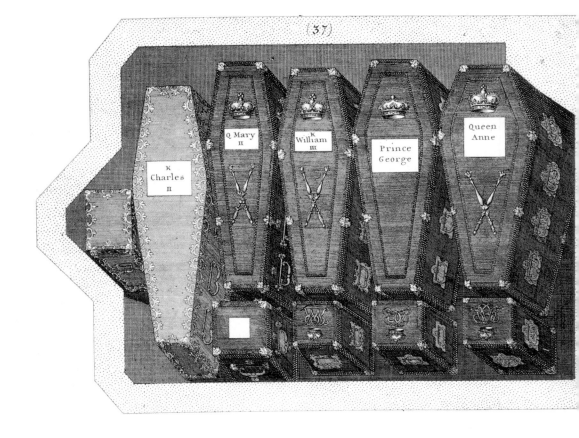

The Elizabethans began to bury their poets in the South Transept, which came to be known as 'Poets' Corner'. Edmund Spenser was the first to be buried here in 1599, followed by Michael Drayton and Ben Jonson.

Right: Dart's engraving of the monument to Ben Jonson, dramatist and poet, who was educated at Westminster School under Camden, the antiquarian, and died in a house which stood between the Abbey and St Margaret's Church. The monument was designed by Gibbs, executed by Rysbrack and presented by the Earl of Oxford in the early eighteenth century.

Lower right: Dart's engraving of the wall monument to Michael Drayton, Poet Laureate. The monument, with a bust by Edward Marshall, was presented by Anne Clifford, Countess of Dorset, Pembroke and Montgomery. The epitaph has been attributed to Ben Jonson.

O RARE BEN: JOHNSON.

Left: Engraving of the royal vault, which lies beneath Henry VII's Chapel, and contains the coffins of Charles II, William and Mary, Queen Anne and her consort Prince George of Denmark.

Wax effigy of William Pitt,
Earl of Chatham, who died in
1778. The effigy was modelled
from life by an American, Mrs
Patience Wright. Pitt is shown
dressed in his Parliamentary
robes.

Church against Low Church, Jacobitism against the Hanoverian Succession. It is said that at the coronation, Princess Anne standing by her sister, the Queen, said 'Madam, I pity your fatigue.' Upon which the Queen rejoined, 'A crown, sister, is not so heavy as it seems.' There was not much love lost between the two sisters; however, Anne's turn was to come.

Hanoverians and Victorians

THE REVOLUTION of 1688 settled the constitution and form of government that had so agitated the seventeenth century and caused Continentals to think of the English as the most mercurial and changeable of peoples. With limited constitutional monarchy, Parliamentary and representative institutions – the governing classes could go forward on an even keel to the immense expansion overseas, the wars for trade and empire, the growth of commercial and industrial prosperity, security and peace at home. Stolid complacency set in. The Abbey reflects it all: the burial (or monuments) of heroes on land, or at sea – Nelson's 'Westminster Abbey, or Victory', before Cape St Vincent; or on the eve of the Battle of the Nile, 'Before this time to-morrow I shall have gained a peerage, or Westminster Abbey' – it was very present in his mind. Coronations are amusing, like those of George IV or Queen Victoria, instead of ominous, like Charles I's; even funerals can be comic, like that of George II, as described by Horace Walpole. Instead of smashing the organs, we have the Handel Festival, with the Hanoverian King on his feet with enthusiasm for the Hallelujah Chorus – setting a nice precedent still adhered to all over the English-speaking world. There is something genial about the Augustan and Victorian Ages – family spirit prevails after so much dissension.

But before this desired consummation and quiet set in there took place a famous episode in the annals of the Abbey – the condemnation and exile of its Dean, Bishop Atterbury, for high treason – which reflects an afterglow of the more combustible conflicts of the previous century. Francis Atterbury was appointed Dean in 1713 (with the bishopric of Rochester, as usual at that time, *in commendam*) at the crest of the High Tory reaction in the last years of Queen Anne. It was in part a reaction against Whiggism in the Church, in part war-weariness after the long succession of Marlborough's victories. Atterbury was a High Church Tory, the most gifted and eloquent, a party-leader. (Poor Swift, who had to content himself with an Irish deanery, and writing an immortal classic, would have liked the job.)

But Atterbury was better connected, and all his life with Westminster. He was a scholar under Busby, went up to Christ Church as a Westminster Student and remained on there as a don, one of the coterie of young wits who thought they had got the better of the great classical scholar, Bentley in the Phalaris controversy. He became the champion of the Tory clergy in convocation, a brilliant ecclesiastical pamphleteer; with his handsome presence and delivery, he made a fine orator. A controversial figure, he was in private engaging, and even endearing.

Atterbury's name is for ever associated with Westminster, the love of his life. He took particular care of the monuments and the fabric, pushing forward Wren's work of re-casing the whole stonework of the Church – even if he did sell the great bell 'Peter' from the decaying belfry to St Paul's, and watched with classic delight the reduction of the rebarbative Gothic sculptures of Solomon's Porch to simpler forms. He commissioned Thornhill to design the figures of Apostles and Evangelists for the rose window in the North Transept. Above all, he was the most intellectual of Deans, and associate of leading writers of the time. There is a description of him preaching, by Steele in the *Tatler*. 'The Dean is an orator. He has so much regard to his congregation that he commits to his memory what he is to say to them; and has so soft and graceful a behaviour that it must attract your attention. His person is no small recommendation . . . adding to the propriety of speech, which might pass the criticism of Longinus, an action which would have been approved by Demosthenes.' And so on.

The Dean was a man of feeling: though Addison was a Whig, Atterbury could hardly conduct the funeral service, he was so much affected by the loss of his friend. But the great Duke of Marlborough was not beloved by the Tories, and we find Pope

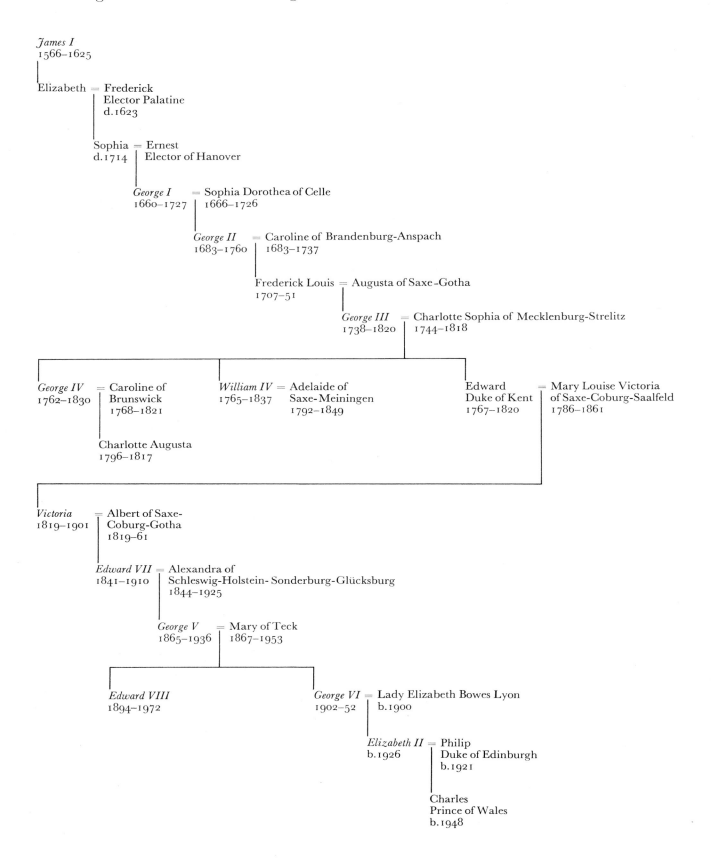

writing to Atterbury, at the time of the Duke's funeral (1722), 'I intend to lie at the Deanery, and moralize one evening with you on the vanity of human glory'. Atterbury replies from rural Bromley, 'I go tomorrow to the Deanery and, I believe, shall stay there till I have said "Dust to dust", and shut up that last scene of pompous vanity . . . I know I shall often say to myself, whilst expecting the funeral:

"O rus, quando ego te aspiciam, quandoque licebit
Ducere sollicitae jocunda oblivia vitae?" '
(O countryside, when shall I behold you, and when
be able to prolong the pleasing forgetfulness of a busy life?)

The Dean's interests had been mainly literary, as befitted a classical scholar; but, plunging into the antiquarian background of his office, he discovered the delights of historical research, and came to prefer it to Virgil and Cicero.

The Hanoverian succession put the Tories out of office and left them discontented; to this the Philistine George I (who knew no English) added a personal rebuff to Atterbury. In addition to his other talents, Atterbury was a good hater and he responded in kind: he had refused to subscribe to confidence in the government upon the Jacobite Rebellion of 1715, he now began to correspond with the exiled Stuarts. At the time of the collapse of the South Sea Bubble, with the new régime at the nadir of public respect, he seems to have inculpated himself in what was regarded as another conspiracy. He was arrested and sent to the Tower where he remained many months. Detested by his Whig colleagues on the episcopal bench, he was a hero to the lower clergy, who were largely Tory and taunted the government by publicly praying for him under the guise of 'one afflicted with the gout'. Verses circulated in his honour, including those by Swift on his little dog Harlequin, which had been an incriminating present from St Germain.

In 1723 he was banished the country: he was given a fine send-off from the Tower, the river crowded with boats and barges, a Tory Duke – one of Charles II's progeny – presenting him with a jewelled sword. Transferring his services to the exiled Stuarts, he found for himself how hopeless they were and quit them for Montpellier to assuage his (genuine) gout. Abroad, he kept up his interest in everything going on at Westminster, particularly his old enemies in the Chapter. (The Dean of St Patrick's and he had formerly exchanged letters about how to keep their respective Chapters in order.) The verses of Westminster Scholars were sent out to him; the Jacobite tendencies he had fostered continued among a minority, particularly the Wesleys. When he died, in Paris in 1732, his body was brought home to be buried privately, at night, with his wife and daughters, in a vault at the west door, 'as far from kings and Caesars as the space will admit of'.

Thus passed the most strongly marked personality, most widely associated with the Abbey in the public mind, until we come to the Victorian Dean Stanley. Perhaps Atterbury's best memorial is the fine book he inspired, John Dart's *Westmonasterium*, or *the History and Antiquities of the Abbey Church*, in two splendid folio volumes with engravings. It came out in the year of Atterbury's exile:

O thou, by pious Anna's favour graced
With holy lawn, and o'er this temple placed.

The book is a monument to eighteenth-century taste as well as scholarship, with its cult of romantic decay:

> Come lead, my Muse, while thoughtful I essay
> To trace thy footings through the cloistered way,
> Where faded guidons, now by age decayed,
> Hang nodding lazy o'er their owner's head:
> Banners, once fierce, now fan some antique tomb,
> Shed showers of dust and wave the spider's loom.
> The painted shield and sword suspended high,
> The cuisses clasping once the manly thigh,
> Ungilt, uncoloured, and devoured with rust,
> Point silently their mouldering owners' dust.

We learn more from the learned prose of these tomes. Dart had Gothic sympathies and deplored the injury to the arches made by some of the classic monuments. Some mediaeval glass has disappeared since his time, and he tells us that a number of the statues round Henry VII's Chapel were taken down by workmen for reasons of safety – so that not all the Abbey's losses are due to Reformation and Civil War.

The range of persons given burial continued to broaden, as did the manners and morals of the time. Consider the Churchills. Marlborough's body was removed to the chapel at Blenheim Palace just before his Duchess's death in 1744. His brother, the Admiral, had been buried in 1710 in the south aisle, on the right hand of the Screen. Twenty years later their sister was laid in the same grave, an old lady who had been James II's mistress – in the odour of sanctity at last. The third brother, General Charles Churchill, had his beautiful actress, Mrs Oldfield, buried in the South Aisle; but successive Deans could not be prevailed on to allow her a monument. On the other hand, the Duke's daughter, Henrietta, second Duchess in her own right, put up a fine monument to her beloved Congreve, the dramatist, commemorating 'the happiness and honour she enjoyed in the sincere friendship of so worthy and honest a man, whose virtue, candour, and wit gained him the love and esteem of the present age, and whose writings will be the admiration of the future'. Her disapproving mother, the redoubtable Sarah, commented: 'I know not what pleasure she might have had in his company, but I am sure it was no honour.'

George I's reign was signalized by the revival of the Order of the Bath at the suggestion of the scholarly, if combative, Cornish herald, John Anstis. Since Charles II's coronation the Order had fallen into desuetude, and Anstis had the idea of organizing it into a company of knights, after the model of the Order of the Garter, limited in number, with its own officers and chapel, for which Henry VII's was chosen in happy rivalry with Windsor. (From mediaeval times, however, it had been associated with the Abbey.) Sir Robert Walpole was delighted, according to his son, with the notion of 'an artful bank of thirty-six ribbons to supply a fund of favours in lieu of places': thus he meant 'to stave off the demands for Garters, and intended that the Red should be a step to the Blue'.

Anstis followed up with a work of research on the history of the Knights, and in 1725 the Order was inaugurated amid a good deal of Georgian ribaldry about the Bath. But it turned out a useful institution for just those purposes, rewards and pro-

Dart's engraving of the Nave of the Abbey in the early eighteenth century, looking up to the high altar. The absence of pews makes the Church look much loftier and unfamiliar to modern eyes. The Choir Screen was replaced by the existing one – the work of Blore – at the beginning of the nineteenth century.

The coronation of George IV took place on 19 July 1821. George was nearly sixty when he eventually became King, and the occasion was celebrated with great magnificence. *Above:* The King wore a crimson velvet train, twenty-seven foot long and decorated by a pattern of gold stars. His hat was vast and decorated with ostrich feathers, so that the painter, Benjamin Haydon, described him as 'like some gorgeous bird of the East'. *Right:* The coronation service of George IV, which lasted for five hours. The Archbishop of York, preached a thunderous sermon on the need for the good ruler to preserve his subjects' morals 'from the contagion of vice and irreligion'.

After the coronation service, the procession made its way from the Abbey to the banquet in Westminster Hall along a special walk raised three feet high, so that the spectators could see the King in his glory.

The coronation banquet in Westminster Hall was attended by 312 peers – the peeresses were obliged to watch hungry from the balcony. This painting by Dighton shows the King's Champion throwing down his gauntlet.

Left: Victoria's coronation on 28
June 1838. The ceremony was
exhausting, lasting from 11.30
in the morning to 6.00 in the
evening. John Martin has
captured the well-known
moment when Lord Rolle, in his
eighties, missed his footing while
paying homage to the Queen
and rolled backwards down the
steps.

Arthur Penrhyn Stanley, the
famous Victorian Dean, and
his wife, Lady Augusta, who
was one of the Queen's
favourite ladies-in-waiting.
Dean Stanley died in 1881 and
is buried in Henry VII's Chapel,
alongside his wife.

COVERED WITH THE HISTORIC "PADRE'S FLAG" AND THE PALL, AND GUARDED BY MEN
OF THE FOUR SERVICES : THE GRAVE AFTER THE ABBEY CEREMONY.

After the Abbey service the grave was enclosed, and within the barrier were posted four sentries, one each from the Army (left foreground
in our photograph), the Air Force (right foreground), the Marines (left background), and the Navy (right background). The grave was
covered with the Abbey pall and over it the historic Union Jack known as "the Padre's flag," presented by the Rev. David Railton, M.C.,
Vicar of Margate, who first suggested to the Dean of Westminster the idea of burying an Unknown Warrior in the Abbey. The flag
was given to Mr. Railton when he went to France as an Army chaplain, and it was used, for purposes many and various, on many
famous battlefields. He brought it back stained with British blood, and it will now hang in Westminster Abbey. Upon it are three
wreaths, including the King's, and others are laid at the end of the grave.—[Photograph by L.N.A.]

Left: At the West End of the Nave hangs the memorial plaque to Franklin Roosevelt, 'A faithful friend of freedom and of Britain, four times President of the United States.'
Right: The memorial to Sir Winston Churchill, which was unveiled by Queen Elizabeth II on 19 September 1965.

Left: After the First World War, an unknown soldier, out of more than three-quarters of a million British dead, was buried in the Abbey as a memorial to them all. The body was brought from France for burial on Armistice Day, 1920. 'They buried him among the Kings because he had done good toward God and toward his House.'
Right: The Choir of the Abbey, before the high altar, showing the damage inflicted upon the Church by bombs during the air-raids of May 1941.

pitiation, as well as ceremonial and decorative. It provided at once an opportunity for the charming colour-drawings of their processions and feasts by Joseph Highmore, engraved by Pyne. Thus we see today the banners providing a gay decorative scheme as we look aloft at the grey walls of Henry VII's Chapel.

George II's coronation was a magnificent affair – perhaps to make a point against his father – Queen Caroline blazing with jewels, most of them hired, it was said. Other figures out of the English past drew more attention: James II's old mistress, Catherine Sedley – to whom he had transferred his favours from Arabella Churchill – now Countess of Dorchester. And there was disapproving Sarah herself. She had tried to dissuade her grandsons abroad from coming home for the coronation, 'only to see some old and odd people walk in red velvet upon green cloth, for handsome figures I know of none'. She herself provided one of the oddest spectacles. The old Duchess took her place, 'if on crutches', in the procession from Palace Yard; when it ground to a lengthy halt, she demanded a drum from the military band nearby, and sat on it in all her finery, to the delight of the crowd who gave her a cheer all to herself.

We have a brilliant description of George II's funeral from the author of *The Castle of Otranto* himself, much in keeping, for it was at night, by torchlight; 'the whole Abbey so illuminated that one saw it to greater advantage than by day; the tombs, long aisles, and fretted roof, all appearing distinctly, and with the happiest chiaroscuro. There wanted nothing but incense, and little chapels here and there, with priests saying mass for the repose of the defunct – yet one could not complain of its not being catholic enough.' The sombreness of the scene was relieved by the burlesque Duke of Newcastle, who could always be trusted to behave ridiculously.

He fell into a fit of crying the moment he came into the Chapel, and flung himself back in a stall, the Archbishop hovering over him with a smelling-bottle – but in two minutes his curiosity got the better of his hypocrisy, and he ran about the Chapel with his glass to spy who was or was not there, spying with one hand and mopping his eyes with t'other. Then returned for fear of catching cold and, the Duke of Cumberland who was sinking with heat, felt himself weighed down and, turning round, found it was the Duke of Newcastle standing upon his train to avoid the chill of the marble.

The Duke of Cumberland himself provided an odd enough spectacle to Horace's brilliant eyes, 'in a dark brown adonis [wig]' and a train five yards long, 'his leg extremely bad, yet forced to stand upon it near two hours, his face bloated and distorted with his late paralytic stroke, which has affected, too, one of his eyes, and placed over the mouth of the vault into which, in all probability, he must himself so soon descend.' He did – and the occasion was attended by an unusual request.

Two ladies present their respectful compliments to the Dean of Westminster, and would take it as a singular favour if his lordship would break through the usual forms observed on these solemn occasions, and permit them to walk and sing in the procession. They were once too intimately connected with His late Royal Highness. They have remarkably fine voices, and are at present sincere penitents and earnestly wish to offer this last tribute of tenderness and respect to his memory.

The dear, delightful eighteenth century! – the Dean solemnly noted that he rejected the request. But no one seems to have suspected that it might have been a hoax, 'Butcher' Cumberland was so unpopular. It sounds too good to be true.

We owe the description of young George III's coronation also to the sharp pen of

The act of homage at the
coronation of Elizabeth II on
2 June 1953.

Horace Walpole. 'What is the finest sight in the world? A Coronation. What do people talk most about? A Coronation . . . Oh! the buzz, the prattle, the noise, the hurry!' Then the genius of Comedy takes over in retailing the incidents of the day. So many mistakes and inadvertences were committed that the Earl Marshal – hereditarily the Duke of Norfolk, for whom another Howard was deputizing – apologized to the young King and said he had taken such care that 'the *next coronation* would be conducted with the greatest order imaginable'. In Westminster Hall the King's Champion 'acted his part admirably and dashed down his gauntlet with proud defiance'. But a misadventure befell his companion Lord Talbot, who 'piqued himself on backing his horse down the Hall and not turning its rump to the King; but he had taken such pains to dress it to that duty that it entered backwards. And at his retreat the spectators clapped, a terrible indecorum, but suitable to such Bartholomew Fair doings.' In the Abbey, 'of all the incidents of the day the most diverting was what happened to the Queen. She had a retiring-chamber, with *all* conveniences, prepared behind the altar. She went thither – in the *most convenient* what found she but – the Duke of Newcastle!'

With the dust of political dissension settled and quiet descending upon the Abbey, we can leaf through its registers to observe how they delineate the whole spectrum of English society in the eighteenth century: from royal persons and great nobles to Abbey servants, or Westminster Scholars drowned in the Thames to a dead child found in the Dark Cloister. The Abbey became a veritable charnel-house for all sorts and conditions of men – though we can observe differences of location according to status: grandees in Henry VII's Chapel or nearby, simpler or less respectable persons in the Cloisters. The naughty novelist, Mrs Aphra Behn, disapproved of by the Victorian Registrar, is in the Cloisters; so is Samuel Foote, actor-dramatist, who was no better a subject. As time goes on one notices something like what economists call 'division of labour' coming about empirically in the English way: poets and writers in the South Transept, politicians in the North, soldiers and sailors about the Nave. But it is not until the Victorian Age that restriction is imposed, and an Abbey burial is only for the eminent.

In the South Transept Poets' Corner was filling up with Dryden, though he died a Catholic, in 1700; Nicholas Rowe, the first biographer of Shakespeare; John Gay, of *The Beggar's Opera*; Dr Johnson, who got a grand send-off suitable to the public figure he was; the popular Thomas Campbell. Among politicians there was the brilliant Halifax, the 'Trimmer', who could have saved James II from himself, given the chance; Lord Treasurer Godolphin, excellent man, who made the Union with Scotland; Chatham – 'I know that I can save my country, and that no one else can' – whose burial in the Abbey displeased the small-minded George III, who saw in him only 'that great trumpet of sedition', because he saw the point of the American Revolution. (General Burgoyne, who surrendered at Saratoga, is here too.) So also are the younger Pitt and his rival, Charles James Fox, both of whom actively sympathized with the American cause. Perhaps one should place Sheridan among the theatre-folk: one cannot take him seriously as a politician.

Among the actors we find Betterton, Mrs Bracegirdle, and Garrick. Most endearing are perhaps the musicians: Henry Purcell, with Byrd and Elgar among the greatest of English composers, who died at only thirty-seven – what he might have achieved if he had only had his full span: the English Handel. But Handel is here too, along with those excellent musicians, John Blow and Dr Croft. Dr Busby has his place, of course; it is no less pleasant to find Thomas Tompion, the clock-maker, and Sir William Chambers, the architect, designer of the most beautiful of London palaces, Somerset House. And, appropriately in a noble spot, in mid-aisle at the west end of the Choir, the grandest luminary of the age, Sir Isaac Newton.

Meanwhile, work on the fabric continued all through these years, from Wren's appointment as Surveyor until the completion of Hawksmoor's Western Towers in the year of the '45, the Young Pretender's attempt to regain the throne for the Stuarts. Thus the Western Front assumed the form so familiar to us. It has been usual not to appreciate the towers simply because they are not mediaeval. This is an aesthetic solecism: in their own terms they provide an admirable resolution of the problem of the Western Front—though both Wren and Hawksmoor considered the Abbey needed spires. (It would have looked more like Lichfield Cathedral.) Hawksmoor had a strain of originality amounting to genius, and in his age had an exceptional understanding of the spirit of Gothic. His towers are of rather smaller proportions than the mediaeval bases they are set upon: but this gives them the more elegance, a feminine grace. This in turn is offset by their emphasis on horizontals, to correct excessive verticality, so that the whole composition has classic solidity as well as Gothic grace.

The Georgian era may be taken to end with the coronation of George IV, which – like everything about him – had an element of the grotesque. Poor George IV, inextricably entangled in his quarrel with Queen Caroline – a German cousin, who was slightly dotty and no better than she should be – laid on a magnificent coronation in 1821 in an effort to counter the popularity the Radical Left had whipped up for her for their party purposes. No expense was spared: the royal robes alone cost £24,000, the crown £54,000. The day was overcast for him with apprehension that the Queen, debarred from the Abbey ceremony, would attempt to force her way in – as she did, trying each entrance in turn. At last she retired defeated to her carriage – once more the Abbey had reflected a piece of the history of the time. The day was oppressively hot, and throughout the homage of the peers, the perspiring monarch made use of innumerable handkerchiefs to wipe his streaming face – and handed them on to the Primate of All England by his side. The Archbishop's secretary had had to revive him with smelling salts; while, during an interval, the King retired to his closet to recline on a sofa, with nothing on but his crown. (He was excessively fat: 'Prinny has let his belly down', a diarist reported; 'it reaches to his knees'.)

Even Queen Victoria's coronation was not without its unrehearsed incidents, though it was the third in seventeen years. In the processions to the Abbey, the biggest cheer went – in the English way – to Napoleon's Marshal Soult, representing France. The Archbishop, the last to wear a wig, did not seem to know his way about the service. At one point the Queen said to a lay official, 'Pray tell me what I am to do, for *they* don't know' – meaning the prelates. The orb was somewhat unexpectedly pressed into her hand, and she found it too heavy to hold; the ring was too small for her finger, but the Archbishop forced it on, giving her pain. The climax of the homage was reached when ancient Lord Rolle missed his footing and rolled from the top to the bottom of the steps.

Perhaps we should regard the event as a postscript to the agreeable eighteenth century with which it had so much in common.

It was in the Victorian Age that the Abbey reached its apogee in the general life of the nation; everyone is agreed that this was the work of the most remarkable of its Deans, 'who more than any other single individual was responsible for making Westminster Abbey what it is today in the eyes of the multitudes who visit it'. Dean Stanley (1864–81) is still a living name to us: what the Abbey is today in the life of the nation was his life's work. The interesting thing is that, though everyone is grateful for it now, it was achieved against constant dissension and opposition from clergy and religious press; for Stanley was regarded with disapproval by the orthodox and was always in the thick of controversy. However, he had powerful friends, and, before his death, was respected as one of the most eminent of Victorians.

Arthur Penrhyn Stanley enjoyed many advantages, in family background – he was a Stanley of Alderley – and in his marriage to Lady Augusta Bruce, a great favourite with Queen Victoria, whose own contribution at Westminster should be mentioned, for she was tactful, warm-hearted, practical and kind: she made the Deanery not only a social and intellectual centre, but opened it wide for children's entertainments and welfare work. Arthur Penrhyn Stanley liked to think that a Welsh marriage had touched his sluggish, steady English stock with 'the imaginative, lively, mercurial character of Celtic parentage'. He evidently exemplified the latter and is depicted as such, 'Arthur' in *Tom Brown's Schooldays*. At Rugby he was a favourite pupil of Dr Arnold, to whose influence at Oxford he succeeded, liberal-minded and tolerant, as Professor of Ecclesiastical History.

He was already marked down as a modernist when he accepted the Deanery, with some misgivings. His appointment was preached against by one of his new colleagues; but the Dean was protected not only by his sense of humour but his natural goodness and sweetness of disposition – the canon, Dr Wordsworth, was to be answered 'by an invitation to dinner on the first opportunity'. The Dean was more bothered by the practical detail of running a Chapter: he was no good at business, and couldn't do arithmetic – an endearing trait. 'To lose one's time in Confirmations is bad, but to lose it in leases and warming-pans [heating the Abbey was being discussed] is worse.' At first Stanley missed the intellectual stimulus of Oxford; the Abbey was in a somewhat somnolent state: he would awake the Sleeping Princess.

At his installation he received his cue: he was immensely struck by the words of the ancient instrument to which he gave assent, that he was set there 'for the enlargement of the Christian Church'. Thenceforth he made that the motto and inspiration of his whole ministry at Westminster. Comprehension, toleration, sympathy for all Christian sects and peoples were his principles – for he was a man of principle, contrary to what his opponents thought. Though a sensitive man, he was a man of indefeasible courage, always defending the defenceless. When Bishop Colenso was hounded for his very apposite criticisms of the Pentateuch, the Dean stood up for him, gave him good counsel, and offered him the Abbey pulpit. When the Ritualists were attacked, he came to their rescue – though he cared nothing about vestments: 'clergymen's clothes', he called them. (Perhaps this, however, was something of an aesthetic defect.) His first attempt at comprehension met with defeat. Bent on making the Abbey, as a national institution, voice as wide a range of religious expression as possible in the Victorian Age, including Nonconformists, he was rebuffed when he also approached the High Church leaders: Keble, Pusey, and Liddon declined to preach. But they could not all hold out against the Dean's persistence and charm: in the end Liddon consented to perform, and shortly Abbey services came to be crowded.

Dean Stanley breathed his own life and vitality into a somnolent institution; he was full of ideas: he initiated children's services, at which he was a favourite preacher, for he gave short and simple addresses. Afterwards, there were games of hide-and-seek all over the hitherto gloomy Deanery – all very unlike the stately and bewigged Augustans. The Dean took delight in showing working-men's parties over the Abbey, and many were the letters and spoken tributes he received. Though curiously insensitive to architecture, he set on foot the restoration of the Chapter House, after centuries of misuse and damage as a storehouse for records. He restored the mediaeval form of the Sanctuary, with its incomparable pavement; in employing Sir Gilbert Scott and J. L. Pearson on the fabric he could hardly have done better. He invented the special services for particular occasions which became a familiar feature of Victorian London. He encouraged Church music: the Abbey had its part in the revival of Bach. When the Passion Music was first performed in Lent 1871, there was a crowd outside unable to get in, besides the vast congregation within.

All was changed, and just-minded contemporaries recognized that it was owing to, and reflected, Dean Stanley's own personality, the width and warmth of his interests. There was a revealing little scene on the last Sunday of 1876 when Disraeli, now Lord Beaconsfield, caught up with the Dean walking down Whitehall. The Prime Minister, his 'head full of telegrams', for that week Queen Victoria was to be proclaimed Empress of India, expressed a wish to go into the Abbey to hear Farrar preach. The Church was crowded, they were not recognized, and there wasn't a seat. So Dean Stanley stood on the pedestal of a monument, Beaconsfield beside him. The ageing Prime Minister could not hear very well, but, as they came away, he said: 'I would not have missed the sight for anything – the darkness, the lights, the marvellous windows, the vast crowd, the courtesy, the respect, the devotion – and fifty years ago there would not have been fifty persons there!'

Archbishop Tait paid tribute to Stanley's achievement: 'no clergyman, perhaps, who ever lived exercised over the public at large, and especially over the literary and thoughtful portion of it, so fascinating an influence.' By the 1870s his public was the nation: 'whatever he wrote or said commanded respectful attention. He was a power, not only in the Church, but in the world'. He had made Westminster Abbey a centre of religious and national life. His home at the Deanery, says his biographer, 'was the coveted resort of all that was best and most distinguished in English and, it may be added, in Continental, life'. Every literary celebrity, European or American, a Renan or a Motley, came to visit him. This was mainly on account of his literary fame, which is not our subject here. But it must be said that this, too, further extended the national and representative character of the Abbey. Dean Stanley was personally responsible for the burial given to Charles Dickens; the ceremony was private, but thereafter crowds streamed through the Church for weeks to pay their respects to the master, many people weeping. The Victorians brought to an end the undiscriminating use of the place for burials that had made Stanley say that 'it seemed to me as if I were going down alive into the sepulchre'. In his time there were only fifteen interments within the Abbey. The Percy family still have an ancient right of burial there, and they continue it; in addition to Dickens there were Bulwer Lytton, Herschel the astronomer, Grote the historian, Palmerston and Lord Lawrence of Indian fame; most popular of all, David Livingstone.

Dean Stanley's chief interest of mind, along with religion, was historical. It was not long before he fell in love with the Abbey; he certainly made the dry bones live, all the monuments and their records were living stories to him – not for nothing was his favourite author Sir Walter Scott. And in time he wrote what is still the most thorough account of it, *Historical Memorials of Westminster Abbey*. (His previous book, *Historical Memorials of Canterbury*, had the good fortune to become the source in our time of T. S. Eliot's *Murder in the Cathedral*.)

Still, to the very end, almost every step Dean Stanley took stirred up controversy or was greeted with abuse:

> And men ignoble harassed him with strife,

as Matthew Arnold wrote. He was sometimes shouted down in Convocation. He arranged a Communion service for the Revisers of the New Testament: these included Nonconformist scholars, one of them a Unitarian. This ecumenical act was described, by the religious press, as 'casting pearls before swine'. He befriended, and defended, a well-known French priest, Père Hyacinthe, who had married. The Dean was well before his time: we have only just caught up with him. He called on Bishop Colenso in trouble, and on Newman at the Oratory, neglected and unconsidered. He was not only irresistible, but a most lovable man.

When he died, all this came clear: he was given the funeral of a national figure himself. When Lady Augusta died, Browning had been a pall-bearer, with Motley to represent America. Since then, in his last disconsolate years, Dean Stanley had had a triumphal tour of the United States. He was an Eminent Victorian. Now, in 1881, among his pall-bearers were the Duke of Westminster; the disapproved (for his liberal views) Dr Temple – to become Archbishop of Canterbury; the President of the Royal Society; W. H. Smith and W. E. Forster, House of Commons leaders for Government and Opposition; Dr Jowett and a faithful Nonconformist divine; Matthew Arnold. There was only wanting a Roman Catholic. Matthew Arnold, in one of his last poems, *Westminster Abbey*, summed up the life and work of his father's most gifted pupil and his place in the Abbey's story:

> What! for a term so scant
> Our shining visitant
> Cheered us, and now is passed into the night?
> Couldst thou no better keep, O Abbey old,
> The boon thy dedication-sign foretold,
> The presence of that gracious inmate, light? –
> A child of light appeared;
> Hither he came, late-born and long-desired,
> And to men's hearts this ancient place endeared:
> What, is the happy glow so soon expired? . . .
>
> Yet in this latter time
> The promise of the prime
> Seemed to come true at last, O Abbey old!
> It seemed a child of light did bring the dower
> Foreshown thee in thy consecration-hour,
> And in thy courts his shining freight unrolled:

Bright wits, and instincts sure,
And goodness warm, and truth without alloy,
And temper sweet, and love of all things pure,
And joy in light, and power to spread the joy.

Epilogue: the Twentieth Century

AFTER DEAN STANLEY the Abbey never lost the ground he had won for it in the general life and common concourse of the nation. The twentieth century added to it and improved upon it in several ways. First on the aesthetic side, where the Victorian Dean was rather defective; an Abbey, as Horace Walpole saw it, requires altars and incense, and any large church demands ritual. The Abbey ceremonial has been rendered far more beautiful in our time than in Dean Stanley's. The House of Commons may have retreated to St Margaret's in the seventeenth century for fear of copes, but now these have increased to sixty or more. (In 1540 there were over three hundred.) Then, too, in an age of mass-civilization, there has been an enormous increase in the tides of visitors swirling through the Abbey, simply to view what Dean Ryle has described as the 'unique and priceless treasure of the English-speaking race'. And the multitudes have become international, so that the Abbey has had to provide guides in foreign languages.

It has not ceased to fulfil its historic functions, or to reflect the history of our time. It has witnessed four coronations, those of Edward VII, George V, George VI, and Elizabeth II – all of them perfectly rehearsed and carried through without anything to mar the spectacle, unlike some previous occasions. Indeed, the last was a technical triumph appropriate to our age, for it was televized and visible over the world. At the same time, to anyone present with historical imagination, looking down upon the scene, the self-same spot that had seen the crowning of the Kings right back to William the Conqueror – the young Victoria and the gay Restoration with Charles II (Mr Pepys looking on), Elizabeth I and her mother, Anne Boleyn, poor young Henry VI looking down 'sagely and wisely' upon the people, or his heroic father Henry V, and so back to the Normans – it did not fail in its effect upon the emotions, the moment of the crowning, the Archbishop raising the crown high for all to see, the guns crashing from the Park all the way to the Tower, and in that same moment the Abbey bells ringing out to the world that the Queen within was safely crowned.

The Abbey itself had come safely through the ordeals of the two German wars that have shaped (or mis-shaped) our time, particularly the terrible dangers of the second war – and this was very present to historically-reflective minds. The first war did not seriously endanger the Abbey, though a bomb struck the Choir School. As the war went on, treasures and movables, like the Coronation Chair and Stone of Scone, were removed to the Crypt for safety, some of the glass taken out, the retable of the High Altar put away. The finest effigies were boarded over and sandbagged against fire and bombs; some two thousand sandbags were used. But, in the second war, sixty thousand were needed. The Abbey registered progress in the art of war – perhaps the most profound development in the civilization of our time.

After the first war there was an affecting mood that some of us still remember – of thankfulness for an almighty deliverance, of relief and hope that the world should not see another such war, of remembrance of the terrible sacrifice in human lives, a dedication to peace. It was in this mood that an inspiration was presented to the Abbey – by an Army chaplain who had served in Flanders – that an Unknown Soldier, out of the more than three-quarters of a million British dead, should be buried in the Abbey as a memorial to them all. 'And some there be that have no name.' This is the memorial that most attracts the eyes and hearts of all entering the Abbey. There are others from that time. The American Ambassador to Berlin, 1914–17, J. W. Gerard, who had done his best for British prisoners in Germany, gave a window in memory of those who died there. The Ambassador to Britain in those years, the Virginian Walter Hines Page – a good friend in time of trouble – has his memorial too, as have James Russell Lowell and Longfellow. A monument of earlier American interest is that put up by the province of Massachusetts, before the Revolution, in honour of the gallant Viscount Howe who fell at Ticonderoga. No less revealing is that to William Wragg, of South Carolina, a Loyalist who was forced to leave home and fortune at the outbreak of the Revolution, and was shipwrecked and drowned off the coast of Holland – there is a vivid relief of the scene, resting on a sagacious dolphin. Inside the West Door we see the memorial to President Franklin Roosevelt, under the spread American eagle, looking across to that of his friend and comrade Sir Winston Churchill, next to the Unknown Warrior.

Alas for the hopes of peace to which this country dedicated itself after 1918! The crest of the second wave in the German attempt to achieve domination that has wrecked the twentieth century – after the civilized hopes of the nineteenth – was reached in 1939–45. This time the Abbey did not escape so lightly. In September 1940 the great West Window was damaged, the Choir School hit by high explosives, houses in the Cloisters struck. Towards the end of the month the East Window of Henry VII's Chapel was blown in. The severest damage came in the great blitz of 10–11 May 1941. In the course of that raid bombs fell all round and upon the Abbey, but most of them were extinguished: by this time fire-watching and dealing with incendiary bombs had become a practised art, the Abbey devotedly served by its staff, air-wardens and fire-service. (What a world for the civilized twentieth century!)

But a fire started in the wooden roof of the Library was difficult to get at, up a tortuous ancient staircase. Water pressure here was insufficient:

... eventually water was obtained from a tank in the south-west tower, but the fire was not quite extinguished before the supply gave out. Such was the situation when further incendiaries pierced the roofs of six houses, the Deanery, Nos. 1, 2, 3, 6 and 7 Little Cloister. No. 6, perhaps the most beautiful of our houses, but old and inflammable, was soon ablaze. The Deanery and No. 3 Little Cloister were the next to go.

Amid so many fires water gave out, and in spite of all efforts only No. 2 The Cloisters and Nos. 4 and 5 Little Cloister were saved, of all the houses in the precincts. The saddest loss, because irretrievable, was Dr Busby's beautiful house of 1681. The incendiaries that fell on the Church were effectively dealt with, all but one that lodged in the timbers of the Lantern and could not be reached. The roof caught fire, 'and flames leaping into the air thirty or forty feet high made many who saw them fear that the church was doomed ... The whole roof broke away from the stone walls to which it was attached and fell some 130 feet on to the pavement below, where it burnt itself out.' And this probably saved the Abbey.

It has taken years since the ending of the war to recover the damage, and an immense sum of a million pounds to repair, rebuild and reconstruct. This has enabled great improvements to be made, in addition to making good the damage. Where the roofing of the Lantern before was temporary, the replacement was permanent and more satisfactory – though the crossing is still without its finishing *flèche*, as it always has been. A vast amount of repairs to stonework, tracery, statuary had to be undertaken, glass and furnishings replaced, the Deanery and prebendaries' houses rebuilt. Within, the Church has come alive with colour, lighting up screens and pinnacles, monuments and coats of arms – the heart of good old John Dart would rejoice to see it. Where there had been much inferior glass, there is now a fine range of Comper windows in the north aisle of the Nave. The good work goes on, and there is more to do – restoring the statues on the North Front, for example.

Among the damaged were some of the mediaeval effigies which are among the Abbey's unique treasures. It was the custom to carry a life-like effigy of the monarch or great personage upon the coffin in the funeral procession, and this went on well into the eighteenth century. Most of these treasures were rescued, so that the Abbey possesses the earliest mediaeval effigy to survive: the wooden one of Edward III, almost certainly a likeness made from a death-mask. A wooden head of Richard II's Queen, Anne of Bohemia, is similarly convincing: a curiously long, though rounded, face with incipient double chin, not at all beautiful, more like a *hausfrau*. But Catherine of Valois, Henry v's Queen, is a beauty, with a long, swan-like neck: of her there is a full figure, painted vermilion. The head of Henry VII is the most remarkable as a character-portrait: a very wide-awake Welsh face, with lined ascetic cheeks, deep-set eyes and scrawny neck.

And so on to the wax effigies, the most remarkable is that of Charles II, of which a contemporary wrote, ''tis to the life, and truly to admiration'. Hardly less so are those of Chatham, modelled by an American, Patience Wright, in 1773; and Nelson, dressed in his own clothes, the shoe-buckles those he was wearing at Trafalgar. This effigy was brought to the Abbey the year after his death, to compete with his tomb at St Paul's in attracting the crowds – another example of the ancient rivalry that appears throughout their long history.

Rivalry of another sort, also going back for centuries, appears in the astonishing story of the theft of the Stone of Scone. After six and a half centuries at Westminster, it was found missing on Christmas Day, 1950. A thrilling detective story in itself, it turned out to be the accomplished, if amateur, work of three young Scottish Nationalists – the jemmy with which they worked is among the Abbey's Museum items. The exploit, if this were the seventeenth century, would make a suitable subject for a marble relief like that of Thomas Thynne, in the South Aisle, being 'barbarously murdered' in his coach in 1682. The historic Stone, successfully concealed for months, was eventually yielded up religiously to Arbroath Abbey in Scotland: whence it was returned in time for the coronation of Elizabeth II.

A saga has grown up around the saving of St Paul's in the blitz of May 1941, Wren's dome floating above the smoke-clouds and the flames of the blazing city below. The survival of the Abbey is no less providential, when the neighbouring House of Commons was burnt to the ground. When the second war, which brought us to a term in our long history, came to an end in 1945, and one saw Churchill lead the Commons across Old Palace Yard to give thanks in St Margaret's, there was the Abbey still standing, with its message of eternity, riding like a great ship over the flotsam and jetsam, the débris and devastation of our time.

George Zarnecki

The Art
and
Architecture

Like most large churches which have been in continuous use for centuries, Westminster Abbey is not a homogeneous structure. When architectural styles changed and as money became available, various parts of it were replaced by what were thought to be more up-to-date forms. However, the conglomeration of parts, built at different times, produces a remarkably harmonious whole, a happy blending of designs by many architects.

Westminster was not an ordinary church. In the first place, it was a Benedictine monastery devoted to prayer, contemplation and work, and thus the Church itself was only a part, admittedly the most conspicuous part, of a range of buildings placed at the four sides of the Cloister. By long tradition in western monastic planning, the arcaded Cloister nestled in the shelter of the Transept and the Nave, on the warmest, south side of the Church. Much of the monks' life was spent in the Cloister in study and in prayer. It was also here that the boy novices received their instruction and played their quiet games, as the board scratched in the stone at Westminster testifies. Of the series of structures adjoining the Cloister, the most sumptuous was the Chapter House, where the monks gathered every morning under their Abbot or Prior, to pray, to listen to a sermon, to be told of their daily tasks and, if need be, for disciplinary action. The Dorter or sleeping quarters were nearby, within easy reach of the Church, for the monastic rule requires frequent processions to the Choir for prayer and singing, even at night. Below, the Refectory or the dining hall was easily accessible from both the Cloister and the Dorter. There followed other buildings such as the Kitchens, the Hospital with its separate chapel, numerous workshops and storerooms, the Abbot's House, the Prior's House, the Guest House and many others.

Monastic life at Westminster came to an end with the Dissolution of the Monasteries under King Henry VIII in 1540, and many of the monastic buildings were subsequently either pulled down or put to a different use from that for which they were originally intended and, in the process, many of them were re-shaped.

Westminster was not an ordinary church for yet another reason. From as early as the second half of the tenth century it had enjoyed royal favour, but the relationship between the Abbey and the Kings became particularly close when, during the eleventh century, the royal residence was moved from Winchester to Westminster, only a short distance from the Abbey along the old Roman road towards the river and its ford. The close physical proximity of the Palace of Westminster to the Abbey eventually led to a unique link. Under Edward the Confessor, and in imitation of the ducal abbeys in Normandy, Westminster became a royal 'private' Abbey, directly dependent upon the King and exempt from episcopal control. At the same time, the Abbey became the Coronation Church of the English Kings as Rheims Cathedral was of the French, and the principal burial place for the Kings and their families, as Saint-Denis Abbey was for the French. This unique rôle of the Abbey assured it of rich endowments and continuous royal patronage throughout the ages, which resulted in splendid building undertakings.

Edward the Confessor (who reigned from 1042 to 1066), who was half Norman by birth and wholly Norman by upbringing and in his tastes, had already financed the rebuilding of the old Church, and his building must have been something of a landmark in the history of English architecture, for it was the first church in England built in the newly emerging Romanesque style. Normandy, under its vigorous dukes and enlightened monasteries, was in the forefront of the new artistic movement in Europe, and King Edward's Abbey was an early example of a Norman Romanesque building outside Normandy. Some features of this Church are known from excavations, and it is clear that the design was modelled on that of the abbey of Jumièges. A schematic view of the Abbey has been immortalized on the Bayeux Tapestry (c. 1070).

The Norman Conquest of 1066 opened the way for the 'invasion' of England by the Norman forms of Romanesque architecture but, before that date, Westminster Abbey stood as a lone forerunner of the new style. The work of Edward was continued under the early Norman kings, for the huge Church had not been completed when King Edward died. There is evidence that even the impious William Rufus – William the Conqueror's second son and successor, who reigned from 1087 to 1100 – was a benefactor of the Abbey, for there existed a mid-twelfth-century capital (now lost, since it was sold to a private collector after its discovery in 1807), which represented the King giving to the monks of Westminster, headed by their Abbot, Gilbert Crispin (who died c. 1121 and whose tomb is in the south walk of the Cloister), a charter of privileges. The rediscovery of this precious early sculpture, and its return to the Abbey would be a happy event. Professor W. R. Lethaby, in his admirable book on the Abbey, informs us that he found identical masons' marks in the Refectory and in Westminster Hall, the gigantic structure erected by William Rufus in the Palace of Westminster. He thus concluded that it was probably William Rufus who financed the building of the Refectory, and even supplied the masons from the royal building site.

Of the Romanesque Church nothing survives, but luckily a fair amount of monastic building from that period can still be seen to the east of the Cloisters. Especially impressive is the undercroft of the Dormitory, supported by sturdy circular piers. From the original Cloister, which was erected sometime around 1120, a few capitals have been miraculously preserved. One of them is particularly worthy of notice, as it is carved with the Judgement of Solomon, a scene rare in Romanesque art. In simple forms, the dramatic moment is shown when the King orders the child to be divided in two, while the real mother implores him to give the child to the pretender rather than to kill it. The use of this subject at Westminster was probably intended not only as an illustration of the well-known Biblical event, but also as an allusion to King Solomon's wisdom which should be an inspiration to all rulers. The meagre ruins of the original Infirmary Chapel dedicated to St Catherine, also survive. This building was enriched with the chevron ornament and it is assumed to have been one of the last to be erected in the Monastery in the Romanesque style, c. 1160.

Opposite: The exterior of Henry VII's Chapel, showing the rich surface of the stonework.

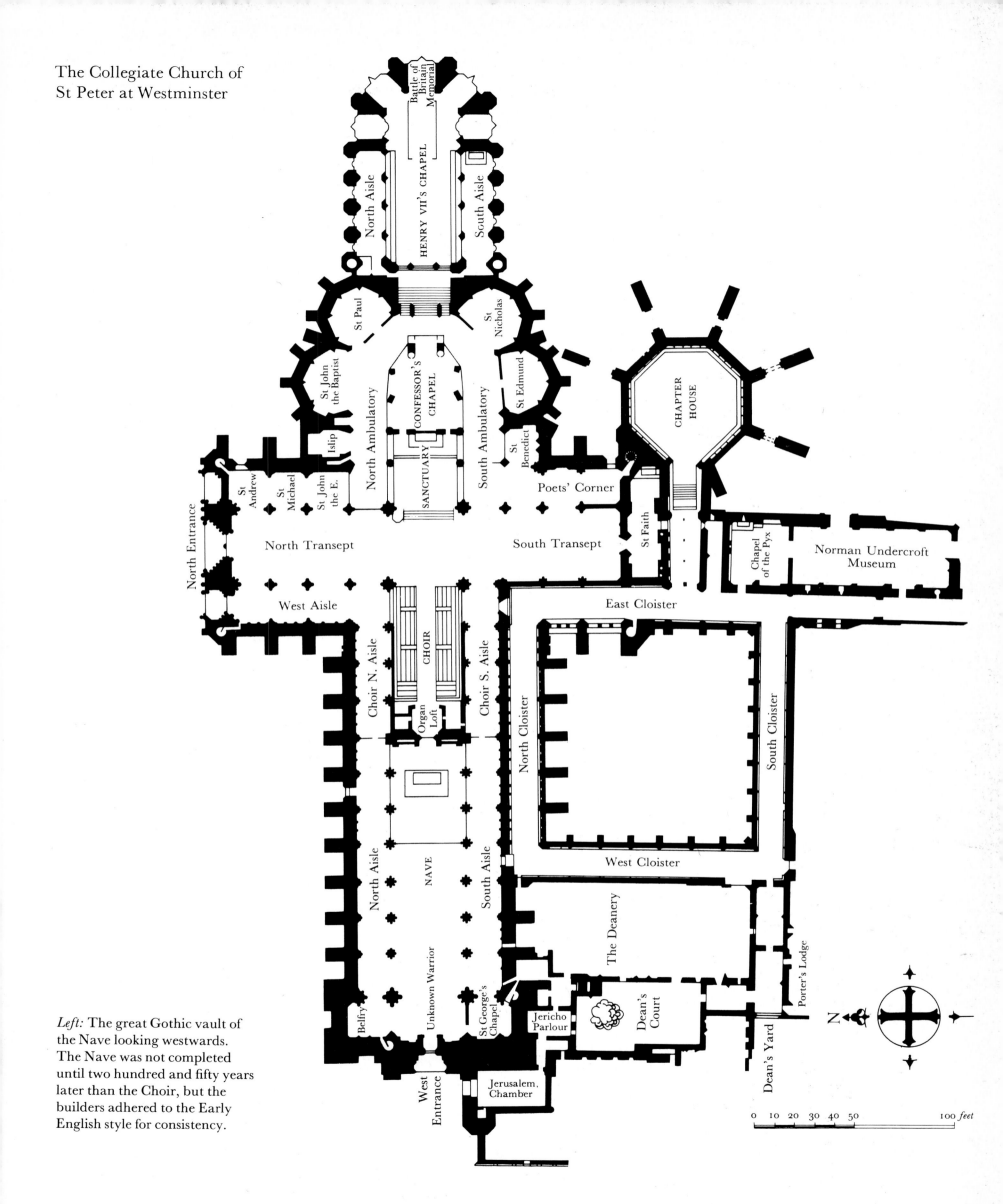

The Collegiate Church of
St Peter at Westminster

Left: The great Gothic vault of
the Nave looking westwards.
The Nave was not completed
until two hundred and fifty years
later than the Choir, but the
builders adhered to the Early
English style for consistency.

Battle of Britain Memorial

HENRY VII'S CHAPEL

North Aisle

South Aisle

St Paul

St Nicholas

St John the Baptist

Islip

St Edmund

CONFESSOR'S CHAPEL

North Ambulatory

SANCTUARY

South Ambulatory

St Benedict

CHAPTER HOUSE

St Andrew

St Michael

St John the E.

Poets' Corner

St Faith

Chapel of the Pyx

Norman Undercroft Museum

North Entrance

North Transept

South Transept

West Aisle

East Cloister

Choir N. Aisle

CHOIR

Choir S. Aisle

North Cloister

South Cloister

Organ Loft

North Aisle

NAVE

South Aisle

West Cloister

The Deanery

Porter's Lodge

Belfry

Unknown Warrior

St George's Chapel

Jericho Parlour

Dean's Court

Dean's Yard

N

West Entrance

Jerusalem Chamber

0 10 20 30 40 50   100 *feet*

Romanesque capital which probably came from the twelfth-century Cloisters. The carvings represent scenes from the story of the Judgment of Solomon. *Above:* The restitution of the child to its true mother. *Below:* Solomon giving his judgment to the two mothers.
Right: General view of the interior, showing the Choir.

Mid-thirteenth century corbels
from St Faith's Chapel.
Above: Negroid head.
Above right: Grotesque head.
Right: Corbel of a lady.

Mid-thirteenth century corbels.
Above: Corbel of a lady in St Faith's Chapel.
Above right: Grotesque head in St Faith's Chapel.
Right: Corbel bust, thought to represent a craftsman, in the East Triforium.

Thirteenth-century roof bosses.
Above: The scene of the
Annunciation in the west aisle
of the North Transept.
Above right: Combat between a
man and a lion centaur, in the
Muniment Room.
Right: Combat between a lion
centaur and a dragon, in the
Muniment Room.

Roof bosses from the Nave.
Above left: Centaur drawing his
bow, from the North Aisle.
Above: Lions attacking a man,
from the North Aisle.
Left: Cock in foliage, from
the South Aisle.

The Nave and Choir looking
towards the east.

Opposite : General view of the
Nave towards the west.

Above: Figures of a pilgrim and a censing angel below the rose window of the South Transept.
Right: The figure of an angel in the spandrel below the rose window of the North Transept.

Far right: The great rose window of the South Transept, with two of the angels below.

Left : Busts of angels on the soffit of a window in the North Transept.
Below : Thirteenth-century falcon capital in the Muniment Room.
Right : General view of the North Transept.

Right: Corbel head of a youthful king, over the door of the North Transept.
Below: Corbel head, thought to represent a master craftsman, in the North Transept below the rose window.
Below right: Lancet window and corbel heads in the Muniment Room.

Details of the wooden misericords in Henry VII's Chapel, carved at the beginning of the sixteenth century. *Right:* A woman exchanging her dead baby for a live one, from the story of the Judgment of Solomon. The main scene is carved to the left, but not illustrated.
Below left: Pig playing the bagpipe.
Below right: Man pulling a face with his fingers.

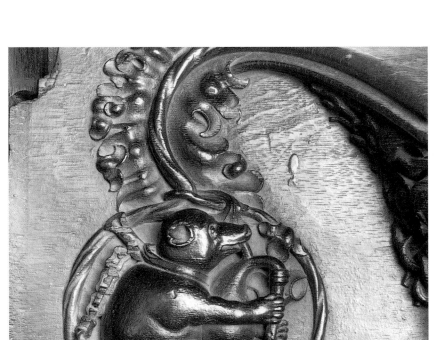

Opposite : Part of the painted sedilia to the right of the high altar, erected during the reign of Edward I. This detail shows one of the kings, possibly Henry III or Edward I.

Three of the shields which decorate the spandrels of the Nave Aisles. They represent the arms of (above), Edward the Confessor (created specially, as heraldry did not exist in the eleventh century), Henry III (lower left) and Richard, Earl of Cornwall, Henry's younger brother who was also King of the Romans (lower right).

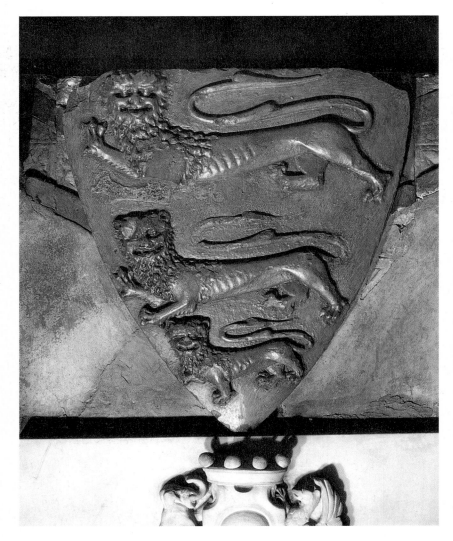

Left : Ackermann's engraving of the thirteenth-century Cosmati-work pavement in front of the high altar. The design is said to represent the world according to the Ptolemaic system. The pavement was made by Pietro di Oderisio, the craftsman sent from Rome to work on the shrine of Edward the Confessor in 1268.

Right: The thirteenth-century doorway of the Chapter House in the East Cloister. This was once decorated with fine sculpture, but it is now seriously decayed. Originally, a statue of the Virgin and Child stood in the centre, flanked by figures of angels. The whole doorway was also brilliantly coloured with vermilion and gold on blue to produce a 'gate beautiful'.

Left: Thirteenth-century tiles from the pavement of the Chapter House. Details showing (above) musicians and (below) rose windows and pike.

Right: The doorway from the Chapter House into the vestibule, which was heavily restored by Sir Gilbert Scott in the mid-nineteenth century. He cut away the dividing column of the double archway and put in a tympanum of Christ in Majesty. He did, however, retain the lovely thirteenth-century statues of the Archangel Gabriel and the Virgin in the scene of the Annunciation in trefoil niches on either side of the doorway. In the spandrels, also in trefoil niches, are reliefs of censing angels similar in style to those in the Transepts of the Church.

Far left: Detail from the thirteenth-century retable showing St Peter. The figure is painted with delicate brush-work, on an ornamental gold background.

Left and below: Wall paintings from the Chapter House, which was executed in about 1400 by the order of John of Northampton. These details are taken from the lower zone of the paintings and show a dromedary, a reindeer and a roe, divided by a tree.

Two panels of the original
thirteenth-century stained glass,
now in the Abbey Museum.
They depict (left) the Descent of
the Holy Ghost and (right) the
Ascension.

King David from the Westminster Psalter, which was written in about 1200 at the Abbey, and is now in the British Museum.

Right: A page from the *Liber Regalis*, one of the Abbey's manuscript treasures. It provided the order for the coronation of a king and a queen, and this illustration shows the crowning of a king. It was written in the reign of Richard II, possibly by a Bohemian artist in the train of Queen Anne.

Overleaf: Part of the thirteenth-century retable believed to be the work of an English painter. This detail shows the feeding of the five thousand, set against a background of painted coloured glass. The surrounding frame is enriched by imitation cameos, gems and precious stones.

Below left: General view of Henry v's Chantry Chapel from the North Ambulatory, showing the coronation ceremony.
Below right: Detail from the Chapel with the King portrayed in full armour, galloping across the battlefield.

Far right: General view of
Henry VII's Chapel looking
eastwards. The tomb of
Henry VII and his Queen,
Elizabeth of York, stands in the
centre of the Chapel behind
the altar.

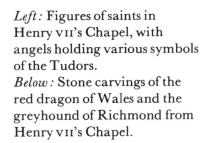

Left: Figures of saints in
Henry VII's Chapel, with
angels holding various symbols
of the Tudors.
Below: Stone carvings of the
red dragon of Wales and the
greyhound of Richmond from
Henry VII's Chapel.

Details of the screen or 'closure' which surrounds the tomb of Henry VII. This was executed in bronze-gilt at the beginning of the sixteenth century, possibly by Thomas Ducheman. *Above:* Many of the figures in the niches have disappeared, but a few survive, including this statue of St Edward the Confessor.

Right: A general view of the screen, which is covered by the badges of Henry VII – the Welsh dragon, the Tudor rose, and the greyhound of Richmond.

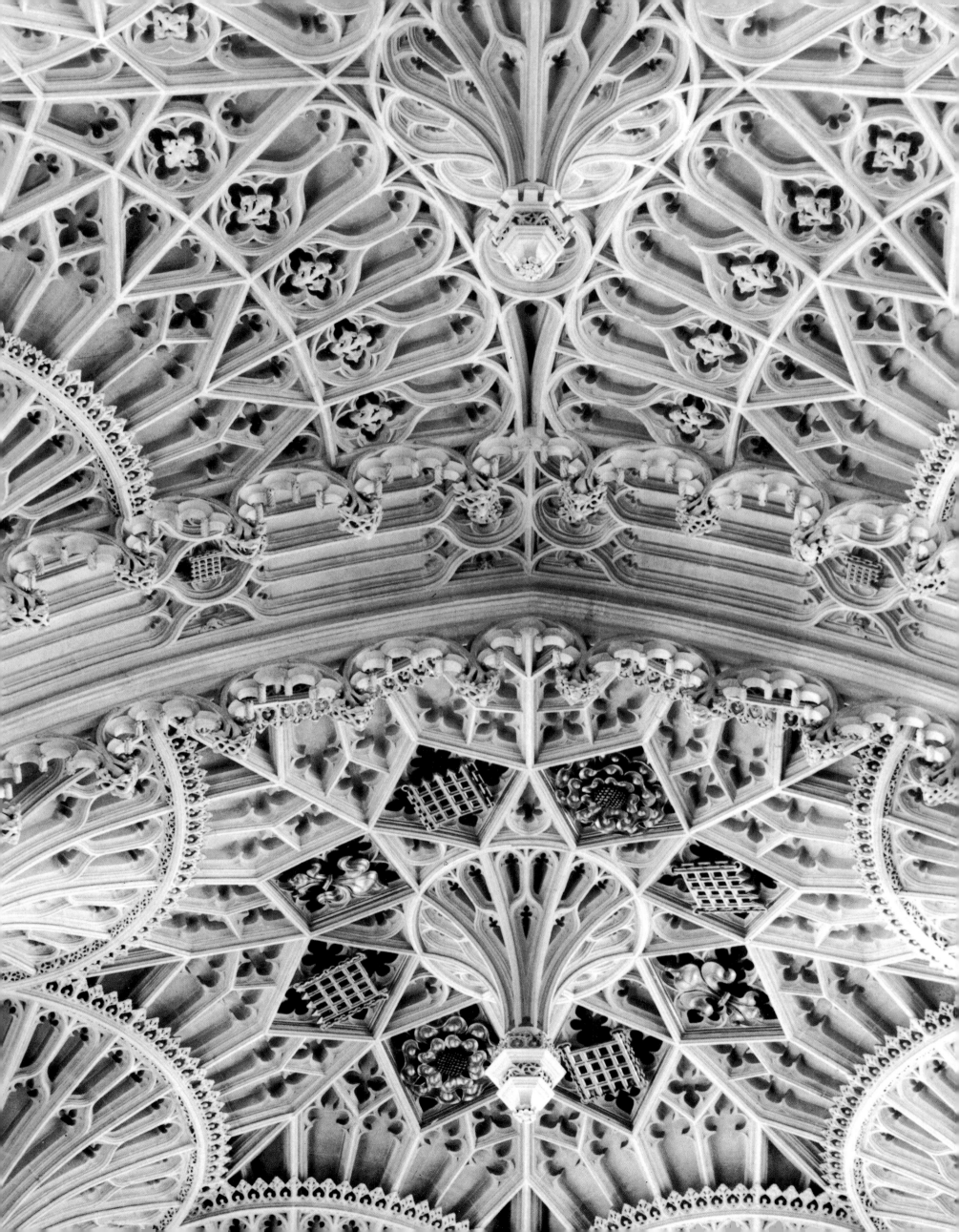

No sooner was the Abbey and all its monastic structures completed than the idea was born of enlarging the Church by an extension towards the east. This was the Lady Chapel, begun under Henry III's patronage in 1220, but it no longer exists, having been replaced by an even larger chapel, that of Henry VII, begun in 1503.

The present Abbey owes everything to King Henry III. There is an obvious parallel between Edward the Confessor's pro-Norman sympathies and the erection by him of the first Norman Romanesque church in England, and King Henry's French connections and his patronage of the new Abbey which, with good reason, is termed the most French of English churches.

Soon after St Catherine's Infirmary Chapel, still entirely Romanesque in style, was completed, a new style, the Gothic, made its first appearance in England – in the celebrated Choir of Canterbury Cathedral, the metropolitan church of England. The fire of 1174 necessitated its rebuilding, and this came at an opportune moment, a year after the canonization of the martyr St Thomas Becket. At one stroke, Canterbury acquired a most up-to-date building and the relics which were to outshine all others in the country, thus becoming a pilgrimage place of European importance.

The decision taken by Henry III in 1245 to rebuild the Abbey Church, the oldest parts of which were at that time not yet two hundred years old, must be regarded as a combination of several motives. First, the cult of Edward the Confessor grew in importance (he was canonized in 1161) and the King, who had a genuine, deep devotion to the saint, obviously wished to give this growing cult as much support as possible by providing a more suitable setting for the shrine. He may have also tried, by these means, to distract attention from Canterbury and St Thomas, for the circumstances of his martyrdom were nothing to be proud of for Henry II's grandson.

The solemn translation of St Thomas's body to the newly dedicated Choir took place in Henry III's presence in 1220, and it was precisely in this year that the building of the Lady Chapel at Westminster was started. But the work on the new Choir and Transepts was not begun until 1245, that is some years after Henry came of age. By that date, many of the large French Gothic cathedrals had been completed or were sufficiently advanced to be already admired and even imitated. The French King Louis IX (1226–70) played a prominent part in these prodigious building operations. St Louis (he was canonized in 1297), because of his reputation as a just and pious monarch and a patron who supported art of all kinds, and created what was, in fact, a court art of the highest quality and refinement, was emulated by many other rulers of his time, not least by Henry III, his English brother-in-law. The buildings so closely connected with French royal ceremonial, Saint-Denis Abbey and Rheims Cathedral, were either partially or entirely rebuilt. The hallmarks of the *rayonnant* Gothic style of these buildings were the rich radiating designs of the rose windows and the traceries of other large windows. The extensive use of flying buttresses enabled the architects to replace the walls by a series of windows filled with stained glass.

King Henry clearly wanted to leave his mark on the Church which was so closely linked with the English royal house at Westminster. By then, the Gothic style was already firmly established in England, with many large churches rebuilt or in the process of being built (such as Salisbury, Lincoln, Wells). In them, an English version of the style was evolved, in which the height of the interiors is by French standards moderate and the vertical two-towered façades of French cathedrals replaced by broad screen façades.

Detail of the fan vault of Henry VII's Chapel. Like all parts of the Chapel, the stonework of the vault is decorated with the badges of the Tudors.

The design of Henry III's Westminster is by far the most French of all the English buildings of the period, and yet it is not a French structure. The royal architect of the time, mentioned in documents between 1243 and 1253, was Henry of Reyns, and it has been suggested that he was a Frenchman from Rheims. On the other hand, there are other names mentioned which are undoubtedly English and, although Westminster owes much to such buildings as Rheims, Amiens, Saint-Denis and Sainte-Chapelle (this last built by St Louis in Paris to house the relics of the Crown of Thorns), these English architects left their mark on the design of Westminster.

In the plan of the Abbey, the Choir, which is terminated by a five-sided apse, is the focal point of the Church, and provides the setting for the shrine of St Edward. The Choir is encircled by an ambulatory, from which project radiating chapels. The Transepts have aisles, the North Transept two, the South only a single aisle, towards the east. Then follows a long Nave with aisles, terminating in a two-towered Western Façade. The four bays of the Nave nearest the Transept were originally enclosed by screens, for the monks' Choir extended as far west as this point, leaving the rest of the Church for the lay congregation. The principal entrance was not from the west but through the North Transept, for this was the shortest route from the Palace of Westminster. The rebuilding of the Church started, as was customary, from the east and proceeded very quickly, so that in the first ten years the eastern bays of the Nave were completed. At the same time, the new Chapter House and the north and part of the east walk of the Cloister were erected. When, in 1269, the relics of St Edward were solemnly translated to the new shrine, the western part of the Nave, built by Edward, was still intact, and it remained in use until 1375. Only then was it pulled down and replaced by the Gothic extension, which was the work of the architect Henry Yevele. He faithfully followed the original thirteenth-century design, introducing only minor modifications. He was not to finish the work, for the existing Western Towers were built to the design of the celebrated architect Nicholas Hawksmoor, between 1735 and 1745. Like Yevele before him, Hawskmoor blended his design with the thirteenth-century work so well that only a few details betray the fact that he was essentially a Baroque architect.

The last great addition to the Abbey was the building of a new Lady Chapel, more sumptuous than that erected by Henry III. The work was started by Henry VII in 1503 and was completed by Henry VIII in 1512, as the burial chapel of his father, and it is, therefore, known as the Chapel of Henry VII.

The history of the Abbey during the last two hundred years, is more concerned with restorations than additions or rebuilding. The aim, since the time of Christopher Wren (1632–1723), who was the first of many famous architects in charge of the restoration of the Abbey, has been to preserve this monument, which is not only a work of art of the highest order, but is also so intimately linked with a thousand years of English history.

The building itself, when examined from the outside, presents numerous and obvious French features: the radiating chapels of the Choir, the forest of buttresses and flying buttresses (three rows of them on the south side, and these should be viewed from the Cloisters), and above all, the windows filled with traceries. Some of these, as for instance the windows of the Choir, are spherical triangles, which repeat the designs of the most up-to-date French models. It is unfortunate that the three-gabled principal entrance to the Abbey in the North Transept is largely the work of restoration, for what little remains of the original work, demonstrates the independence of this feature from French portals, with their concentration of figure sculpture upon the tympana and door-jambs. The English portals, whether Romanesque or Gothic, gave preference to ornamental, purely decorative motifs.

The original decoration is much better preserved in the interior of the Church. Here, the elevation, the slender proportions and the general design are based on such French buildings as, for instance, Rheims Cathedral, but the gallery is an English feature taken over from Romanesque buildings. In comparison with French High Gothic churches, there is yet another, more fundamental difference. In France, the interiors are sober, rational, often devoid of sculpture. At Westminster, the English taste for a rich, luxuriant, colourful surface pattern is carried to extremes. Not only are the shafts made of Purbeck stone, different in texture and colour from the rest of the fabric, not only are all the arches adorned with complex, delicate mouldings, but all the available wall-surface is enriched with carved diaper or floral patterns. Many of the spandrels of the wall-arcades, whether in the aisles, Choir chapels, the Transepts or the Nave are, or were, filled with the most intricate sculpture, some of the best that was produced in mid-thirteenth-century England. Unfortunately, much of this sculpture was obliterated by the later wall-monuments. In many cases, the decoration consists merely of conventional foliage but, not infrequently, there are also scrolls of naturalistic foliage, birds, animals and even figural motifs, some religious, which miraculously survived the iconoclastic zeal of the Reformation. The most beautiful of them all, and the best preserved because beyond easy reach, are the angels in high relief in the spandrels, below the magnificent rose windows of the Transepts. Here, Gothic sculpture displays the newly-discovered naturalism, still tentative, occasionally awkward, but full of lyrical grace. The angels' outstretched wings and the rich draperies of their robes, fill the triangular spandrels in a most skilful way. Parallels exist for such spandrel angels in France, for instance in Sainte-Chapelle, but none compare in beauty with those of Westminster. That these sculptures were admired by contemporaries can be deduced from the fact that the same scheme, on an even larger scale, was repeated shortly afterwards in what is known as the Angels' Choir of Lincoln Cathedral. In the aisles of the Nave, the spandrels are decorated with armorial shields of great decorative merit and of great importance as early examples of heraldry. The arms include those of Edward the Confessor (imaginary, since heraldry did not exist in the eleventh century), Henry III, St Louis of France and Richard, Earl of Cornwall (Henry's younger brother). The work was certainly completed before 1264, for one of the shields is that of Simon de Montfort, who rebelled against the King in that year and was killed the following year.

The inventiveness of Henry III's sculptors can further be seen in the delightful and unconventional enrichments applied to such features as, for instance, the soffits (lower surfaces) of the windows (North Transept). Carved corbel heads or busts abound, even in the less accessible parts of the Church. Lavish bosses display naturalistic leaves and plants, monsters, or religious figures or scenes. Amongst the most beautiful is the Annunciation (the west aisle of the North Transept), showing the Virgin Mary about to turn the page of a book on a reading desk and in a pose of humble submission on hearing the words of the Archangel Gabriel. Equally beautiful are the bosses representing combats between men, centaurs and beasts found in the Muniment Room, which is above the north-eastern Cloister walk, and which was probably originally the Royal Pew, from which the King could watch the Mass. Even some ribs of the vaulting are enriched with sculpture and these have now been restored in their original colours. For it should be remembered that most mediaeval sculpture was painted, and at Westminster many traces of bright colours and of gilding still survive, uncovered by recent cleaning. Thus the effect of the interior must have been truly sumptuous and jewel-like.

The sculptors employed at the Abbey were kept exceptionally busy. The octagonal Chapter House, lit by large windows and supported in the centre by a slender compound column, is, in spite of severe restoration, architecturally a superb work, in which French features, such as traceried windows, are blended with an overwhelmingly English over-all design. It was built between 1245 and 1253, and combines graceful architectural forms with subtle decoration in which, originally, vast expanses of stained glass must have played a prominent part. The colour effect extended on to the walls, enriched with trefoil arcading, decorative sculpture on the spandrels and painting at the back of the seats. On five sides of the octagon these paintings are still quite well preserved: they were added in about 1400 at the expense of John of Northampton, a monk of Westminster, and represent the Last Judgement and scenes from the Apocalypse. The decorative scheme further extended to the floor, which preserves the superb decorative tiles of about 1255. In style and in motifs, they resemble contemporary tiles in the royal abbeys at Chertsey in Surrey and in Hailes in Gloucestershire, and were probably designed by Master William, 'the King's beloved painter'. Traces of a charming inscription (the south-eastern part of the floor) survive: '*Ut rosa flos florum, sic est domus ista domorum.*' ('As the rose is the flower of flowers, so this House is the house of houses.') The Chapter House is linked with the Cloister by a long vestibule divided into two chambers. The outer doorway, facing the Cloister, was originally decorated with delicate sculpture, now largely decayed, but the doorway facing the interior of the octagon contains much original work. Unfortunately, the restorers of the nineteenth century inserted, quite unnecessarily and wrongly, a Christ in Majesty, where there was originally an open-work tympanum above the door, supported by a slender trumeau, or stone pier. Flanking the doorway in trefoil niches, are the original mid-thirteenth-century statues of the Archangel Gabriel and the Virgin in the scene of the Annunciation. Stylistically, these sculptures are so close to the angels of the Transept spandrels that they must have been the work of the same artist or workshop. In the trefoiled fields, reliefs of censing angels complete the composition. This doorway includes on both its faces, towards the Chapter House and towards the vestibule, delicate, almost filigree sculptures on the arches and the jambs. The open-work, pierced tympana, the placing of statues in niches or on brackets, rather than their use as column-figures of door-jambs, the small scale decorative sculpture instead of monumental figure sculpture, all these are characteristics which make English Gothic so different from French.

The rebuilding of the Abbey was intended to provide a worthy setting for the shrine of St Edward. The shrine itself, made of gold set with precious stones, was commissioned in 1241, even before the rebuilding began. Such shrines, with gabled roofs, were often quite large; that of St Edward must have been particularly splendid, for it was praised as incomparable by foreigners, even as late as the early sixteenth century, shortly before its destruction at the time of the Reformation. The shrine was probably of English workmanship, and when the Choir was ready, it was placed behind the Altar, as was the custom, on a high pedestal, which luckily survives. It is decorated with twisted colonettes at the corners and originally it was flanked by two columns carrying the statues of St Edward and the Pilgrim (for according to legend, Edward gave a ring to a poor pilgrim who was, in fact, St John the Evangelist in disguise; he was supposed later to have returned the ring to the King, through English pilgrims visiting the Holy Land). The making of the pedestal as well as of the pavement around the shrine and in front of the High Altar, was entrusted to Italians, who were masters of the technique known as Cosmati work, a kind of mosaic made of coloured materials, such as red and green porphyry, marble and glass. The materials were brought from Rome, and the work was carried out between 1267 and 1272. The pedestal was executed by Petrus Romanus and the pavement by Odericus. Cosmati work, of which many examples, chiefly of the twelfth and thirteenth centuries, survive in Rome and elsewhere in Italy, relies for effect on geometric patterns, often made by continuous bands forming circles and rectangles, skilfully interlaced and linked together, with the background filled with small, multi-coloured stones, cut into intricate, geometric shapes. It has been pointed out that the tomb of Pope Clement IV at Viterbo, which includes Cosmati work, was made by Petrus Romanus. The Pope died in 1268, while Odericus and his son were in London, and it was the son Petrus who carried out the work at Viterbo, returning to Westminster to complete the work there. In addition to the shrine and the pavement, the Italian team executed the base for the future tomb of Henry III, and the tomb of the royal children.

At the same time as the Italian artists were busy in the Abbey, embellishing it with works in techniques hardly ever seen before outside Italy, the main retable (or perhaps merely the antependium of the High Altar), was commissioned to be painted on a wooden panel. No documents exist to throw light on its precise function, its author or its date. Most recent scholarship believes it to be a work of about 1270, and its style can be paralleled by the finest illuminated manuscripts of the period. No comparable panel painting survives anywhere in Europe, so obviously King Henry spared no effort to have everything in his Church of unsurpassed quality. Unfortunately the panel is very damaged, but the portions which survive testify to the exceptional artistic level and the elaborate iconographic programme. In the centre, Christ, with the globe in his hand, blesses. He is flanked by the Virgin and St John the Evangelist, as in representations of the Crucifixion. This central group was, in turn, flanked by small scenes of Christ's miracles, contained in star-shaped fields, but only those on the left side survive. The composition was finally flanked by two figures, those of the principal apostles, St Peter (the patron saint of the Abbey) and St Paul. The painted scenes are placed against a background of painted, coloured glass and the frames are enriched with imitation cameos, gems and precious stones. The figures are elongated and graceful, rendered with an obvious love of minute detail, suggesting that the artist was trained as a miniature painter.

Little is known of earlier painting at Westminster. As far as manuscripts are concerned, the earliest surviving book, decorated with five full-page miniatures, is the so-called Westminster Psalter, now in the British Museum (Royal MS. 2A.XXII). It was produced towards the end of the twelfth century, and represents the distinctive 'classical' style, which characterized the transition from Romanesque to Gothic. To this manuscript, a mid-thirteenth-century artist added five drawings, which are very close in style to the drawings of the historian and monk of St Albans, Matthew Paris.

King Henry knew Matthew Paris well, and one wonders whether these pages added to the Psalter have anything to do with the close relationship between the two men. Incidentally, in the *Historia Anglorum* by Paris (British Museum, Royal MS. 14C. VII, folio 9v.), there is a representation of King Henry, holding in his hand a model of Westminster Abbey, as if the historian considered it the King's greatest achievement.

The very high artistic standard of the service books in the Abbey can, of course, be assumed, but there are two outstanding manuscripts surviving from a later century, which demonstrate it vividly. These manuscripts, still in the possession of the Abbey, are the Missal of Abbot Nicholas Litlyngton and the *Liber Regalis*, giving the order for the coronation of a king and a queen. Both these books were produced in the early 1380s, but they differ from each other very strikingly. The first contains a well-known page with the Crucifixion, painted in a heavy style and dominated by exuberant decorative devices. The other, in subtle, beautiful colours, is believed to have been influenced by the art of Bohemia, through the contact established between that country and England by the marriage of King Richard II in 1382 to Anne of Bohemia.

The high quality of wall-painting in England during the years of Henry III's reign and in the century that followed, can be illustrated by other surviving examples in the Abbey. The very tall figure of St Christopher and the Incredulity of St Thomas, are remnants of wall-paintings on the south wall of the South Transept, and are roughly contemporary with the retable, but in contrast with the delicate and detailed treatment of the retable's figures, the wall-paintings are summary and monumental. There is also a late thirteenth-century wall-painting surviving over the altar in St Faith's Chapel (entrance from the South Transept) and the sedilia in the Presbytery south of the High Altar, painted in the early years of the fourteenth century.

The important part played by painting in the general effect of the interior must be guessed rather than experienced. The same can be said of the stained glass, so dominant in Gothic buildings with their large windows. Of the original thirteenth-century glass, alas, little survives. A document of 1272 mentions William le Verrer (glass-maker), and it is tempting to attribute to him the excellent glass representing scenes from the life of Christ and episodes from the lives of the saints, framed by mandorlas, quatrefoils and roundels which is preserved in the Abbey Museum in the Dark Cloister. These small scenes were undoubtedly originally used in the Abbey Church and date from before the consecration of the building in 1269.

At the time of the consecration, the Abbey was still full of artists and craftsmen completing their tasks and for at least a generation work continued, to provide furnishings and adornments. In fact, since then the work has been unceasing. Each century, each generation, has made further additions and changes. Chantry chapels were added, new windows inserted and tombs began to crowd the interior, while repairs must have been made almost constantly. Thus, the Abbey is a complex and wonderful monument to the artistic aims and fashions of many ages.

Of the chantry chapels, the most important is undoubtedly that of Henry V in the easternmost bay of the ambulatory, incorporating a bridge which contains an altar. Two open-work spiral stair-turrets lead to the upper storey. The general idea of the design, it is believed, was derived from the delicate structure housing the relics in the upper church of Sainte-Chapelle, in Paris. The author of the design was John Thirske, the King's master mason, who was also responsible for the eastern screen in the Presbytery. King Henry died in 1422, but the actual execution of the design, which had been made in 1415 and approved by him, was not carried out at once and the work was not completed till some thirty years later. The Chantry is enriched by numerous statues of various sizes, heraldic devices, canopies, friezes and, above all, by reliefs representing the King's coronation and his military exploits. The sculpture is perhaps not of the highest order, but it is quite up-to-date, for it displays the extensive use of deeply under-cut angular draperies, which appeared first in Flanders and Germany in the second quarter of the fifteenth century.

The most striking contribution to the Abbey's appearance since the thirteenth century was made, however, at the waning of the Middle Ages, when Henry VII decided to erect a new Lady Chapel to house the tomb of Henry VI, who, it was hoped, would eventually be canonized, and by whose side he wished to be buried. This mausoleum extends the Abbey eastwards to contain its richest embellishments. It is preceded by a comparatively plain vestibule, so that the surprise on entering the Chapel itself is the greater. By the time the Chapel was built, in the first years of the sixteenth century, the English Perpendicular style had developed its most extravagant and sophisticated features, which the Chapel gave the opportunity to display. Not surprisingly, it was described by contemporaries as the *miraculum orbis* – the wonder of the world.

The plan of the Chapel consists of a 'nave' with aisles, and a 'chancel' with a three-sided apse and five radiating chapels. Externally, the structure is punctuated by octagonal buttresses crowned by bulbous pinnacles, decorated with panelling and, in their upper parts, originally adorned with statues. Between them are bow windows, which give the surface its undulating appearance. The curving flying buttresses, anchored to the octagonal buttresses, give support to the high walls of the main structure, which is pierced by large windows. The interior is full of light because of this abundance of windows. No part of the wall surface is plain, all is ornament and enrichment. Above the bronze gates and the arcades, a row of carved angels support shields with royal arms. Below the windows and in the chapels, there are statues placed in niches and surmounted by rich canopies. The elaborately carved wooden stalls are only in part original. Enclosing it all, from above, is the fan vaulting, audacious and at the same time delicate – 'a triumph of geometry and stone cutting' (Lethaby).

In Henry VII's will, there is provision for ten thousand Masses to be said for the salvation of his soul, in honour of the Trinity, for the Five Wounds of Christ and the Five Joys of the Virgin, the Nine Orders of Angels, the Patriarchs, the Twelve Apostles and for All Saints. Something of this is reflected in the iconography of the Chapel's statuary, though many figures, lacking inscriptions, and which were originally painted, are impossible to identify. They were carved in stone by several artists, and no wonder, since they amount to nearly one hundred. In spite of certain stylistic differences between them, they all display that late Gothic love of realism in their expressions, costumes, accessories and the extreme agitation of the deeply under-cut draperies, forming a complicated play of light and shade. Stylistically, they are connected with the late Gothic sculpture of the Low Countries, and it is not without interest that many craftsmen employed during that time at Westminster have Dutch names.

In spite of the Chapel's foreign-inspired sculpture, this *miraculum orbis* is as thoroughly English as is the thirteenth-century French-inspired Abbey. Reflecting as they do the tastes and aspirations of their founders, their piety as well as their worldly pride, they are as much their own creations as of the artists whom they employed.

John Pope-Hennessy

The Tombs and Monuments

'TIS CERTAIN there is not a nobler amusement in the world, than a walk in Westminster Abbey, among the tombs of heroes, patriots, poets and philosophers,' writes James Ralph in his *Critical Review of the Publick Buildings ... in and about London.* 'You are surrounded with the shades of your great forefathers; you feel the influence of their venerable society, and grow fond of fame and virtue in their contemplation; 'tis the finest school of morality, and the most beautiful flatterer of the imagination in nature.' In 1733, when Ralph's book was published, the message of the monuments at Westminster was less confused and less confusing than it is now. The most recent of them, those to Sir Isaac Newton (1731) and Lord Stanhope (1733), were designed by Kent and carried out by Rysbrack, and faithfully reflected, in their Augustan style, the moralizing predilections of the time. Beyond them stood a number of Stuart tombs, in the most notable of which a foreign artist, Hubert Le Sueur, celebrated the unheroic figure of George Villiers, Duke of Buckingham, in the symbolic language of Northern Baroque art. Moving back in time, there were a number of Jacobean and Elizabethan monuments, of which the finest commemorated Queen Elizabeth I and the largest, typical in its diffuseness and polychromy, was dedicated to her Chamberlain, Lord Hunsdon. These tombs had it in common that their spirit, if not their imagery, was secular. In so far as they possessed a common factor, it was that the artists who produced them looked on the Abbey as a vast container for sepulchral monuments. But across the caesura of the Reformation lay a host of memorials which conformed to the ethos of the Church, stretching back from the tomb of King Henry VII in the King's own Chapel to that of Edward the Confessor. In 1733 it would have been impossible to visualize the great mid-eighteenth-century examples of the tomb as drama, still less the point at which the fever of these monuments abated, at the classicizing hands of Flaxman and of Westmacott, as the noble stoicism of the eighteenth century succumbed to a prosaic tide of Victorian civic piety.

The monuments at Westminster reflect not only changes in commemorative practice, but changes in the policy governing burial in the Church. The Abbey was designed by Edward the Confessor as his own burial place, and when he died, in January 1066, his body was interred, as he intended, near the High Altar. In the century that followed, the tomb became a place of pilgrimage, the cult reaching its climax when he was canonized in 1161. When the Abbey was rebuilt under King Henry III, St

Edward's body was reinterred at the east end of the new building, and the King chose a site for his own grave to the north of the shrine. The artists responsible for the shrine and royal tomb, and for the mosaic pavements of the Presbytery and of the Chapel of the Confessor, came from Rome and are known by the generic name of the Cosmati; they were Odericus, who in 1268 signed the Presbytery pavement, and Petrus Romanus (or Pietro di Oderisio), who was responsible for the Confessor's shrine. The magnificent geometrical design of the pavement can be associated with those of pavements in the neighbourhood of Rome at Farfa Sabina and Anagni, while the Confessor's shrine makes use of related decorative motifs that recur in Roman monuments. The Confessor's body was translated to the new shrine in 1269, carried by King Henry III, his sons, and his brother, Richard Earl of Cornwall, King of the Romans. Immediately after, work began on the tomb of the King, which is in the form of a rectangular tomb-chest resting on a high platform decorated with mosaic.

In its present state the tomb of the Confessor gives a sadly inadequate impression of the shrine that pilgrims in the Middle Ages would have visited. What is preserved is the base, which originally supported the feretory of the Confessor. At the time of the Dissolution of the Monasteries the feretory was stripped of its gold casing, and the base seems to have been levelled to the ground. In the winter of 1556, after the accession of Queen Mary I, it was hastily rebuilt, but much of the glass mosaic inlay had been damaged beyond repair. An inscription in mosaic round the top had been prised out and the matrices (which are still visible at the east end of the shrine) were plastered over. The painted inscription dates from this time. In looking at this part of the shrine it must be remembered that the interior of the niches, three on each side, and the whole outer surface were covered with mosaic, and that the present effect of the effulgent glass tesserae in the spiral columns, the tesserae in the niches and the geometrical marble slabs let into the surface would have been greatly magnified. Though the gold feretory was destroyed, the Confessor's coffin survived, and in 1556 it was set once more in its old position, covered with a wooden canopy with glass pilasters. It is in this much mutilated form that the shrine survives today.

Pietro di Oderisio, the author of this work and of the tomb of King Henry III, was also responsible for the wall-monument of Pope Clement IV at Viterbo, which, like the royal tomb, is planned on two levels, and consists of a deep plinth supporting a tomb chest. The plinth of the Henry III tomb is once more decorated in mosaic, and has three apertures for relics; close parallels for these occur in Cosmatesque altars in Rome and especially in the ciborium of San Giorgio in Velabro. The sarcophagus above is a work of great distinction; it terminates at the corners in paired spiral columns, and its sides are formed of huge oblong panels of red porphyry framed in mosaic. Small porphyry slabs occur on episcopal thrones made by the Cosmati for Santa Sabina and San Lorenzo fuori le mura, in Rome, but nowhere else was this prized material used on so generous a scale as it is here. There is a tradition that the porphyry was brought back by King Edward I from the Crusades, but it is more probable that, like the material for St Edward's shrine, they were procured in Rome.

The Henry III tomb is very high, and from the floor of the Chapel or from the ambulatory the gilt bronze effigy of the King on top of the sarcophagus is practically invisible. Perhaps it was originally intended that the tomb, like the adjacent tomb of Edward I, should consist simply of a sarcophagus. The effigy dates from nineteen years after the King's death (1272), and was commissioned by his son Edward I, at the time of the death of his first wife, Eleanor of Castille, whose tomb, with a gilt bronze effigy by the same artist, William Torel, also stands nearby in the Confessor's Chapel. Both effigies were in course of manufacture in 1291. In the tomb sculpture of the thirteenth century, Torel's two figures have a place apart. Other thirteenth-century bronze effigies are known – the whole conception of the royal mausoleum in the Abbey seems to derive from the group of commemorative monuments commissioned by Louis IX of France in 1263–4 for Saint-Denis – but none are modelled with such elegance or chased with such refinement as these figures. Though Torel, who practised as a goldsmith, appears to have been English, the two effigies, with their idealized features and their smoothly articulated robes, make use of the *lingua franca* of French Gothic art. This is the less surprising when we read, as we can do only in photographs, the inscription in Lombardic letters that runs round the top of the King's tomb-chest: '*Ici gist henri jadis rey de engletere seygnur de hirlaunde educ de aquitayne lefiz lirey johan jadis rey de engletere akideu face merci amen.*' ('Here lies Henry, formerly King of England, Lord of Ireland and Duke of Aquitaine, son of King John, formerly King of England, on whom God have mercy. Amen.') Both figures were studded with jewels; in the effigy of the King there are holes for jewels in the crown, and in that of Queen Eleanor there were jewels in the necklace held in the left hand. The right hand of the Queen originally held a sceptre, and the hands of the King held a sceptre and orb. The two effigies have one peculiarity which was important for later tombs at Westminster – each was framed in a gilt bronze tabernacle which covered the head and ran down alongside the figure. The canopy and sections of the sides of the tabernacle of the Eleanor of Castille tomb are preserved, and holes for fixing on the upper surface of the Henry III tomb show that the figure of the King was framed in the same way. This practice continued in the royal monuments at Westminster until the early sixteenth century.

Almost a century separates the tomb of Eleanor of Castille from that of Queen Philippa of Hainault (1369) on the south side of the Confessor's Chapel. This was entrusted to one of the most highly prized marble sculptors of the time, Hennequin de Liège, whose reputation had been made in Paris. Originally Queen Philippa's tomb was a work of great complexity, with thirty small portrait figures round the sarcophagus and a total of seventy subsidiary figures. With one exception these have disappeared, but the marble effigy, with strongly marked features that must be based upon a death-mask, is a work of extraordinary accomplishment. Despite Queen Philippa's wish that her husband should 'not choose any other sepulchre than mine, and that you will lie beside me in the Cloister at Westminster,' Edward III has a separate monument in the centre of the south side of the Chapel. When he died, in 1377, a mask was taken of his features; the head of the resulting funeral effigy is still preserved at Westminster. Presumably the mask, which reveals traces of the stroke suffered by the King before his death, was made available to John Orchard, the putative author of the gilt bronze effigy, but if so it was rejected in favour of a conventionalized head with few of the characteristics of a portrait. Orchard (if the effigy be his) undertook work for the tomb of Philippa of Hainault and seems also to have been responsible for the tomb of the Black Prince at Canterbury, and his stiff hieratic style (which can be seen again in the six small gilt bronze figures in relief on the side of the tomb facing towards the ambulatory) would be impressive in any other context than that established by Torel's earlier and more sensitive bronze sculptures.

Orchard was also responsible for one of the strangest and most touching of the Abbey monuments, that to William of Windsor and Blanche of the Tower (died 1340), children of Edward III who died in infancy and are commemorated in the Chapel of St Edmund by minuscule alabaster effigies. This tomb forms a middle term between the little altar tomb in the south ambulatory, originally decorated with marble and mosaic, which commemorates four children of Henry III and four children of Edward I and may have been made after the death of Henry III's daughter Catherine (1257), and the small monuments in the Confessor's Chapel to Margaret, daughter of Edward IV, who died at the age of nine months in 1472, and Elizabeth, daughter of Henry VII, who died in 1495 at the age of three. In the north aisle of the Henry VII Chapel is a sarcophagus containing bones identified in 1674 as those of Edward V and Richard, Duke of York (murdered in 1483). The remains of the Duke of York's child bride, Anne Mowbray, who died in 1480–1, have recently been reinterred in the Chapel. Some of the most striking of these child monuments are those erected by Maximilian Colt to two children of King James I, Princess Sophia, who died in 1606 when three days old, and Princess Mary, who died in 1607 aged two.

The great series of gilt bronze royal effigies is resumed, at the west end of the south side of the Chapel, with the double tomb commissioned in his own lifetime by King Richard II for himself and his Queen, Anne of Bohemia. Anne of Bohemia died in 1394, and the tomb must have been made between this date and the King's death six years later. The effigies were ordered in 1395 from two London bronze-workers, Nicholas Broker and Godfrey Prest. In this tomb the supporters beneath the feet and the cushions under the heads are missing (the latter were replaced in the nineteenth century), and the figures lack the hands, which were cast separately. According to the contract, the King and Queen were to be shown 'clasping their right hands together and holding sceptres in their left hands'. The head of Anne of Bohemia was adapted from a funeral effigy (which is still preserved at Westminster), and that of the King is also strongly realistic and seems to have been based on drawings from life. The impact of the two effigies is due not only to their intrinsic sculptural quality, but to the engraving of the surfaces. Common to both are the repeated crowned initials A and R; in addition the Parliament robe of the King bears the badges of the broom-pod, tree-stock, sunburst and the chained and couched hart, while the dress of the Queen carries the emblems of knots and of chained ostriches, holding nails in their beaks and wearing crowns. The sarcophagus is considerably larger than those of the earlier royal monuments, and the figures are set far down towards its foot; presumably this would have been compensated when the elaborate gilt bronze canopy was in place.

Burial in the Abbey was not confined to monarchs. William de Valence, the stepbrother of Henry III, was buried in St Edmund's Chapel (it has been suggested that this tomb was originally in the Chapel of the Confessor, but there is no proof of this), and a son of Henry III, Edmund Crouchback, Earl of Lancaster, was buried, with his wife, Aveline, Countess of Lancaster, on the north side of the Presbytery. Thirty years later the Lancaster tombs were joined by that of Aymer de Valence, Earl of Pembroke (died 1324), son of William de Valence, and the tomb of William de Valence by that of the second son of Edward II, John of Eltham, Earl of Cornwall (died 1336). Under Richard II, tradition was broken, when, at the King's insistence and seemingly amid protests, his friend and adviser the Lord Treasurer, John of Waltham, Bishop of Salisbury (died 1395), was interred in the Confessor's Chapel and commemorated by

The tomb of Henry III which
was commissioned by his son,
Edward I, in about 1291.
William Torel's gilt-bronze
effigy of the King is set upon
a high plinth made by Pietro
di Oderisio, and decorated
with mosaic and set with slabs
of porphyry. The three niches
in the base were probably
designed for relics.

Detail of the gilt-bronze
canopy and head of Eleanor of
Castille, Edward I's Queen,
made by William Torel. The
cushions and top of the tomb
are decorated with heraldic
lions for Leon and castles for
Castille. In the background is
the iron grille made for the tomb
by Master Thomas of Leighton
Buzzard.

The canopy and head of
Edward III, made in gilt-
bronze by John Orchard.
The King reclines on a
Purbeck marble tomb chest
designed by the architect
Henry Yevele.

Right above: The head of Henry III, from the gilt bronze effigy by William Torel. According to the account for payments, Torel made the portrait 'in the likeness of King Henry'.
Below: Detail of the head of William de Valence, Lord of Pembroke, half-brother to Henry III, who died in 1296. The tomb is of great interest as the only example in England which retains its Limoges *champlévé* enamelwork. This can be seen on the diapered cushion beneath William's head, and on the great shield at his side. William's arms appear on small shields powdering his surcoat.

The south side of the tomb of Edward III, seen from the Ambulatory, showing the small effigies of six of his children, including Edward, the Black Prince. The fine oak canopy over the tomb was made by Hugh Herland.

Overleaf: Detail of the effigy of Lady Margaret Beaufort, Countess of Richmond, mother of Henry VII. The gilt bronze effigy executed by Pietro Torrigiano in 1511, a master-piece of portraiture, shows the aged Countess in widow's robes with hands raised in prayer.

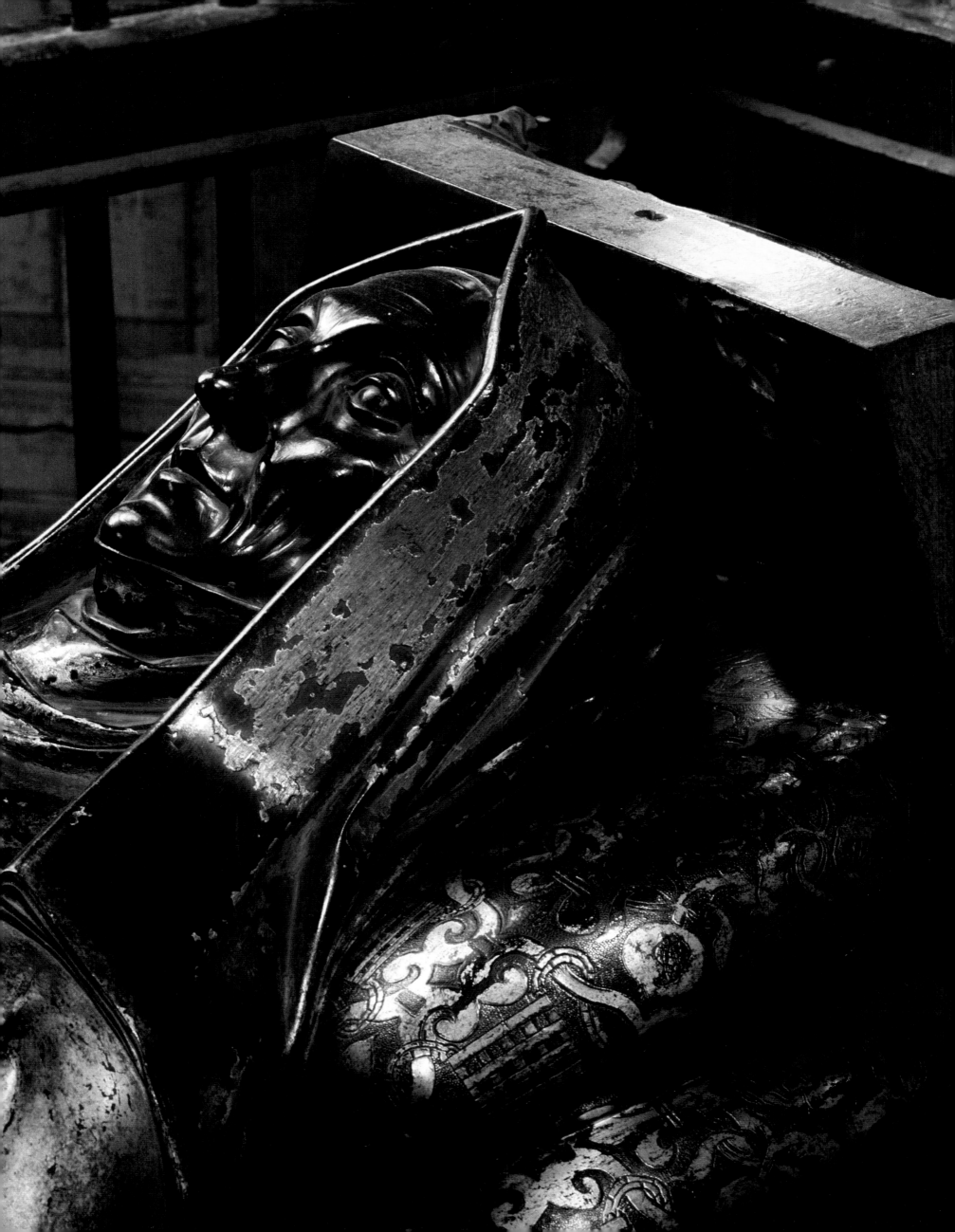

Left: The large wall monument in the Chapel of St Nicholas erected by Lord Burghley, Elizabeth I's great minister, to his second wife Mildred and their daughter Anne, Countess of Oxford. It is composed of different kinds of marble with effigies of the two ladies and a kneeling figure of Lord Burghley at the top.

Right: The canopy and coloured monument to Aymer de Valence, Earl of Pembroke, son of William de Valence and cousin to Edward I. The figure is dressed in armour and a surcoat decorated with the arms of Valence. Behind, across the ambulatory, is the monument to General Wolfe.

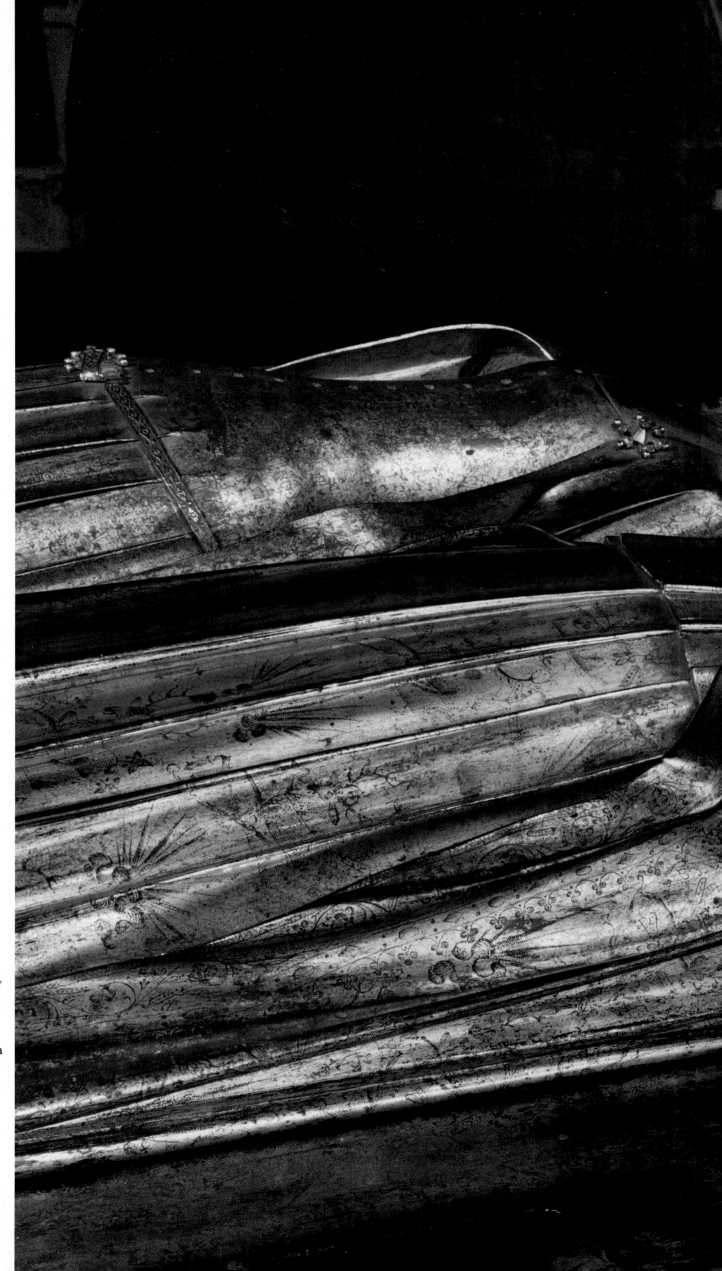

The effigies of Richard II and his first Queen, Anne of Bohemia, which were made by Nicholas Broker and Godfrey Prest. Originally they were portrayed holding hands. Their robes are decorated with engraved initials and heraldic badges, including the broom-pod of the Plantagenets and the white hart.

Detail of the alabaster effigy of John of Eltham, the second son of Edward II. His head is supported by two angels, while the shield is carved with the royal arms of England, differenced by a border of fleurs-de-lys.

a memorial brass. Soon after, the King's tutor, Robert de Waldeby, Archbishop of York (died 1397), was buried in St Edmund's Chapel. This practice was extended by Henry IV, who permitted the body of Geoffrey Chaucer to be buried in the Transept. Chaucer was thus the first poet to be interred at Westminster, though permission seems to have been given because he was Clerk of the King's Works, not for his literary eminence. No monument to Chaucer was built before the middle of the sixteenth century.

One other royal tomb of note stands in the area of the Confessor's Chapel, that of King Henry V (died 1422), which is set to the east of the shrine of St Edward, on the same axis, under the Henry V Chantry. Only the wooden core, lacking its plating and its original cast silver hands and head (recently replaced in polyester resin), can now be seen. The pedigree of this tomb type can be traced back to the much earlier William de Valence monument, where the wooden effigy is plated with copper and partly covered with Limoges enamel. In this magnificent heraldic tomb, which seems to have been made in France, the shield charged with the arms of Valence is intact and the head rests on a cushion decorated in enamel with rosettes and the arms of Valence and England.

The colouristic impact of those tombs in the Abbey which were not furnished with gilt bronze effigies and were not enriched with mosaic and enamelling must also have been very great. The three tombs on the north side of the Presbytery differ from the royal tombs in the Chapel of the Confessor in that they have elaborate marble canopies (parts of them broken and restored), and enough pigmentation survives to show that not only the faces and bodies of the effigies but also the architecture was

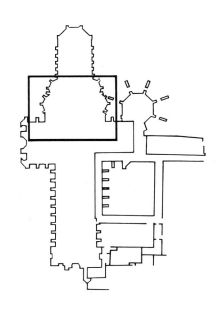

Plan of Sanctuary
and Chapels

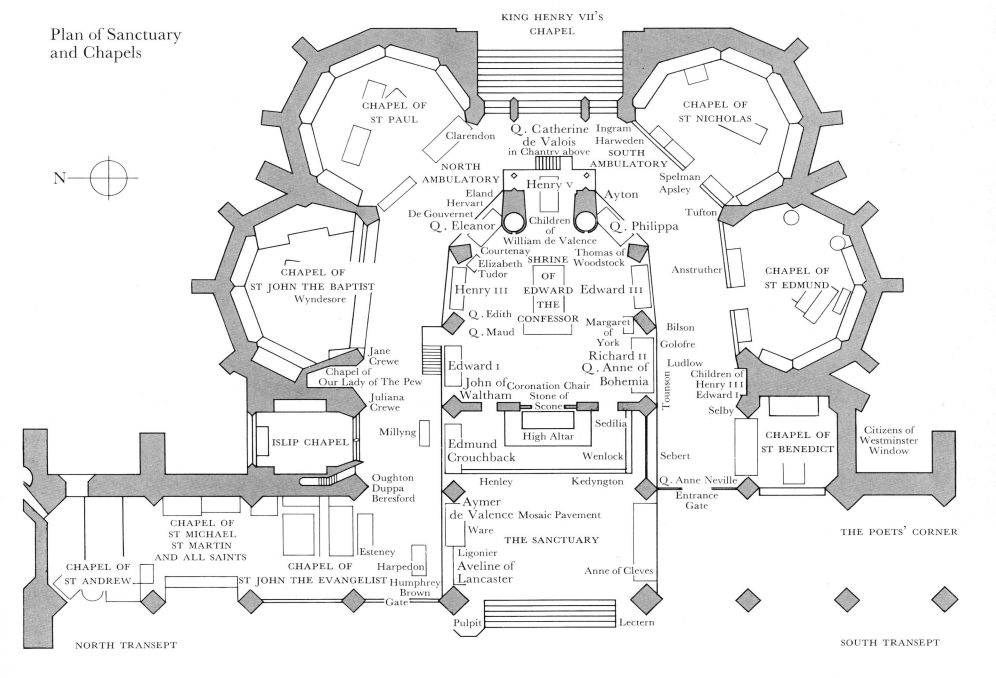

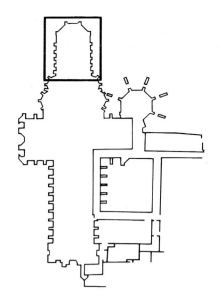

Plan of Henry VII's
Chapel

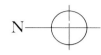

N

painted naturalistically. In the Crouchback tomb the buttresses are decorated with a minute brick pattern and there are traces of upwards of a hundred and fifty small painted coats-of-arms, while the interior of the canopy of the tomb of his wife, Aveline, is decorated with painted flowers and coats-of-arms. This colouristic tradition explains certain features of the earliest of the Renaissance monuments at Westminster, the tomb of Lady Margaret Beaufort by Pietro Torrigiano.

Torrigiano was born and trained in Florence, but in 1492 he left his native town for Rome, where two great papal monuments in bronze by Antonio Pollajuolo in St Peter's, the tomb of Pope Sixtus IV (completed 1493) and that of Pope Innocent VIII (completed 1498), must have left an indelible impression on his mind. In 1509–10

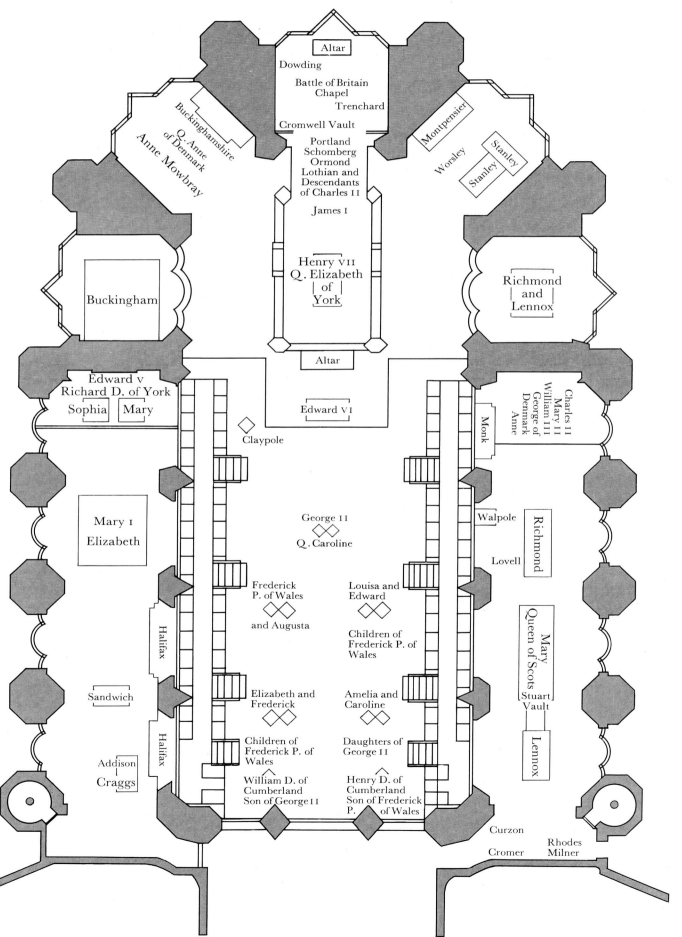

he was in the Netherlands, in the service of Margaret of Austria, and from the Netherlands, by a natural progression, he came to London, where he was awarded first the commission for the tomb of Lady Margaret Beaufort, mother of King Henry VII (1511), and then, eleven months later, a contract for the tomb of the King and of his Queen, Elizabeth of York. The tomb of Lady Margaret Beaufort reveals what can only be regarded as some measure of resistance to Renaissance style. Though the black touch tomb chest is articulated with Renaissance pilasters and carries the Renaissance motif of wreaths enclosing a crowned coat-of-arms, the effigy, like those of the earlier royal tombs, is framed in a Gothic gilt bronze tabernacle. The figure is clad in a gilt bronze robe, but the veil was painted and so, seemingly, were the head and hands. There is no precedent for pigmentation in any Italian Renaissance bronze monument, and colour must have been employed to bring the tomb into conformity with the earlier monuments. The head, which is based on a death mask, is treated with consummate sensibility. In his second work at Westminster, the double monument which stands in the centre of the Henry VII Chapel, Torrigiano seems to have been granted full autonomy, and achieved the finest Renaissance tomb north of the Alps. Its singularity is emphasized by the Gothic grille surrounding it, which, like the bronze doors of the Chapel, appears to be English or Flemish work, probably the latter since its author is referred to as Thomas Ducheman. The bronze component of the tomb is much larger than in that of Lady Margaret Beaufort; the sides of the sarcophagus are decorated with circular gilt bronze reliefs with paired saints, which reveal the residual influence of Donatello; round them are gilt bronze roses, and at the foot are two large putti in half relief supporting the royal arms. Above at each end of the tomb are pairs of seated angels holding up the arms of England encircled by the Garter; these are some of the most beautiful bronze sculptures of their time. The two effigies, like that of Sixtus IV in St Peter's, are set on the upper surface of the tomb without an architectural frame, their strongly modelled heads, more vivid than that of Lady Margaret Beaufort because less literal, contrasting with the bold movement of their robes. These figures continued to exert some influence at Westminster more than a century after they were installed, and are the source of the paired effigies in the adjacent tomb of George Villiers, Duke of Buckingham, by Hubert Le Sueur.

However beneficial an effect the Reformation may have had in other spheres, its consequences for the fine arts, and especially for the art of sculpture, were regrettable. The tomb of Henry VII and Elizabeth of York is indeed the last monument at Westminster which is, and can be seen to be, in harmony with the purpose and tradition of the Church. With the death of Queen Mary I, the brief attempt of Abbot Feckenham to repair the damage which reformers had inflicted on the Abbey came to an end, and under Queen Elizabeth it was tacitly recognized that the chapels in the Chevet, on the north and south sides of the Chapel of the Confessor, had become redundant, and had no further use save as sites for sepulchral monuments. Gradually they were filled with large architectural wall-monuments or with free-standing tombs to the Queen's relations and to members of the Court, most of them women. Thus there were introduced the tombs of Frances Brandon, Duchess of Suffolk (died 1559); Margaret, Countess of Lennox (died 1578); Winifred, Marchioness of Winchester (died 1586); Anne, Duchess of Somerset (died 1587); Mildred, Lady Burghley (died 1589); Frances, Countess of Sussex (died 1589); Frances, Countess of Hertford (died 1598); and Elizabeth Russell (died 1601), as well as John, Lord Russell

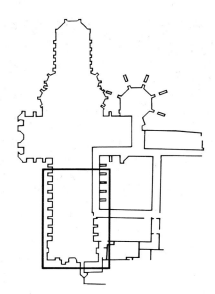

Plan of the Nave

N

(died 1584); the Lord Keeper Sir Thomas Bromley (died 1587); Sir John Puckering, Speaker of the House of Commons (died 1596); and Lord Hunsdon (died 1596). In no case can a sculptor's name be attached to any of these monuments. They vary greatly in quality, and the finest of them is also the earliest, that of Frances, Duchess of Suffolk. The wall-monuments are conceived as autonomous architectural units, which employ with magnificent abandon the rather inorganic forms of late Tudor mannerism. The limited naturalism of their effigies was from the first designed to be redressed with pigmentation, and in a number of the monuments the garish polychromy has been renewed.

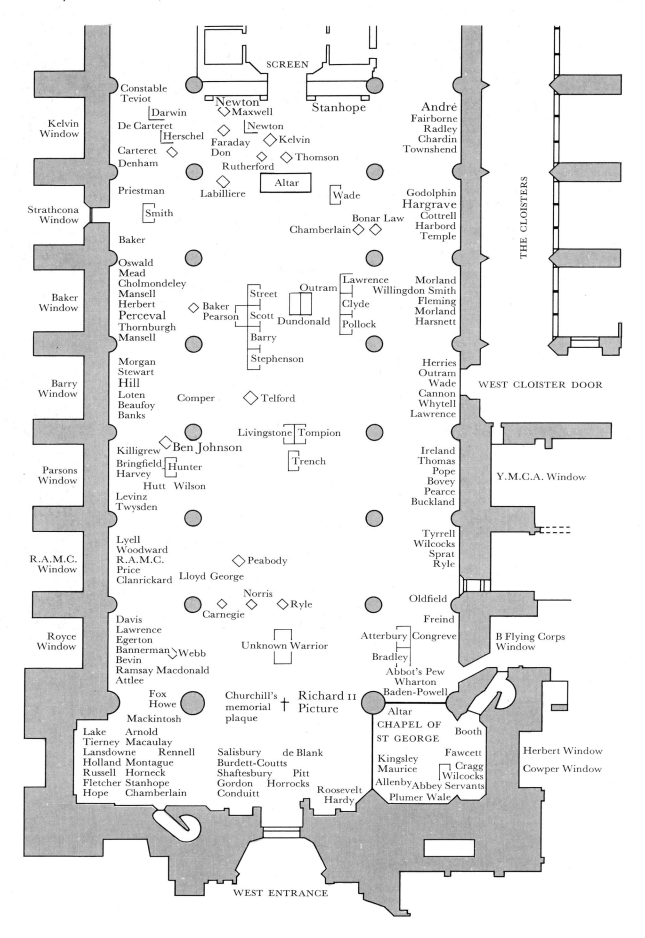

Monument in Poets' Corner to
Geoffrey Chaucer, who died
in 1400. This simple tomb
chest and canopy of Purbeck
marble was erected by the
Tudor poet, Nicholas Brigham,
in 1556.

The tomb of Henry VII and
his Queen, Elizabeth of
York, which stands in the
middle of Henry VII's Chapel.
Executed by Pietro Torrigiano,
it is the finest Renaissance
tomb north of the Alps.

Left: The gilt-bronze effigy of
Lady Margaret Beaufort, the
mother of Henry VII. The
monument was commissioned
in 1511, two years after her
death, from the Florentine
sculptor, Pietro Torrigiano.

The east end of Henry VII's
tomb, showing the superb
gilded bronze detailing by
Torrigiano.

Right: The late Elizabethan monument to Frances Seymour, Countess of Hertford, who died in 1598.
Below: Detail of the finely-carved alabaster effigy of Frances Brandon in the Chapel of St Edward. Frances Brandon was the daughter of Mary Tudor, Henry VIII's younger sister, and the mother of Lady Jane Grey.

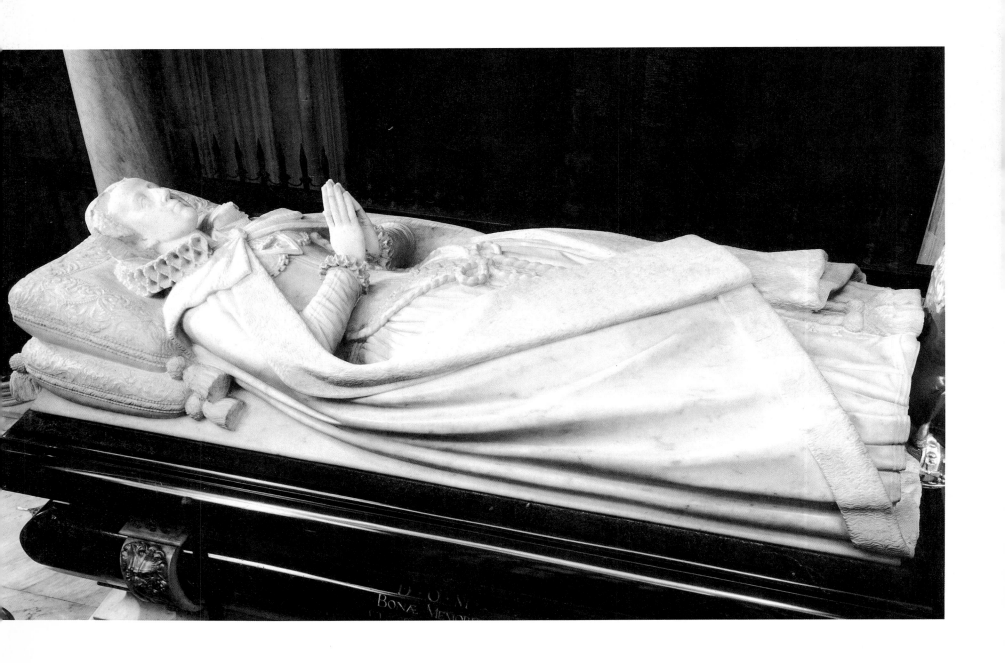

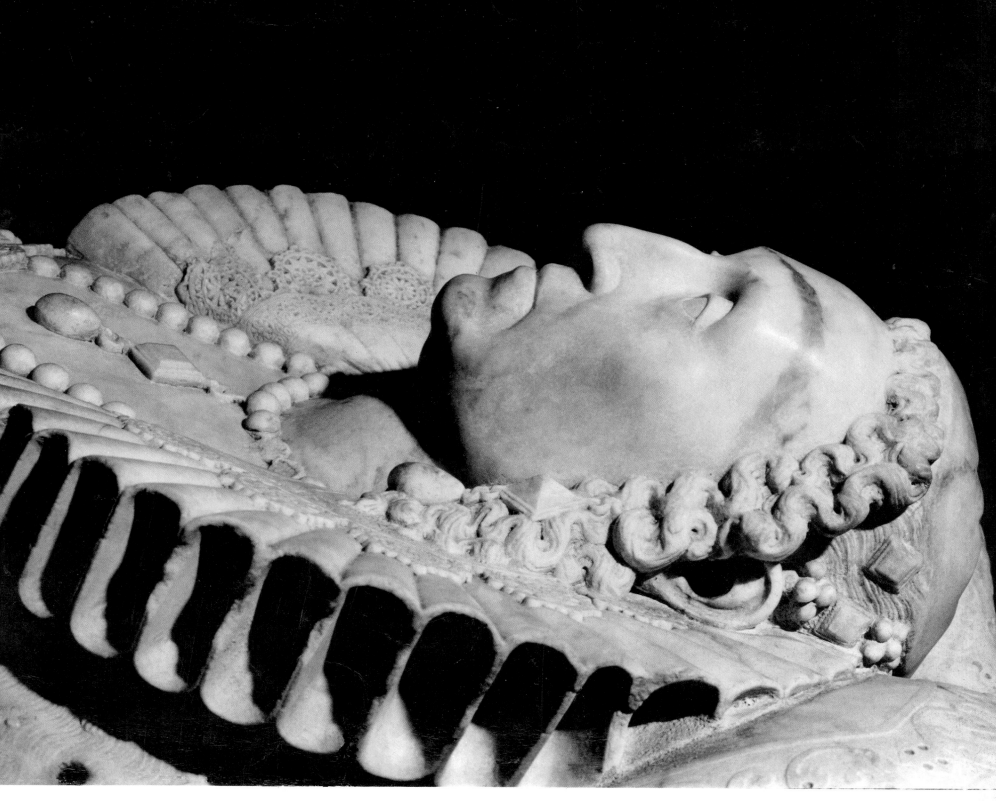

Detail of the head of Elizabeth
I from her white marble tomb,
also erected by James I. It was
executed by Maximilian Colt
and was completed in 1607.

Left : The effigy of Mary
Queen of Scots, made in white
marble by William and
Cornelius Cure. The tomb was
commissioned in memory of
his mother by James I.

Monument to Henry Carey, 1st Baron Hunsdon, Elizabeth I's first cousin through the Boleyn connexion. This monument, of which only the lower part is shown, rises to 36′ in height and is the largest in the Abbey. It is a prime example of the lavish display of heraldic and allegorical ornament of the period.

The monument to Sir Francis
Vere, a famous soldier of
Elizabeth I's reign, who spent
much of his career fighting the
Spanish in the Netherlands.
The tomb is attributed to
Maximilian Colt and is
clearly inspired by the contemporary monument to a
count of Nassau, at Breda in
Holland. The effigy reclines
beneath a marble slab with
military accoutrements,
supported on the shoulders of
four kneeling men.

Right: The bronze bust of Sir Robert Ayton by the Italian sculptor, Francesco Fanelli. Ayton was a poet and philosopher, and also secretary to Anne of Denmark and Henrietta Maria.

The tomb of George Villiers, 1st Duke of Buckingham, the great favourite of James I and Charles I. He was assassinated in 1628, and buried by Charles I in Henry VII's Chapel – hitherto reserved for those of royal descent. The monument was erected by his Duchess, whose effigy lies beside his, and was the work of Hubert Le Sueur, the sculptor of the equestrian statue of Charles I in White-hall.

Left: The standing wall monument to Thomas Thynne of Longleat, murdered in Pall Mall in 1682 by assassins employed by Count Königsmarck, who wished to marry Thynne's wife. The monument was executed by the Netherlandish sculptor, Arnold Quellin, who portrayed Thynne's assassination in a relief on the plinth.

Right: Detail of the monument to Major John André, Adjutant-General to the British forces. He was hanged as a spy during the American War of Independence and the relief shows General Washington receiving a petition for clemency. The monument was erected at the expense of George III, designed by the architect Robert Adam and carved by Peter Vangelder.

SACRED to the MEMORY,
of
MAJOR JOHN ANDRÉ,
who raised by his Merit at an early period of Life to the rank of Adjutant General
of the British Forces in America,
and employed in an important but hazardous Enterprise
fell a Sacrifice to his Zeal for his King and Country
on the 2ᵈ of October A:D 1780
Aged 29,
universally Beloved and esteemed by the Army in which he served
and lamented even by his
FOES.
His gracious Sovereign KING GEORGE the Third
has caused this Monument
to be erected.

The Remains of Major JOHN ANDRÉ
Were, on the 10ᵗʰ of August 1821, removed from Tappan,
By JAMES BUCHANAN ESQ,ʳ
His Majesty's Consul at New York,
Under instructions from His Royal Highness
The DUKE of YORK,
And, with the permission of the Dean and Chapter,
Finally deposited in a Grave
Contiguous to this Monument.
On the 28ᵗʰ of November 1821.

To the Memory of
IOHN HOLLES, DUKE of NEWCASTLE, Marquis and Earl of CLARE, Baron Haughton of Haughton,
And Knight-Companion of the most Noble Order of the GARTER. Whose Body is here deposited under
the same Roof with many of his Noble Ancestors and Relations of the Families of VERE, CAVENDISHE,
and HOLLES, whose Eminent Virtues he inherited and was particularly distinguished for his Courage,
Love to his Countrey, and Constancy in Friendship, which Qualities he very duely wrought his Ford for

Sr. CLOUDESLY SHOVELL Knt.
Rear-Admirall of Great Britain
And Admirall and Commander in Chief of the Fleet
The just rewards
Of his long and faithfull Services
He was
Deservedly beloved of his Country
And Esteem'd tho dreaded by the Enemy
who had often experienc'd his Conduct and Courage
being Shipwreckt
On the Rocks of Scilly
In his Voyage from Thoulon
The 22d. of October 1707 at Night
In the 57th Year of his Age
His fate was lamented by all
But Especially the
Sea faring part of the Nation
To whom he was
A Generous Patron and a worthy Example
His body was flung on the shoar
And buried with others in the sands
But being soon after taken up
Was placed under this Monument
Which his Royall Mistress has caused to be Erected
To Commemorate
His Steady Loyalty and Extraordinary Vertues.

Far left : The monument to John Holles, Duke of Newcastle, who died in 1711. It was designed by the architect James Gibbs and carried out by the sculptor Francis Bird, who completed it in 1723.

Left : The standing wall monument to Sir Cloudesley Shovell, executed by Grinling Gibbons who is better known for his virtuosity in wood-carving. At the bottom is a relief showing the wreck of Shovell's ship off the Scilly Isles in 1707.

The standing marble figure of
James Craggs, Secretary of
State to George I. This is all
that remains of a much larger
standing wall monument,
designed by the architect
James Gibbs and carved by
the Roman sculptor Giovanni
Baptista Guelfi. The epitaph
is written by Craggs' friend,
Alexander Pope.

The monument in the South
Transept to John Campbell,
Duke of Argyll and of
Greenwich, who died in 1743.
It was carved in 1745–9 by
Louis François Roubiliac.
Minerva and Eloquence
stand below the recumbent
figure, while History inscribes
his titles, stopping short at
Gr . . . . to show that the
dukedom of Greenwich
expired with him.

The monument to the scientist,
Sir Isaac Newton, on the
north side of the Nave Screen,
forming a companion piece
to Earl Stanhope's monument
on the south side. It was
designed by William Kent and
carved by Michael Rysbrack.

Details from the monument showing the head of Newton, children playing with a telescope and two putti with a diagram relating to the solar system.

Right : Poets' Corner, in the
South Transept, showing on the
left-hand wall, the monuments
of Samuel Butler, John Milton,
Edmund Spenser and Thomas
Gray. The large standing wall
monument on the right is to
Matthew Prior, designed by
James Gibbs and carved by
Michael Rysbrack. The bust
is by the French sculptor
Antoine Coysevox, made in
about 1700 and presented to
Prior by Louis XIV.

Peter Scheemakers' monument
to William Shakespeare,
erected by public subscription
in 1740, and designed by
William Kent. On a pedestal
are busts of Elizabeth I,
Henry V and Richard III.

Roubiliac's dramatic monument to Lady Elizabeth Nightingale, who died from a miscarriage brought on through fear of a thunderstorm. Her husband, Joseph, attempts to ward off the spear aimed at his wife by Death.

The death of General Wolfe at Quebec in 1759 is represented on his monument by Joseph Wilton. This was erected by King and Parliament in 1772.

Sacred to the Memory
of Sir PETER WARREN
Knight of the Bath,
Vice Admiral of the Red Squadron
of the Britiſh Fleet,
and Member of Parliament
for the City and Liberty of Weſtminſter.

Roubiliac's monument to
Admiral Sir Peter Warren,
who died in 1752. Hercules is
portrayed placing the
Admiral's bust upon his tomb.

GEORGE FREDERICK HANDEL Esqr
born February XXIII. MDCLXXXIV.
died April XIV. MDCCLIX.

L.F.Roubiliac inv^t et sc^t.

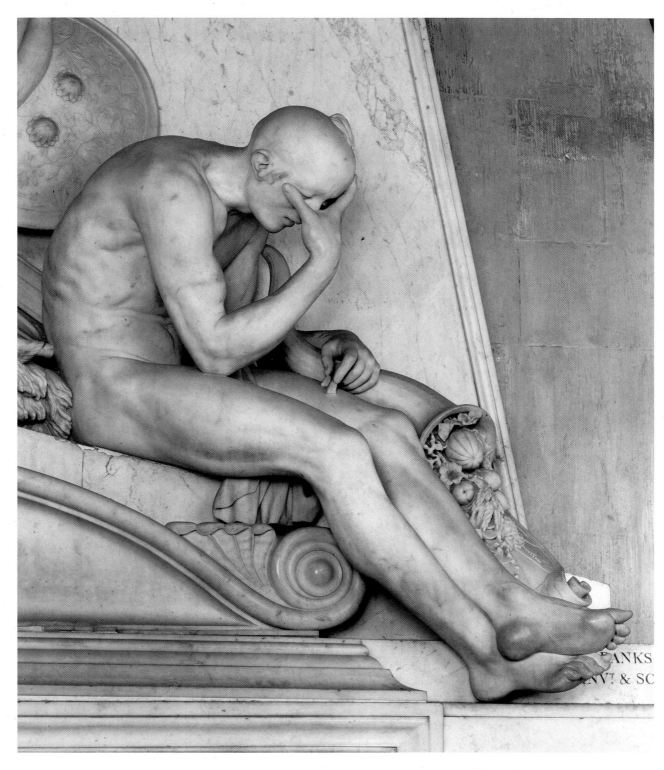

Above: Detail of a mourning Hindu captive from the monument to Sir Eyre Coote, the British general who drove the French out of the Coromandel Coast and who died in 1783. The monument was carved by Thomas Banks at the request of the East India Company.

Left: Set high up in the South Transept is Roubiliac's portrayal of Handel holding the score of an aria from the *Messiah*. A tablet above recalls the first Handel Festival held in the Abbey in 1784.

TO THE MEMORY OF
DAVID GARRICK,
WHO DIED IN THE YEAR 1779,
AT THE AGE OF 63.

TO PAINT FAIR NATURE, BY DIVINE COMMAND,
HER MAGIC PENCIL IN HIS GLOWING HAND,
A SHAKSPEARE ROSE, THEN TO EXPAND HIS FAME
WIDE O'ER THIS "BREATHING WORLD" A GARRICK CAME
THOUGH SUNK IN DEATH THE FORMS THE POET DREW
THE ACTOR'S GENIUS BADE THEM BREATHE ANEW;
THOUGH, LIKE THE BARD HIMSELF, IN NIGHT THEY LAY,
IMMORTAL GARRICK CALL'D THEM BACK TO DAY:
AND 'TILL ETERNITY WITH POWER SUBLIME,
SHALL MARK THE MORTAL HOUR OF HOARY TIME,
SHAKSPEARE & GARRICK LIKE TWIN STARS SHALL SHINE,
AND EARTH IRRADIATE WITH A BEAM DIVINE.
S. J. PRATT.

THIS MONUMENT, THE TRIBUTE OF A FRIEND,
WAS ERECTED IN 1797.

WEBBER
FECIT.

Left: David Garrick taking a curtain call: from the monument to the actor by Henry Webber.

Right: Detail from the enormous monument to William Pitt the Elder, Earl of Chatham, who died in 1778. It was executed by John Bacon and cost £6,000 to erect.

Monument by Joseph Nollekens to three naval captains, William Bayne, William Blair and Robert Manners, who died in sea battles between Admiral Rodney and the French fleet in 1782.

William Murray, 1st Earl of Mansfield, Lord Chief Justice of England for thirty-two years, who died in 1793. The figure on his monument by John Flaxman is based on a portrait by Sir Joshua Reynolds. On either side stand the figures of Justice and Wisdom.

Left: Detail of the monument by Sir Richard Westmacott to the Whig statesman, Charles James Fox, who died in 1806. He is shown dying in the arms of Liberty.

Sir Richard Westmacott's monument to Spencer Perceval shows the figure of the dead Prime Minister lying beneath a representation of his assassination in the lobby of the House of Commons in 1812.

IN MEMORY OF THE RIGHT HON.ᴮˡᴱ SPENCER PERCEVAL
Chancellor of the Exchequer _ First Lord of the Treasury
THIS MONUMENT WAS ERECTED BY THE PRINCE REGENT AND PARLIAMENT
TO RECORD THEIR DEEP SENSE OF HIS PUBLIC AND PRIVATE VIRTUES
AND TO MARK THE NATION'S ABHORRENCE OF THE ACT BY WHICH HE FELL

Born 1 Nov.ᵗ 1762 _ Affaſſinated within the walls of the Houſe of Commons _ 11 May 1812

By the nineteenth century,
space in the Abbey for large
wall monuments had become
exhausted, and Victorian
statesmen are represented by
large standing statues, such
as this by John Gibson to Sir
Robert Peel.

ROBERT PEEL
BORN FEB. 5.1788 DIED JULY 2.1850

With the accession of James I, new and more critical attention seems to have been given to the quality and purpose of the Abbey monuments. This is first apparent in the tomb of Queen Elizabeth. It was entrusted to Maximilian Colt, a native of Arras who had come to London late in the Queen's reign, seemingly at the instance of Lord Salisbury, and was completed in 1607. If the tomb is compared with late sixteenth-century monuments nearby, the superior quality of thinking that was devoted to it can be in no doubt, and its noble architectural frame combines with careful carving of the effigy and a powerful, highly realistic head to lend it a dignity that is not unworthy of its theme. The tomb of Mary Queen of Scots (1607–12) in the south aisle of the Henry VII Chapel was entrusted by James I to Cornelius Cure, a sculptor of Dutch extraction, and his son William; its architecture is related to that of the tomb of Queen Elizabeth, but the effigy, by William Cure, is very different, an ideal image carved with much delicacy and restraint.

Under James I and Charles I the links between the Abbey monuments and sculpture in the Netherlands progressively increase. The tomb of Sir Francis Vere (died 1609), conjecturally by Colt, shows the effigy beneath a marble slab with military accoutrements which is supported on the shoulders of four kneeling men, and was inspired either by the well-known monument of the Count of Nassau at Breda, or by an engraving of Ducerceau from which the Dutch tomb depends. When George Villiers, Duke of Buckingham, the favourite of James I and Charles I, was assassinated in 1628, he was buried in the Henry VII Chapel, in a tomb by Hubert Le Sueur, a French sculptor who seems to have been brought to London by Buckingham. Le Sueur had already executed the tomb of Ludovic Stuart, Duke of Richmond and Lennox (died 1624) on the south side of the Chapel, which includes a figure of Fame based on a late sixteenth-century French statue. The bronze Virtues on the Lennox tomb and the bronze mourning figures at the foot of that of Buckingham make use of the conventional imagery of Northern Baroque sculpture. By the elevated standards of Hendrik de Keyser's tomb of William the Silent at Delft, neither is a monument of first-rate consequence, and their interest is rather as by-products of the taste which led to the commissioning of the Rubens ceiling at Whitehall and of the great royal portraits of Van Dyck. Some small marble figures on the Buckingham tomb are by an Englishman, Nicholas Stone, who worked in Holland with De Keyser, and who after his return to England carved the seated figure of Francis Holles (died 1622) in the Abbey, where a motif derived from the Medici Chapel of Michelangelo in Florence is transposed into the timid language of Anglo-Netherlandish alabaster carving. Against this background it is easy enough to understand the vogue of the Italian bronze sculptor Francesco Fanelli, who was patronized by Charles I and is represented at Westminster by the highly accomplished bust of Sir Robert Ayton on the Ayton monument (1638). About this time the Nave of the Abbey, which had hitherto been free of monuments, received its first memorial, that of Mrs Jane Hill (1631), whose claim to fame was that her son was gentleman-in-waiting to the King.

Until the burial of Buckingham the Henry VII Chapel was what the Chapel of the Confessor originally had been, the preserve of royalty. Under the Commonwealth, however, when burial in the Abbey was for the first time treated as a national honour, and Ireton, Pym, Strode and Bradshaw were buried there, the body of Admiral Robert Blake (died 1657) was placed on Cromwell's order 'amongst the Kings, with all the solemnity possible'. After the Restoration his body, and those of the other

Commonwealth leaders interred there, were removed by order of King Charles II, and reinterred between the Abbey and St Margaret's, Westminster. In one case, that of Colonel Edward Popham (died 1651), whose father-in-law had been groom of the bedchamber to James I and whose wife had Royalist connections, the monument (and a wretched work it is) was allowed to remain in the Abbey, in the Chapel of St John the Baptist, though the body was removed and the epitaph erased.

In a more general sense the Commonwealth had a disruptive influence on British art, and the sculptors at work in England between the return of Charles II and the death of Queen Anne were an undistinguished band. The Abbey monuments provide a fair, even a favourable, picture of their work. The finest of these monuments is the historically unimportant but strikingly dramatic tomb of Thomas Thynne (1682), a courtier who was pilloried by Dryden and later murdered in Pall Mall. Above is the figure of Thynne, with a putto pointing to an inscription, and below is a relief of his assassination. This is the first of a series of narrative reliefs on the monuments at Westminster. When a monument was erected to Major John André (1780) by King George III, it contained a relief showing André, after an interview with Washington, on the way to execution; and when a monument was erected in 1812 to the Prime Minister Spencer Perceval, it included a relief of the murder of Perceval in the House of Commons. These reliefs may not be great sculpture, but are historically of much interest.

The most ambitious monuments projected at this time were never carried out. Planned by Grinling Gibbons, they celebrated Queen Mary II (died 1694) and King William III (died 1702), and are known only from drawings. An impression of the sculptor's intentions can be formed, however, from a work in which some of the same motifs are used, the tomb of the Duke of Beaufort at Badminton, and from a monument at Westminster, that of Admiral Sir Cloudesley Shovell (died 1707). Addison, writing of this tomb, objected that 'instead of the brave rough English admiral, which was the distinguishing character of that plain gallant man, he is represented on his tomb by the figure of a beau, dressed in a long periwig, and reposing on velvet cushions under a canopy of state'. 'The Dutch,' continued Addison, 'show an infinitely greater taste of antiquity and politeness in their buildings and works of this nature, than we meet with in those of our own country.' Addison had returned to England in 1703 after four years of travel on the Continent, and to him, as to anyone with practical experience of Italian and Netherlandish monumental sculpture, the inadequacy of Gibbons's monument must have been clearly evident. But within two decades this unhappy period of transition came to a close, and gave way to a commemorative style in which the classicizing aspirations of Pope and of Addison himself found a close sculptural equivalent.

In so far as the change is ascribable to any single cause, it is the introduction about 1720 of the architect-designed memorial. The first architect to exercise a decisive influence on sculptural style was Gibbs, initially with the Borromini-like monument of John Holles, Duke of Newcastle (1723), then with the monument of Matthew Prior (died 1721), which was carved by Rysbrack and incorporates a bust by Coysevox presented to the poet by Louis XIV, and a year later with that of James Craggs (1724). The practical merits of these monuments vary with the sculptors who worked on them, in the case of the Newcastle monument Francis Bird, who fails to meet the challenge of Gibbs' fine design, and in that of the James Craggs monument Giovanni

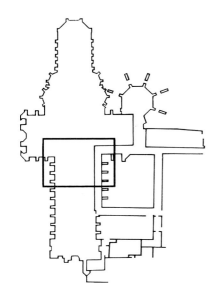

N

Plan of Choir and Aisles

Baptista Guelfi, whose beautiful standing figure of Craggs dressed in a toga and leaning on an urn, above a celebrated epitaph by Pope, is the only part of the tomb to be preserved.

The second architect to set his stamp on sculpture in the Abbey is William Kent, who had the advantage over Gibbs that his designs were carried out by Rysbrack and Scheemakers, two of the most serious and accomplished sculptors of their time. Encumbered though they now are by the brightly coloured Victorian Gothic Choir Screen of Blore, the monuments by Kent and Rysbrack to Sir Isaac Newton (1731) and Earl Stanhope (1733) register, as we approach them up the Nave, as the greatest of the later monuments at Westminster. As we might expect, the Newton monument was planned with special care. On the sarcophagus are children playing with a prism (in allusion to Newton's work on light and colour), a telescope, a stilliard (referring to a proposition in the *Principia*), and a furnace (alluding to Newton's post as Master of the Mint). Above, on the level of the effigy, are two putti with 'a remarkable diagram relating to the solar system', and above them again is a globe showing the path predicted by Newton for the comet of 1681. At the top is the lamenting figure of Astronomy. The visionary head of Newton is perhaps the finest of the later portraits in the Abbey. Lord Stanhope had made his reputation as a general in the Peninsula, and in his monument, which was designed as a counterpart to that of Newton, he is shown in classical armour beneath a grey-veined marble tent. The programme of the third of the great Kent monuments, that to William Shakespeare erected by public

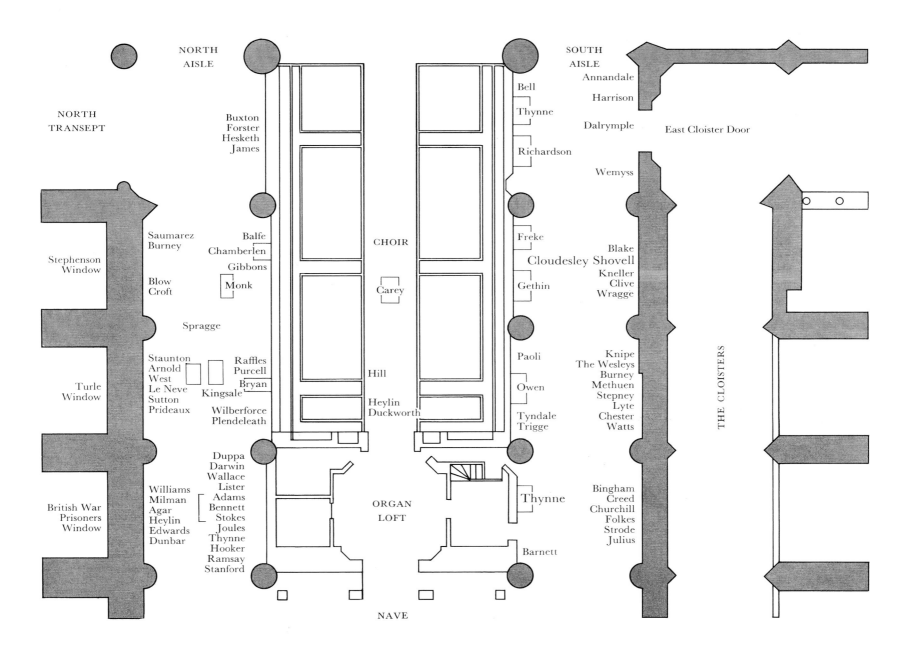

subscribers in 1740, is more romantic; on the plinth are busts of Queen Elizabeth, Henry V and Richard III, and above them is a quotation from *The Tempest*. The growing popularity of the concept of a literary pantheon or Poets' Corner also gave rise to wall-monuments to Milton (1737) and Ben Jonson, carved by Rysbrack and designed by Gibbs.

After the death of Kent the architect-dominated monument fell into disfavour. The leader of the reaction was Louis François Roubilliac, and its manifesto is the monument to John, Duke of Argyll (1745–9), of which a contemporary writer declared that it 'outshines for nobleness and skill all those before done, by the best sculptors, this fifty years past'. Superficially the Argyll monument has a good deal in common with Rysbrack's Stanhope tomb, but to a far greater extent it is dominated by figure sculpture. Above the reclining statue of the Duke, a figure Muse of History inscribes his titles on an obelisk, while at the foot on the right the seated figure of Pallas looks up at the scene, and on the left Eloquence, a standing female figure symbolizing the attribute for which Argyll achieved renown, addresses the spectator. The imagery is more insistent than that of Rysbrack, and the emphasis on movement is more pronounced, both in the inscription, which is cut short at the initial letters of the second part of the Duke's title, Greenwich, and in the Eloquence, one of the most admired sculptures in the Abbey, which breaks out of its containing frame. The quality of Roubilliac's imagination is evident once more in the tomb of Sir Peter Warren, where Hercules places the bust of Warren on his monument, under the approving gaze of Britannia, who is seated at one side, a conceit that must have been even more striking

South Transept

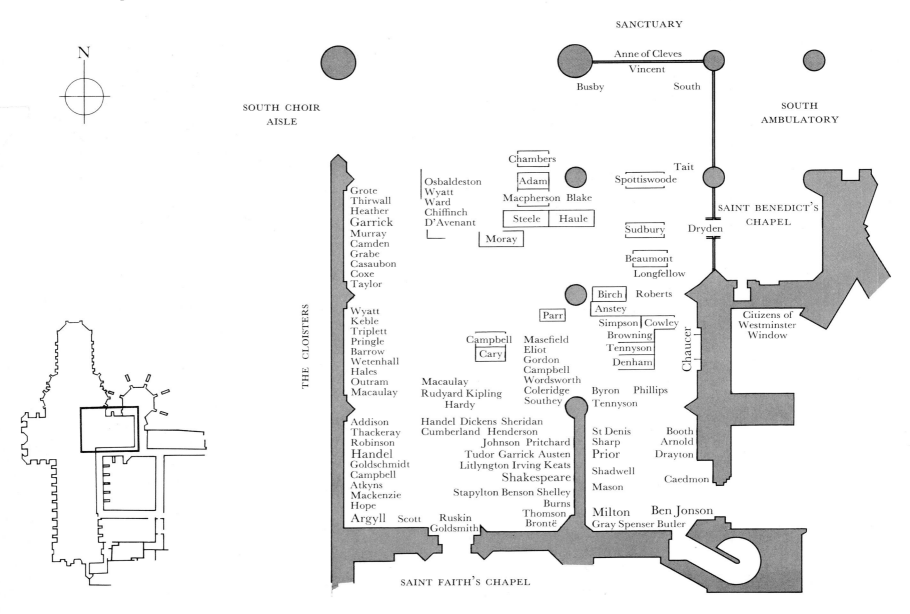

[252]

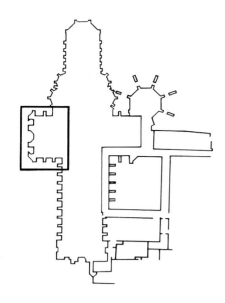

before the tomb was docked of its upper section, a 'large Flag hanging to the Flagstaff, and spreading in natural folds behind the whole Monument'. In the still later monument of General Hargrave, Governor of Gibraltar (1751), an angel sounds the trump of doom as a pyramid behind collapses and the General, freeing himself from his shroud, starts up from the tomb. The most overtly theatrical of Roubiliac's monuments was also the most popular, that of Lady Elizabeth Nightingale (1761), who had died in 1731 of a miscarriage caused by a thunderstorm. Here we see Lady Elizabeth protected by her husband from the assault of Death, who appears from a doorway at the bottom of the tomb.

With the advent of Neo-Classicism the style of the memorials in the Abbey becomes more staid. The first symptom of change is Joseph Wilton's monument to General Wolfe (1772), where the subject, an angel bringing the palm of victory and a laurel wreath to the dying general in his tent, is one Roubiliac might well have carved, but the figures are less extravagant and less emotional. In Thomas Banks's monument to Sir Eyre Coote (1789) the imagery is simplified, and is indeed reduced to two figures, of Victory who attaches the portrait of Sir Eyre Coote to a palm tree, and of a mourning Hindu captive on the right. The latter is one of the finest Neo-Classical sculptures at Westminster. The change of taste in the seventies and eighties of the century is most evident in the contrast between the monuments in the South and North Transepts. In the South Transept Gothic arcading supplied the sculptor with a frame, and the space within the arch presented itself as a stage; it is so used by Roubiliac, in his portrayal of Handel with the score of the *Messiah*, and by Webber, who depicts David

North Transept

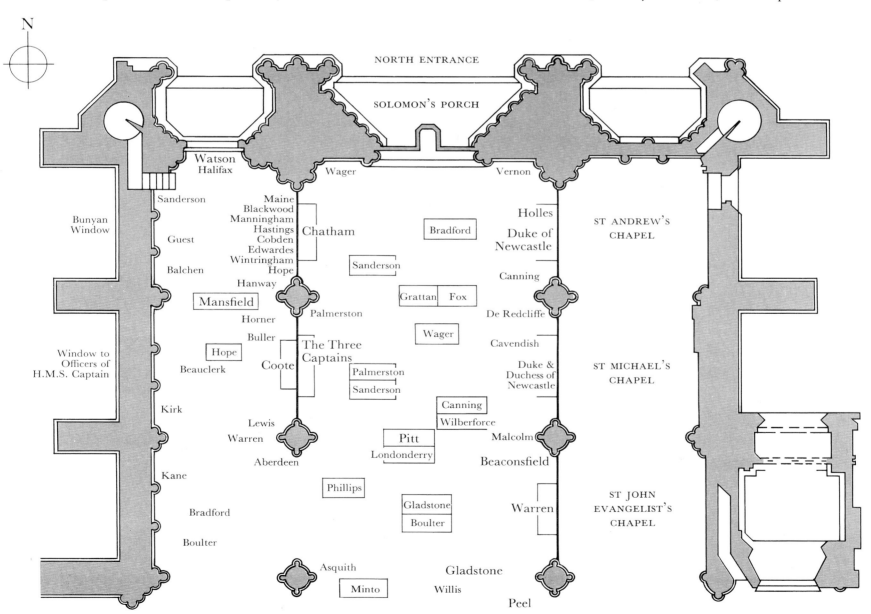

NORTH CHOIR AISLE

NORTH AMBULATORY

Garrick taking a curtain call. In the North Transept, on the other hand, free-standing monuments could be introduced under each arch, and sculptors and their patrons showed no hesitation in availing themselves fully of the substantial space that was available. The first to do so was John Bacon, whose huge monument to William Pitt, Earl of Chatham (1779–83), shows Chatham standing in a niche with five large allegorical figures beneath. Bacon was followed by Nollekens, whose monument to three naval captains was planned as a counterpart of that to Chatham and was allegedly based on a drawing by Sir Joshua Reynolds. Though these two tombs are technically free-standing, the scheme in both cases is that of a wall-monument. One tomb in the North Transept avoids this inconsistency, that of the Earl of Mansfield by John Flaxman (1801), which was designed in Rome under the influence of Canova. Here the three main figures, the seated Lord Chief Justice and the standing figures of Wisdom and Justice, are united in a coherent, fully circular design.

By some fatality the greatest English monumental sculptor of the first half of the nineteenth century, Chantrey, is represented in the Abbey only by secondary works. More prominent is Westmacott, a reputed pupil of Canova, who brings the eighteenth-century commemorative tradition to a close with the monuments to William Pitt (1807–13), triumphant over Anarchy; Spencer Perceval (1816), lamented by Power, Truth and Temperance; and Charles James Fox (1810–23), who dies, mourned by Peace and by a negro slave, in the arms of Liberty. In the Perceval monument, the narrow space of a window ledge is used with consummate ingenuity. Thereafter the great political leaders of the nineteenth century are commemorated not by allegories but by descriptive statues, of which the most distinguished is Gibson's toga-clad figure of Sir Robert Peel and the least worthy are Boehm's Disraeli and Brock's Gladstone.

For the two hundred years which separate Le Sueur's monuments at Westminster from Westmacott's the sculptors of the Abbey monuments seem to have been unperturbed by the patent incongruity between the tombs that they erected and the building in which they were set. In the second half of the nineteenth century, however, renewed interest in Gothic architecture led to a change of view in which the monuments, and especially the monuments to forgotten figures, were regarded not with pride but with embarrassment. It was repeatedly suggested that they should be moved to a new building, and though this was not done – the historical objections to such a course were obvious – some of them were treated with great ruthlessness. The monuments of General Wolfe and Captain Cornewall were reduced in height; Dean Stanley made an unavailing effort to remove the monument to Spencer Perceval; Le Sueur's tomb of the Duke and Duchess of Richmond and Lennox was 'barbarously demolished' and was only reinstated under pressure from Lord Darnley; later the Craggs monument by Gibbs was pulled down and the effigy by Guelfi, the only part to be retained, was transferred to a window ledge, and 'Athenian' Stuart's monument to Rear-Admiral Charles Watson was treated in somewhat the same way, though in this case three figures by Scheemakers were preserved. In all these circumstances we must be grateful that so many of the monuments survive, and that the Abbey remains not simply a unique repository of English sculpture, but the living record of achievement that it was long designed to be.

Epilogue
by
Kenneth Clark

Westminster Abbey is often referred to as the national shrine of England, but its architecture and sculptured monuments are, for the most part, not done by Englishmen. Architecturally, the Abbey is the most French building in England, and was almost certainly designed by a French mason. Its central feature, the shrine of Edward the Confessor, of which, alas, only fragments remain, was the work of a Roman mosaicist, Pietro di Oderisio. The magnificent series of mediaeval recumbent figures are nearly all by French or Flemish craftsmen. The only exception is William Torel, whose figure of Henry III is in a Gothic style indistinguishable from that of the tombs of Saint-Denis. Torrigiano's tomb of Henry VII and his Queen is a masterpiece of Renaissance sculpture which could be equalled only in Rome or Florence. The gaudy monumental sculpture of the next century is chiefly by Flemings, and even in the early eighteenth century, when England was speaking with her own voice in architecture, the chief sculptors in the Abbey are Scheemakers, Rysbrack and Roubiliac. What a refutation of the theory that art, if it be fully expressive of a national feeling, must be consciously national! The great periods of art which have set their stamp on the Abbey – Gothic and Baroque – were international, part of cultures that stretched from England or Sweden to Czechoslovakia. We do not need the marriage of Richard II to Anne of Bohemia to explain the ruined, but still splendid, portrait of the King that faces us as we enter the Abbey. We need only to keep in mind the unity of European culture at its finest moments.

And yet Westminster Abbey is essentially English, how English we can judge by comparing it with the 'national shrine' of France, Saint-Denis. Approached through a sordid suburb, the Abbey of Suger, the fountain-head of Gothic, has an unwelcoming aspect, and the visitor is compelled to wait his time until a peremptory guide has collected enough people to make it worthwhile showing them round. This he does with the utmost strictness, not allowing them to stray by a foot from the prescribed route, or pause to look at a monument. Visiting Nôtre-Dame de Paris is less of an ordeal, but there is no joy of discovery or feeling of participation. Westminster Abbey is welcoming and inexhaustible. I suppose that someone entering it for the first time might be shocked by the clutter of monuments that fill almost every available inch of wall and floor, seeming to drown, like a babble of discordant voices, the soaring notes of the architecture; and I confess that for many years I felt that some of the large white marble statesmen in the North Transept would be better off in a Neo-Classic building. Today almost the only one I would wish elsewhere is the enormous, obstructive monument to Captain Montague in the Belfry Tower. There are also places where the wall monuments become over-assertive, but on the whole it is extraordinary how well Baroque designers have adapted themselves to their Gothic setting. Perhaps this is partly due to the fact that the outburst of eighteenth-century sculpture in the Abbey came at a date when Gothic was being looked at with an amused affection, and the leading architects of the time, Wren, Hawksmoor and Kent, had experimented in the Gothic style. Kent was, in fact, one of the first English-born designers to set his stamp on the interior of the Abbey, and his settings for Rysbrack's sculpture in the monuments to Newton and Stanhope dominate even the elaborate nineteenth-century Screen by Blore. But this is not the whole answer, because such a confirmed classicist as Gibbs could place a Classical pediment in a Gothic trefoil arcade and achieve a kind of harmony. Rococo, of course, is half-way to Gothic, and at a time when Chippendale was veering between the two styles, it was not difficult for such a resourceful designer as Sir John Cheere to fit in perfectly with his Gothic surroundings. One of his most successful designs is the tomb of Joseph Wilcocks, the Dean of Westminster who commissioned Wren's office, and ultimately Hawksmoor, to build the towers of the west end. What a disaster they might have been, as depressing as the eighteenth-century Gothic towers of Orléans! But in fact they are a complete success, both as design and as a means of situating the Abbey in the context of eighteenth-century Westminster. They are reasonable, and reassuring, like the red brick houses that were to grow up beyond Ashburnham House and Dean's Yard; and they confirm, at the outset, the feeling of unbroken tradition of which the Abbey is, outside of Rome, the greatest example in the world.

Burke, in a famous passage, compared the English constitution to a Gothic castle. He meant thereby that it had evolved according to necessity rather than plan, and gained its strength from the good sense with which its architects had met each new demand of legal and political history. Westminster Abbey has this feeling of organic growth, assimilating and reflecting every change of society. It has been a royal chapel, the shrine of a saint, a monastery, the seat of an order of chivalry and the place of solemn festivals. The tombs of Kings and Queens have been followed by the tombs of powerful statesmen, soldiers and churchmen, so that almost unconsciously people began to look at it as the mausoleum of great Englishmen. The excellent official guide to the Abbey reads like a short Dictionary of National Biography. No one knows who first suggested that great writers should be buried in the South Transept; Chaucer seems to have been buried there as an outstanding clerk of the Works and not as a poet, and if the idea of a 'poets' corner' had been put to a committee it would probably have been turned down. Looking round the Abbey it is indeed hard to know by what arguments the Dean and Chapter were swayed when they granted permission for a monument to be erected; some of the names, like those of Harvey and Hutt, commemorated in one of Bacon's most graceful works, evoke very faint memories in the average educated visitor; and there are many others considerably more obscure, like Johannes Smith, *armiger*. This seems to be in keeping with the quality of the Abbey, at once royal and popular. The thousands of visitors who stream through every day are not, after all, so far removed from the very mixed collection of soldiers, deans and merchants whose memorial tablets line the walls.

And yet in spite of this feeling that all men can enter, feel closer to their fellow men, and enjoy, under the crystal candelabra, an almost festive atmosphere, such as must often have existed in the mediaeval Church, Westminster Abbey is essentially a religious place and a place of ancient beliefs; the belief in sanctity and the sacred annointing of Kings, and a place that was for centuries devoted to prayer and contemplation. To experience this aspect of the Abbey it is better not to go in between the four-square Western Towers, but to approach it through the dark tunnel that leads from the yard of Westminster School, past the pretty Fountain Court, which seems to offer a contemplative life to the age of reason, and into the Cloister. A cloister is one of those architectural forms which expresses a spiritual need so perfectly that even in an age of materialism it suggests the possibility of peace and seclusion. As we pass through it on our way to the small south door of the Church we are already in a different frame of mind. We should then turn into the Choir and its surrounding chapels, for there we are once more in a Gothic world, in which the exuberant eighteenth-century confidence in reason and pleasure, and the nineteenth-century belief in material progress, have left less evidence. It is true that the chapels surrounding the sanctuary are even more crowded than the aisles of the Nave, or at least give that impression, since the Elizabethan and Jacobean tombs, recently restored in bright colours with a lavish use of gold, seem to proclaim themselves more loudly. We feel the pride and push of sixteenth-century English families, their arrogant heads belying their folded hands, a vainglory that culminates in the enormous monument to Lord Hunsdon in St John the Baptist's Chapel. Festive in a provincial sort of way, it shows how little art and taste had evolved in England in the hundred years after Torrigiano's tomb of Henry VII. These assertions of insular prosperity are often what is called 'amusing', although this was certainly not their original intention; but they are of a very different order to the beautiful works of Gothic art, many of which they must have displaced. We cannot blame the courtiers, when the King himself had allowed the destruction of what was undoubtedly one of the most precious and beautiful monuments in England, the shrine of Edward the Confessor.

But in the Abbey it is a mistake to dwell on what we have lost. For a few minutes we may try to picture it in the mid-fifteenth century, the monuments gleaming with gold tesserae and crystal inlays (as on that fascinating ruin, the painted retable), the pavement inlaid with serpentine and porphyry, the walls covered with paintings and hangings, the windows filled with painted glass. All around us are scraps of evidence, even some big scraps, like the wall-paintings in the South Transept, or the enamelled shield of William de Valence, to furnish our mental picture. But if we tried to carry the dream into actuality, as has been done in the Sainte-Chapelle, the whole character of the Abbey would be lost.

In fact, if we consider how much has been lost in most English churches it is surprising how much of the Abbey has survived the activities of zealots, restorers and mere hooligans. Thieves (for what purpose?) took away the head of Henry V; what a miracle that they left the gilt effigies of Henry III and Eleanor of Castille, two of the most beautiful bronze figures of the Middle Ages, the stern, depersonalized Edward III, the source perhaps of Blake's Jehovah, and the all too personalized likeness of his grandson, Richard II. Presumably they felt some veneration for these royal monuments, and, as so often with iconoclasts, there was an element of luck. They seem to have been distracted on the threshold of St Edmund's Chapel, sparing not only the tomb of William de Valence but the effigy of John of Eltham, surely the work of that same delicate craftsman who carved an untouched masterpiece of Gothic art, the tomb of Edward II in Gloucester Cathedral. Even the most zealous reformers shirked the labour of erecting a scaffolding that would have enabled them to destroy the censing angels high up in the Transepts, which thus remain the finest pieces of sculpture to survive from Henry III's Abbey. What happened to the North Portal? One would suppose that the carving would have been protected by a building called Solomon's Porch, that seems to have abutted on to it, and probably a great deal could have been preserved. But, with true nineteenth-century confidence, it was decided to build an entirely new portico, designed by Sir Gilbert Scott and Pearson. It is almost the last major work to have transformed the appearance of the Abbey, and the lovers of mediaeval art may deplore it. But how many of the visitors who stream through it are conscious that it is not yet a hundred years old?

But then, how much can they see of the Abbey in a crowded visit? After almost fifty years I still find it full of surprises. On some visits one thinks only of the Baroque tombs; and sees a masterpiece of portrait sculpture that one had passed a dozen times without pausing; on others one discovers unexpected Gothic details in mouldings which the reformers or restorers had overlooked. One realizes what a concentration of skilled craftsmen Henry III had brought together in order to achieve a project which was, perhaps, the chief occupation of his mind. He was certainly one of the most devoted patrons of art of the Middle Ages, less forcefully creative than Suger, but with a refinement and consistency of taste that appears in every surviving fragment, and with a feeling that he was undertaking a sacred duty which in some measure has communicated itself to almost all of those who have followed him in the adornment of the Abbey, even those whom we may consider misguided, like Blore and Gilbert Scott.

The truth is that Westminster Abbey, when the last visitor has gone and the chandeliers are extinguished, is an awe-inspiring place. The weight of so much history, the resonance of so many moving ceremonies, must touch even the most prosaic mind. Even Addison, the embodiment of deist common sense, was moved to write his once-famous essays on the tombs. No wonder that the youthful Blake, who could see the prophet Ezekiel in Peckham Rye, found in the hours spent drawing the royal effigies for the engraver Basire a confirmation of his belief in 'a reality which always and eternally exists', and kept these solemn figures in his mind's eye for the rest of his life.

Chronology

	Dates of Reign	Crowned
Edward the Confessor	1042–66	3 April 1043 (at Winchester)
Harold	1066	6 January 1066
William I	1066–87	25 December 1066
William II	1087–1100	26 September 1087
Henry I	1100–35	5 August 1100
Stephen	1135–54	22 or 25 December 1135
Matilda (declared Queen)	1135	—
Henry II	1154–89	19 December 1154
Richard I	1189–99	3 September 1189
John	1199–1216	27 May 1199
Henry III	1216–72	28 October 1216 (at Gloucester)
Edward I	1272–1307	19 August 1274
Edward II	1307–27	25 February 1308
Edward III	1327–77	29 January 1327
Richard II	1377–99	16 July 1377
Henry IV	1399–1413	13 October 1399
Henry V	1413–22	9 April 1413
Henry VI	1422–61 and 1470–1	6 November 1429
Edward IV	1461–70 and 1471–83	28 June 1461
Edward V	1483	—
Richard III	1483–5	6 July 1483
Henry VII	1485–1509	30 October 1485
Henry VIII	1509–47	24 June 1509
Edward VI	1547–53	20 February 1547
Mary I	1553–8	1 October 1553
Elizabeth I	1558–1603	15 January 1559
James I	1603–25	25 July 1603
Charles I	1625–49	2 February 1626
Commonwealth	1649–60	—
Charles II	1660–85	23 April 1661
James II	1685–8	23 April 1685
William and Mary	1688–1702 (Mary d. 1694)	11 April 1689
Anne	1702–14	23 April 1702
George I	1714–27	20 October 1714
George II	1727–60	11 October 1727
George III	1760–1820	22 September 1761
George IV	1820–30	29 July 1821
William IV	1830–37	8 September 1831
Victoria	1837–1901	28 June 1838
Edward VII	1901–10	9 August 1902
George V	1910–36	22 June 1911
Edward VIII	1936	—
George VI	1936–52	12 May 1937
Elizabeth II	1952–	2 June 1953

The Very Rev. Eric S. Abbott was Dean of Westminster from 1959 to 1974. He was born in 1906, and attended Nottingham High School, from which he went on to Jesus College, Cambridge. He spent the early part of his life as an ordained priest in London – as curate of St John's, Smith Square, Westminster, as Chaplain to King's College, London, and Chaplain to Lincoln's Inn. He then became Warden of the *Scholae Cancellarii* in Lincoln, and for twenty years from 1940 was a Canon and Prebendary of Lincoln Cathedral. In 1945 he returned to King's College, London, as Dean, an office which he held for ten years. He was Chaplain to King George VI from 1948 until his death in 1952, and to the Queen until 1959. He was Chaplain and Sub-prelate to the Order of St John of Jerusalem from 1969 and served as Extra Chaplain to the Queen from 1974. He was made an Honorary Fellow of Keble College, Oxford, in 1960, and of Jesus College, Cambridge, in 1966. In the same year he received an honorary doctorate of Divinity from London University. He died in the summer of 1983.

Sir John Betjeman, Poet Laureate from 1972 until his death in 1984, was also well known as a lover of ancient buildings, particularly churches. As a poet, he wrote serious and often profound verse which was read and admired by an unusually wide audience. He had a considerable influence on the growing awareness of the need to conserve Britain's historic buildings, and on the revival of interest in Victorian architecture. He was born in 1906 and educated at Marlborough College and Magdalen College, Oxford. As a young man he worked as a journalist. During the war he was UK Press Attaché in Dublin and then at the Admiralty. He was a Royal Fine Art Commissioner and a member of the Royal Commission on Historical Monuments, set up in 1969. He held honorary degrees from the universities of Aberdeen, Reading, Birmingham, Exeter and the City of London, and was an Honorary Associate of the Royal Institute of British Architects. His volumes of poetry include *First and Last Loves* (1952), *A Few Late Chrysanthemums* (1954), *Collected Poems* (1958), *Summoned by Bells* (an autobiography in verse, 1960), *High and Low* (1966), *A Nip in the Air* (1974), *Church Poems* (1981) and *Uncollected Poems* (1982). He has also published several anthologies of poetry, and a number of county guides and books on architecture.

A. L. Rowse is a leading historian and man of letters, poet, biographer and essayist. His combination of historian and poet, with his lifelong research into the Elizabethan Age, resulted in the foremost biography of William Shakespeare. His many works on Shakespeare include a modern edition of the Sonnets solving their problems. Among his historical works are *The Elizabethan Renaissance* in two parts, *The Life of the Society* (1971) and *The Cultural Achievement* (1972), and, more recently, *Reflections on the Puritan Revolution* (1986). Born in Cornwall in 1903, he has written extensively about his county and fellow countrymen in works such as *A Cornish Childhood* (1942) and *A. L. Rowse's Cornwall* (1988). A Fellow of All Souls College for many years, Dr Rowse divides his time between writing and researching at his home near St Austell and lecture tours, particularly in the USA.

Dean Eric Abbott

John Betjeman

A. L. Rowse

Professor George Zarnecki is a leading scholar of the field of Romanesque art, especially Romanesque sculpture. His books include *English Romanesque Sculpture 1066–1140* (1951), *Later English Romanesque Sculpture 1140–1210* (1953), *Art of the Medieval World* (1975) and *Studies in Romanesque Sculpture* (1979). He was born in 1915 and educated at Cracow University, where he was a Junior Assistant at the Institute of Art from 1936 to 1939. During the war he served in the Polish army in France and Britain. From 1945 to 1982 he was on the staff of the Courtauld Institute of Art in London, and was Deputy Director from 1961 to 1974. Between 1960 and 1961, he was Slade Professor of Fine Art at Oxford. He was Vice-President of the Society of Antiquaries of London from 1968 to 1972 and Professor of History of Art at London University between 1963 and 1982. Professor Zarnecki lives in London.

Sir John Pope-Hennessy is a leading authority on the history of sculpture, and has written extensively on Italian sculpture of the Gothic, Renaissance and Baroque periods. Since 1977, he has been Professor of Fine Arts at New York University. He was born in 1913 and was educated at Downside and Balliol College, Oxford. In 1938 he joined the staff of the Victoria and Albert Museum, becoming Keeper of the Department of Architecture and Sculpture in 1954 and then Director from 1967 to 1972. He has held a number of academic posts, including the Slade Professorships of Fine Art at both Oxford and Cambridge and the Clark Professorship of Art at Williams College, Massachusetts. From 1974 to 1976 he was Director of the British Museum and from 1977 to 1986 he was Consultative Chairman to the Department of European Paintings at the Metropolitan Museum, New York. He has published many books, among them *Italian Gothic Sculpture* (2nd ed. 1972), *Italian Renaissance Sculpture* (2nd ed. 1971), *Italian High Renaissance and Baroque Sculpture* (2nd ed. 1970), *The Portrait in the Renaissance* (1967), *The Study and Criticism of Italian Sculpture* (1980) and *Cellini* (1985). Sir John Pope-Hennessy lives in Florence.

Lord Clark was one of Britain's best-known art historians. As well as publishing a number of celebrated books including *The Gothic Revival* (written at the age of twenty-two), *Landscape into Art* (1949), *The Nude* (1955), *Looking at Pictures* (1960), *Ruskin Today* (1964), and *Civilisation* (1969), he made over sixty television programmes, the most acclaimed being the series 'Civilisation', broadcast in 1969. He was born in 1903 and educated at Winchester College and Trinity College, Oxford, becoming Keeper of the Department of Fine Art at the Ashmolean Museum in Oxford. At the age of thirty he was appointed Director of the National Gallery in London, where he remained until 1945. During the War he organized the War Artists' Scheme, and with Dame Myra Hess arranged the National Gallery Concerts. From 1949 to 1950 he was Slade Professor of Fine Art at Oxford and again from 1961 to 1962. He was Chairman of the Arts Council of Great Britain from 1953 to 1960, and became the first Chairman of Independent Television Authority in 1954. He was a Trustee of the British Museum and a member of the advisory council of the Victoria and Albert Museum. He held honorary degrees from thirteen universities in Britain and America, and was Chancellor of the University of York from 1969 to 1979. In his later years he wrote two volumes of autobiography, *Another Part of the Wood* (1974) and *The Other Half* (1977). Lord Clark died in May 1983.

George Zarnecki

John Pope-Hennessy

Kenneth Clark

Index

Ackermann, Rudolf, engravings by, *24, 25, 30, 41, 168*
Adam, Robert, *229*
Addison, Joseph, 16, 126, 250, 258
Argarde, Arthur, 46
Alberic, Master, *44*
Alfred, King, 37
Almonry, the, 71
Altarpiece (originally in Whitehall), 108, *116*
Amiens Cathedral, 190
Ampulla and Anointing Spoon, *59*
André, Major John, *229, 250*
Andrewes, Lancelot, Dean of Westminster 1601–5, 102
Anne, Queen, 47, 103, 125, 250
Anne of Bohemia, 48, 145, 200, *210, 211*
Anne Boleyn, *80*, 91–2, 97, 143
Anne of Cleves, 94
Anne Neville, 68, 69
Anstis, John, Garter King of Arms, 128
Apse, 8, 9, 42
Argyll, John Campbell, Duke of, *233, 252*
Armigil of Plöermel, St, 71
Arnold, Matthew, 142
Arnold, Thomas, 140
Arras, Bishop of, 94
Arthur, King of Britain, 37
Arthur, Prince of Wales, 69
Arundel, Richard Fitzalan, Earl of, 48
Atterbury, Francis, Dean of Westminster·1713–23, *120*, 125–7
Ayton, Sir Robert, *227, 249*

Bach, Johann Sebastian, 141
Bacon, Sir Francis, 97, 256
Bacon, John, *243, 254*
Bacon, Sir Nicholas, 97
Baillie, 104, 105
Banks, Thomas, *240, 253*
Barry, Sir Charles, 25
Basire, James, 258
Bayeux Tapestry, 40, 48, *50, 51*
Bayne, William, *244*
Beaufort, Joan, 65
Beaufort, Margaret, Countess of Richmond, 66, 68, 69, 71; tomb of, *35*, 70, 72, *206–7*, 214, 215, *218*
Beaumont, Francis, 98
Beauneveu, André, *90*
Becket, Thomas, Archbishop of Canterbury, 40, 189
Beerbohm, Sir Max, 25
Behn, Mrs Aphra, 138
Belfry Tower, 255
Bentley, John Francis, 15
Bentley, Richard, 125
Betterton, Thomas, 138
Bingham, Sir Richard, 98
Bird, Francis, *230, 250*
Biron, Charles de Gontaut, Duc de, Marshal of France, 101
Black Prince, the, 199, *204*
Blagrave, Thomas, 107
Blair, William, *244*
Blake, Admiral Robert, 106, 249
Blake, William, 257, 258
Blanche of the Tower (daughter of Edward III), 200
Blore, Edward, 26, *42*, 251, 255, 258
Blow, John, 139
Boehm, Sir Joseph Edgar, 254
Bonner, Edmund, Bishop of London, 95
Bosses, 26, *156, 157*, 191
Bourchier, Thomas, Cardinal Archbishop of Canterbury, 67, 69
Bower, Stephen Dykes, 26
Bowle, John Edward, 25
Bracegirdle, Anne, 138
Bradley, George Granville, Dean of Westminster 1881–1902, 16
Bradshaw, John, 106, 249
Brigham, Nicholas, *217*

Broker, Nicholas, 200, *210, 211*
Bromley, Sir Thomas, Lord Chancellor, 216
Buckingham, George Villiers, Duke of, 102, 197, 215, *226, 249*
Buckingham, Henry Stafford, Duke of, 68
Bulwer Lytton, Edward, 141
Burghley, Mildred Cooke, Lady, 97, *208, 215*
Burghley, William Cecil 1st Baron, 97, *208*
Burgoyne, General, Sir John, 138
Burnet, Gilbert, Bishop of Salisbury, 108
Busby, Dr Richard, 106, 107, *118*, 125, 139, 144
Butler, Samuel, *237*
Byrd, William, 103, 138

Cabot, John and Sebastian, 70, 71
Camden, William, 46, 96, 97, 98, *110, 111*
Campbell, Thomas, 138
Canova, Antonio, 254
Caroline of Anspach, 137
Caroline of Brunswick, 139
Carpenter, Canon Edward, Archdeacon of Westminster, 16, 35
Catherine (daughter of Henry III), 200
Catherine of Aragon, 71, 91, 92
Catherine of Valois, *63*, 65, 69, 145
Caxton, William, 71, *75*
Cecil, Robert, 1st Earl of Salisbury, 97, 101, 249
Cecil, Thomas, 2nd Baron Burghley and 1st Earl of Exeter, 97
Cecil, William *see* Burghley
Cerdic, King of Wessex, 39
Chantrey, Sir Francis, 254
Chantry Chapels: 93, 194–5; *see also* Henry V Chantry Chapel and Islip, Abbot John
Chapels: St Anne, 71; St Benedict, 97; St Catherine, 93, 120; St Edmund, 200, 257; St Edward *see* Edward the Confessor; St Erasmus, 67; St Faith, 35, *154, 155*, 194; Henry VII *see* Henry VII; St John the Baptist, 26, 250, 257; St Nicholas, 97; of the Pyx, 45, 103
Chapter House, 15, 26, 35, *44*, 46, 65, 141, 147, *169, 170, 171, 173*, 190, 192
Charles I, 102, 103, 106, 108, 125, 249
Charles II, 106–8, 127, 128, 143, 145, 250; coronation of, *114, 115*; wax effigy of *116*
Chatham, William Pitt, Earl of, monument to, 138, *243*, 254; wax effigy of *124*, 145
Chaucer, Geoffrey, 37, 47, 98, 213, *217*, 256
Cheere, Sir John, 256
Chevet, 45, 215
Chippendale, Thomas, 256
Choir, 26, *42*, 65, 107, 135, 139, *153, 158*, 189, 190, 192, 256
Choir School, 143, 144
Choir Screen, 26, *42*, 255
Churchill, Arabella, 137
Churchill, General Charles, 128
Churchill, Admiral George, 121, *128*
Churchill, John, *see* Marlborough
Churchill, Sir Winston, 38, *135*, 144, 145
Clarendon, Edward Hyde, Earl of, 107
Clement IV, Pope 1265–8, 193, 198
Clifford, Anne, Countess of Dorset, 98
Cloisters, 15, 25, 35, *43*, 47, 107, 138, 144, 147, 148, 190, 192, 194, 199, 256
Colenso, John William, Bishop of Natal, 140, 142
College Hall (Great Hall), 71, 96, *119*
Colt, Maximilian, *100*, 101, 200, *223*, 225, *249*
Confessor *see* Edward the Confessor
Congreve, William, 128
Cooke, Sir Anthony, 97
Coote, General Sir Eyre, *240, 253*
Corbels, *31, 154, 155, 164*, 191
Cornwall, Janes, 254
Cornwall, John, Earl of, *see* John of Eltham

Cornwall, Richard, Earl of, *166*, 191, 198
Coronation Chair, 48, *89*, 143
Cosmati, Peter, 45
Cosmati work, 26, *168*, 193, 198
Cotton, Sir Robert, 46, 98
Coverdale, Miles, 93
Cowper, William, 96
Cox, Richard, Dean of Westminster, 1549–53, 96
Coysevox, Charles Antoine, *237, 250*
Craggs, James, *232*, 250, 251, 254
Cranmer, Thomas, Archbishop of Canterbury, 92, 93, 94, 95
Crispin, Gilbert, Abbot of Westminster 1085–1117, 148
Croft, William, 139
Cromwell, Elizabeth, 106
Cromwell, Oliver, 25, 47, 104, 105, 106, 108, *113*, 249
Cromwell, Richard, 47
Crouchback, Edmund Plantagenet, Earl of Lancaster, 200, 214
Crypt, 143
Cumberland, William, Duke of, 137
Cure, Cornelius, *222, 249*

Dacre, Thomas, 9th Baron, 95
Daniel, Samuel, 98
Darnley, Henry Stuart, Earl of, 70, *88*, 101
Darnley, John Stuart Bligh, Earl of, 254
Darnley Cenotaph, *88*
Dart, John, 127, 128, 145; engravings by, *121, 123*, 125; *see also West-monasterium*
De Keyser, Hendrik, 249
Dickens, Charles, 35, 141
Dighton, Robert, *131*
Disraeli, Benjamin, Earl of Beaconsfield, 141, 254
Dolben, John, Dean of Westminster, 1662–83, 107
Donatello, 215
Donne, John, Dean of St Paul's, 101, 102
Drayton, Michael, 98, *123*
Dryden, John, 96, *122*, 138, 250
Ducerceau, Jacques Androuet, 249
Ducheman, Thomas, 28, 29, *186*, 215

Earles, John, Dean of Westminster, 1660–2, 107
Edgar the Atheling, 37
Edward I, 46, 47, 66, *167*, 198, 200
Edward II, 46, 200, 257
Edward III, 46, 145, 200; tomb of, 199, *203, 204*, 257
Edward IV, 66–7, 68, *73, 74*, 92, 200
Edward V, 15, 40, 67–8, *73, 122*, 200
Edward VI, 70, *82–3*, 92–4, 97
Edward VII, 143
Edward VIII, 15, 40
Edward, Prince of Wales (son of Henry VI), 66
Edward, Prince of Wales (son of Richard III), 69
Edward the Confessor, *30*, 37, 39–40, *49, 50, 51, 56*, 147–8, 166, *186*, 189; shrine of, 15, 45, 47, 48, *52*, 65, 66, 92, 95, 108, 189, 190, 192, 193, 197–8, 199, 200, 213, 215, 249, 255, 257
Effigies, *63, 78, 88, 110–11, 116, 124*, 145, 198, 199, 200, *206–7, 218, 221, 222*
Egbert, King of Wessex, 49
Eleanor of Castille, 66, 199, *202*, 257
Elgar, Sir Edward, 138
Eliot, Sir John, 102, 103
Eliot, T.S., 142
Elizabeth I, 15, 70, 91, 93, 94, 95–8, 101, 143, 197, 215, 249, 252; bust of, *236*; coronation of, *86–7*; funeral cortège of, *110–111*; genealogy of, *49*; tomb (detail) of, *223*
Elizabeth II, *136*, 143, 145
Elizabeth (daughter of Henry VII), 200
Elizabeth of York, 38, 69; tomb of, 215, *219*, 255
Escorial, 37
Estney, John, Abbot of Westminster, 1474–98, 71

Evelyn, John, 106, 107, 108

Fanelli, Francesco, *227, 249*
Farrar, Frederick William, Dean of St Paul's, 141
Feckenham, John, Abbot of Westminster, 1556–9, 94–5, 96, 215
Ferdinand, King of Aragon, 70
Fisher, John, Bishop of Rochester, 72, 92
FitzJames, Richard, Bishop of London, 68
Flaxman, John, 197, *245*, 254
Flying buttresses, *34*, 189, 190
Foote, Samuel, 138
Forster, E.E., 142
Fox, Charles James, 138, *246*, 254
Foxe's *Book of Martyrs*, woodcut from, *84*

Gardiner, Stephen, Bishop of Winchester, 94, 95
Garrick, David, 138, *242*, 254
Gate House, 101, 102
Gaveston, Piers, 46
Gay, John, 138
George I, 127, 128
George II, 125, 137
George III, 137–8, 250
George IV, 125, *130, 131*, 139
George V, 143
George VI, 143
Gerard, J.W., U.S. Ambassador to Germany, 144
Gibbons, Grinling, *231*, 250
Gibbons, Orlando, 102, 103
Gibbs, James, *123*, *230, 232, 237*, 250, 251, 252, 254, 255
Gibson, John, *248*, 254
Gill, Eric, 26
Gladstone, W.E., 254
Goldolphin, Sidney, Earl of, Lord Treasurer, 138
Goodman, Gabriel, Dean of Westminster 1561–1604, 97, 101, *109*
Gray, Thomas, *237*
Grey, Sir Richard, 68
Grote, George, 141
Guelfi, Giovanni Baptista, *232*, 251, 254

Halifax, George Savile, Marquess of, 138
Handel, George Frederick, 125, 138, *241, 253*
Hargrave, General, Governor of Gibraltar, *253*
Harley, Sir Robert, Earl of Oxford, 103
Harold II, 40, *51*
Hastings, Warren, Governor-General of India, 96
Hastings, William 1st Baron, 68
Hawksmoor, Nicholas, *10*, 26, 27, 139, 190, 255, 256
Heath, Nicholas, Archbishop of York, 95, 96
Hennequin de Liège, 199
Henri III of France, 101
Henri IV of France, 101
Henrietta Maria, 102, 108
Henry I, 37, 40
Henry II, 40, 189
Henry III, 15, 26, 45, 46, 47, *53, 54, 55, 166*, 189, 190, 191, 197, 200, 258; head of, *205*; tomb of, 193, 198, 199, 201, 255, 257
Henry IV, 48, *58*, 65, 213
Henry V, 48, *62, 63*, 65, 143, 145, 213, 252, 257
Henry V Chantry Chapel, *8, 9, 30, 62*, 65, *182, 183*, 194–5, 213
Henry VI, *64*, 65–6, 67, 70, 143, 195
Henry VII, 37, 38, 65, 69–71, 92, 101, 145, 190, 195, 197, 200, 215
Henry VII Chapel, 15, *24, 25, 28, 29, 35*, 40, 65, 67, 69, 70, 71, *77, 78, 99*, 101, 103, 104, 106, 107, 108, 128, 137, 138, 144, *150, 184, 185, 186, 187, 188*, 189, 190, 197, 200, 215, *219, 220, 226*, 249, 255, 257
Henry VIII, 46, 71–2, *79, 80*, 91 2, 94, 96, 147, 190
Henry, Prince (son of Henry II), 40
Henry of Reyns, 190
Herland, Hugh, *204*

Herschel, Sir J. F. W., 141
Hertford, Frances Seymour, Countess of, 215, 221
High Altar, 25, 102, 103, 125, 134, 143, 193, 197
Highmore, Joseph, 137
Hill, Mrs Jane, 249
Historia Anglorum, 53, 194
Holden, Charles, 26
Hollar, Wenceslaus, 21, 112
Holles, Francis, 249
Hornebolt, Gerard, 81
Howe, George 3rd Viscount, 144
Hunsdon, Henry Carey, 1st Baron, 26, 197, 216, 224, 257
Hyacinthe, Père, 142

Impey, Sir Elijah, Chief Justice of Bengal, 96
Innocent VIII, Pope 1484–92, 214
Ireton, Henry, 106
Irving, Washington, 96
Isabella, Queen of Castille, 70
Islip, John, Abbot of Westminster 1500–32, 71, 72, 79, 81

James I, 38, 71, 101, 102, 200, 249, 250
James II, 108, 117, 128, 137, 138
James IV of Scotland, 38
Jerusalem Chamber, 48, 60, 104, 194
John of Eltham, 200, 212, 257
John of Gaunt, 48, 66
John of Northampton, 173, 192
Johnson, Samuel, 138
Jonson, Ben, 46, 96, 98, 123, 252
Jowett, Benjamin, Master of Balliol, 142
Jumièges Abbey, 148
Juxon, William, Archbishop of Canterbury, 108

Keble, John, 140
Kent, William, 197, 234, 236, 251, 252, 255
Killigrew, Sir Henry, 97
Kitchin, Anthony, Bishop of Llandaff, 95
Kneller, Sir Godfrey, 120

Lady Chapel, 65, 67, 189, 195
Lancaster, Aveline, Countess of, 200, 214
Lancaster, Edmund, Earl of see Crouchback
Lanfranc, Archbishop of Canterbury, 37
Langham, Simon, Cardinal Archbishop of Canterbury, 47
Lantern, the, 144, 145
Latimer, Hugh, Bishop of Worcester, 84, 94
Laud, William, Archbishop of Canterbury, 102, 103
Lawes, 35
Lawrence, John 1st Baron, Viceroy of India, 141
Lennox, Margaret Douglas, Countess of, 70, 88, 215
Lennox and Richmond, Ludovic Stuart, Duke of, 249
Le Sueur, Hubert, 197, 215, 226, 249, 254
Lethaby, Professor W.L., 16, 26, 148, 195
Lichfield Cathedral, 139
Llewelyn, Prince of Wales, 37, 47, 92
Liber Regalis, 177, 194
Library, the, 96, 97, 102, 144
Liddon, Henry Parry, Canon of St Paul's, 140–1
Lincoln Cathedral, 120, 191
Litlyngton, Nicholas, Abbot of Westminster 1362, 86, Missal of, 180, 194
Livingstone, David, 141
Longfellow, Henry Wadsworth, 144
Louis IX (St) of France, 189, 190, 191, 199
Lowell, James Russell, 144

Manners, Robert, 244
Mansfield, William Murray, 1st Earl of,

Lord Chief Justice, 245, 254
Margaret of Anjou, 66, 67
Margaret of Austria, 215
Margaret (daughter of Edward IV), 200
Margaret Tudor, Queen of Scots, 38
Margaret of York, Duchess of Burgundy, 75
Marlborough, John Churchill, Duke of, 108, 121, 125, 126, 127, 128
Marlborough, Henrietta Churchill, Duchess of, 128
Marlborough, Sarah (Jennings), Duchess of, 128, 137
Martin, John, 132
Mary I, 70, 85, 91, 94–5, 101, 198, 215
Mary II, 108, 125, 250
Mary Queen of Scots, 71, 101, 222, 249
Mary (daughter of James I), 100, 200
Matthew Paris, 53, 54, 55, 194
Maud (wife of Henry I), 37
Michelangelo, 70, 249
Milton, John, 104, 105, 237, 252
Missal of Abbot Lytlington see Lytlington
Misericords in Henry VII Chapel, 165
Monk, George, Duke of Albemarle, 107, 108, 115
Montagu, Edward, 1st Earl of Sandwich, 106, 108
Montague, Captain, 255
Montfort, Simon de, 191
Monstrelet, Enguerrand de, 58
Moore, Henry, 26
More, Sir Thomas, Lord Chancellor, 68, 69, 92
Morgan, William, 97
Morley, 103
Motley, John Lothrop, 141, 142
Mowbray, Anne (wife of Richard Duke of York), 200
Muniment Room, 191; bosses in, 156; capital in 162; lancet window and corbel heads in, 164

Nassau, Count of, 249, 255
Nave, 15, 17, 25, 26, 35, 45, 65, 71, 125, 145, 147, 149, 158, 159, 190, 191, 249, 251, 257
Nelson, Admiral Horatio, 1st Earl, 125, 145
Newcastle, John Holles, Duke of, 230, 250
Newcastle, Thomas Pelham Holles, Duke of, 137, 138
Newman, Cardinal John Henry, 142
Newton, Sir Isaac, 139, 197, 234, 235, 251, 255
Nightingale, Lady Elizabeth, 238, 253
Noailles, Antoine de, 94
Nollekens, Joseph, 244, 254
Norfolk, Edward Howard, 9th Duke of, 138
Norfolk, John Howard, 1st Duke of, 68
Norris, Henry, 1st Baron, 97
Norris, Sir Henry, Usher of the Black Rod, 97
Norris, Sir John, 97
North Aisle, roof bosses in, 157
North Portal, 20, 257
North Transept, 48, 126, 138, 190, 191, 253–4, 255; busts and figures of angels in, 160, 162; corbel heads in, 164
Nowell, Alexander, Dean of St Paul's, 97

Odericus, 193, 198
Oglethorpe, Owen, Bishop of Carlisle, 95
Oldfield, Anne, 128
Orchard, John, 199, 200, 203
Oxford, Anne (Cecil), Countess of, 97, 208

Page, Walter Hines, U.S. Ambassador, 144
Painting, 53, 54, 55, 56, 57, 58, 73, 86, 88, 90, 132, 167, 168, 172, 173, 174, 175, 176, 177, 180, 181, 193–4, 209
Palace Yards, 39, 137, 145
Palgrave, Sir Francis, 16, 47

Palmerston, Henry John Temple, 3rd Viscount, 141
Pantheon (Paris), 37
Pavement (Cosmati work), 168, 193, 196
Pearson, J.L., 141, 257
Peel, Sir Robert, 248, 254
Pepys, Samuel, 65, 106, 107, 108, 143
Perceval, Spencer, 247, 250, 254
Perkins, Canon Jocelyn, 15
Petrus Romanus, see Pietro di Oderisio
Philip II of Spain, marriage of, 85, 94
Philippa of Hainault (wife of Edward III), 199
Pietro di Oderisio, 168, 193, 198, 201, 255
Pitt the Younger, William, 138, 254
Poets' Corner, 16, 98, 123, 138–9, 217, 237
Pole, Reginald, Cardinal Archbishop of Canterbury, 94, 95
Pollajuolo, Antonio, 214
Pope, Alexander, 126, 232, 250, 251
Popham, Colonel Edward, 250
Prest, Geoffrey, 200, 210
Prior, Matthew, 237, 250
Puckering, Sir John, Speaker, 216
Purcell, Henry, 138
Pusey, E.B., 140
Pym, John, 102, 106, 249
Pyne, 137

Quellin, Arnold, 228

Rahere, Edward, 35
Ralegh, Sir Walter, 101, 102–3
Ralph, James, quoted, 197
Renan, Ernest, 141
Retable, 178–9, 193, 194, 257
Reynolds, Sir Joshua, 245, 254
Rheims Cathedral, 148, 189, 190, 191
Richard I, 45
Richard II, 47–8, 57, 65, 90, 145, 194, 200, 210, 255, 257
Richard III, 40, 66, 68–9, 76, 236, 252
Richard, Duke of York, 62–8, 69, 122, 200
Rivers, Anthony Woodville, 2nd Earl, 68, 71
Rochester, John Wilmot, 2nd Earl of, 108
Rolle, John, 1st Baron, 132, 139
Rolls Ofice, 46
Romanesque capital, 148, 152
Roosevelt, F.D., 135, 144
Rose windows, 160, 161, 191
Roubiliac, Louis François, 25, 233, 238, 239, 241, 252, 253, 255
Rowe, Nicholas, 138
Rubens, Sir Peter Paul, 249
Russell, Lord John, 97, 215
Ryle, Herbert Edward, Dean of Westminster 1911–25, 143
Rymer, Thomas, 47
Rysbrack, Johan Michael, 123, 197, 234, 237, 250, 251, 252, 255

Saint-Denis, Church of (France), 37, 148, 189, 190, 199, 255
St Margaret's, Church of (Westminster), 26, 32, 33, 48, 70, 102, 143, 145, 250
Sainte-Chapelle (Paris), 190, 191, 194, 257
Salisbury see Cecil, Robert, Earl of
Sancroft, William, Archbishop of Canterbury, 108
Sanctuary, the, 67, 68, 71, 72, 103, 141, 257
Scheemakers, Pieter, 236, 251, 254, 255
Scott, Sir Gilbert, 26, 35, 141, 157, 258
Scott, Sir Walter, 142
Sedilia, 167
Sedley, Catherine, Countess of Dorchester, 137
Selden, John, 104–5
Seymour, Jane, 92
Shakespeare, William, 48, 138, 236, 251
Sheridan, Richard Brinsley, 138
Shovell, Admiral Sir Cloudesley, 231, 250
Sixtus IV, Pope 1471–84, 214, 215
Shelton, John, 72, 91

Smith, W.H., 142
Snorri Sturluson, quoted 39
Solomon's Porch, 20, 22, 23, 48, 125, 257
Somerset, Anne, Duchess of, 215
Somerset, Edward Seymour, Duke of, 93
Sophia (daughter of James I), 100, 200
Soult, Nicholas, Marshal of France, 139
South, Dr Robert, 108
South Aisle, 145
South Transept, 25, 35, 138, 190, 194, 253, 257; rose window in, 161; wall paintings in, 176; see also Poets' Corner
South-west Door, 35
South-west Tower, 106
Spenser, Edmund, 98, 237
Sprat, Thomas, Dean of Westminster 1683–1713, 107, 108
Stained glass, 26, 29, 35, 69, 103, 144, 145, 174, 175, 176, 189, 257
Stanhope, James, 1st Earl, 197, 251, 252, 255
Stanley, Arthur Penrhyn, Dean of Westminster 1864–81, 16, 46, 127, 133, 140–2, 143, 254
Stanley, Lady Augusta, 133, 140, 142
Stephen, King, 40
Stone, Nicholas, 98, 249
Stone of Scone, 37, 47, 56, 89, 106, 143, 145
Strode, William, 249
Suffolk, Frances Brandon, Duchess of, 215, 216, 221
Suger, Abbot of Saint-Denis, 255, 258
Sussex, Frances, Countess of, 215
Swift, Jonathan, Dean of St Patrick's, 125, 127

Tait, Archibald Campbell, Archbishop of Canterbury, 141
Talbot, William, Earl, 138
Tallis, Thomas, 103
Tanner, Lawrence, 16
Temple, Frederick, Archbishop of Canterbury, 142
Thirlby, Thomas, Bishop of Westminster 1540–50, 92, 93
Thirske, John, 30, 194
Thomas, Master, 202
Thornhill, Sir James, 126
Thynne, Thomas, 145, 228, 250
Tiles, thirteenth-century, 170
Tompion, Thomas, 139
Torel, William, 47, 199, 201, 202, 205
Torrigiano, Pietro, 70, 78, 103, 206–7, 214–15, 218, 219, 220, 255, 257
Townson, Robert, Dean of Westminster 1617–20, 103
Transepts, 26, 45, 147, 189, 190, 191, 192, 257 see also North Transept and South Transept
Tudor, Edmund, Earl of Richmond, 69
Tudor, Jasper, Earl of Pembroke, 69–70
Tudor, Sir Owen, 65
Tudor, Owen, 69, 70
Tunstall, Cuthbert, Bishop of Durham, 95

Undercroft, the, 40, 116
Unknown Soldier, Tomb of, 26, 134, 144
Usher, James, Archbishop of Armagh, 102, 106

Valence, Aymer de, Earl of Pembroke, 200, 209
Valence, William de, Lord of Pembroke, 200, 205, 213, 257
Van Dyck, Sir Anthony, 249
Vangelder, Peter, 249
Van Wyngaerde, Anthony, 112
Vere, Sir Francis, 97, 249, 255
Vergil, Polydore, 20
Vertue, Robert and William, 99
Victoria, Queen, 125, 132, 139, 140, 141, 143

Waldeby, Robert de, Archbishop of York, 213
Wall monuments, 191, 208, et seq, 221, 228, 231, 232, 237, 254
Wall paintings, 173, 176, 192, 194, 257

Walpole, Horace, 125, 137–8, 143
Walpole, Sir Robert, 128
Waltham, John, Bishop of Salisbury, 72
Warham, William, Archbishop of Canterbury, 72
Warren, Sir Peter, *239, 252*
Warwick, Richard Neville, Earl of, 67, *74*
Watson, Rear-Admiral Charles, 254
Webber, Henry, *242*, 253
Webster, Daniel, 38
Wells Cathedral, 190
Wesley, Charles and John, 127
West Window, 26
Western Towers, *10, 26, 27, 32, 33*, 71, 139, 140, 256
Westlake, H. F., 16
Westmacott, Sir Richard, 197, *246, 247*, 254
Westminster, Hugh Lapus Grosvenor, 1st Duke of, 142
Westminster Abbey: aerial view of, *7*; exterior (sixteenth century), *112*; (mid-seventeenth century), *22, 23*; (eighteenth century), *32, 33*; interior (general view), 153; plan of, *21*
Westminster Hall, 25, 35, 39, 47, 66, 68, 94, 108, *112, 131*, 138, 148
Westminster Psalter, *181*, 193–4
Westminster School, 15, 16, 46, 71, 96, 102, 107, *119*, 125, 127, 128, 256
Westmonasterium or the History and Antiquities of the Abbey Church, (Dart), *122*, 127
Weston, Hugh, Dean of Westminster 1553–6, 94
Weelkes, Thomas, 35, 103
Wilcocks, Joseph, Dean of Westminster 1731–56, 256
William I, 15, 37, 40, *49, 51*, 143, 148
William II, 40, 148
William III, 47, 108, 250
William le Verrer, 194
William, Master, 192
William of Windsor (son of Edward III), 200
William the Silent, Prince of Orange, 249
Williams, John, Dean of Westminster 1620–44, 102, 103 *see also 60*
Williams, Roger, 104
Wilton, Joseph, *238*, 253
Wilton, Diptych, *56, 57*
Winchester, Winifred, Marchioness of, 215
Windows, 26, *29*, 35, 144, *162, 174, 175*; rose, 126, *160, 161*
Windsor (St George's Chapel), 66, 73, 92
Wiseman, Sir Richard, 103
Wolfe, James, *209, 238*, 253, 254
Wolsey, Thomas, Cardinal Archbishop of York, 72, 91
Woodville, Elizabeth, 67, 68, 71
Wordsworth, Canon, 140
Wragg, William, 144
Wren, Sir Christopher, 26, 69, 106, 108, *117, 122*, 125, 139, 145, 190, *255*, 256
Wren, Matthew, Bishop of Ely, 106
Wright, Patience, *124*, 145

Yevele, Henry, 190, *203*
Young Pretender, the (Charles Edward Stuart), 139

Acknowledgments

The publishers would like to thank Mrs E. D. Nixon and Miss C. Reynolds of Westminster Abbey Library for their help, and the following for supplying photographs and for granting permission for them to be reproduced.

Batsford Ltd: 170/t; BBC Hulton Picture Library: 133/r, 261/c; Bodleian Library, Oxford: 75/b; British Library, London: 64/t; British Museum, London: 21/t, 32–3, 53, 54–5, 58/t, 58/b, 61, 74/t, 74/b, 80/b, 84, 86–7, 110–11, 112/t, 112/b, 113, 118, 120, 130/b, 131/t, 131/b, 181; Camera Press: 260/c, 261/r; Courtauld Institute of Art, London: 49/t, 49/bl, 135/tl, 135/tr, 159, 163, 169, 176; Dean & Chapter of Westminster: 22–3, 24, 30, 31, *41*, 49/br, 52/t, 52/b, 56/t, 63/t, 63/br, 64/b, 77, 78/b, 79/t, 79/b, 81, 109, 115, 116, 117/t, 117/b, 119, 121/t, 121/b, 122/tl, 122/tr, 122/b, 123/t, 123/b, 124, 129, 133/l, 153, 154/tl, 154/tr, 154/b, 155/tl, 155/tr, 155/b, 156/tl, 156/tr, 156/b, 157/tl, 157/tr, 157/b, 162/t, 162/b, 164/t, 164/bl, 164/br, 165/t, 165/bl, 165/br, *168, 177, 178–9, 180*, 182/r, 184/t, 184/bl, 184/br, 188, 201, 212, 217; Dean & Canons of Windsor: 73; Department of the Environment (Crown Copyright Reserved): 59; Stanley Eost and P. Macdonald: 202, 203, 210–11, 218, 220, 221/b, 222, 226, 227, 228, 230, 231, 232, 234, 235/t, 235/bl, 235/br, 236, 237, 239, 240, 241, 242, 243, 244, 245, 246, 247, 248; Werner Forman: *8–9*, 28/t, 28/bl, 28/br, 29/tl, 29/tr, 29/b, *42, 44*, 60, 88/t, *89, 99, 100*, 152/t, 152/b, 160/t, 160/b, *167*, 170/b, 204, *205/t, 205/b, 206–7, 208*, 219; John Hedgecoe: *7, 10, 17, 18, 19, 20, 27, 34, 149, 150*; Michael Holford: *90*; Henry Huntington Library, California: 75/t; Jarrolds Ltd: *43*, 183, 224; A. F. Kersting: 62, 158, 171, 172, 185; Keystone Collection: 135/b, 136; Mansell Collection: 114; 130/t, 134; National Gallery, London: 56/b, 57; National Portrait Gallery, London: 76, 86; Press Association: 260/l; Public Record Office: 85; Reproduced by Gracious Permission of H. M. The Queen: 88/b; Royal Commission on Historical Monuments of England (Crown Copyright): 161, 173/t, 173/b, 174, 175, 182/l, 186, 187, 225, 238/r; Society of Antiquaries of London: 82–3; Staatliche Museen, Berlin: 80/t; Tate Gallery, London: 132; Victoria and Albert Museum, London 21, 50/t, 50/b, 51/t, 51/b; Warburg Institute, London: 63/b, 78/t, 166/t, 166/bl, 166/br, 238/l; George Zarnecki: 261/l.